PENGUIN CLASSICS

THE BIRDS AND OTHER PLAYS

ADVISORY EDITOR: BETTY RADICE

ARISTOPHANES was born, probably in Athens, *c.* 448–445 BC and died between 386 and 380 BC. Little is known about his life, but there is a portrait of him in Plato's *Symposium*. He was twice prosecuted in the 420s for his outspoken attacks on the prominent politician Cleon, but in 405 he was publicly honoured and crowned for promoting Athenian civic unity in *The Frogs*. Aristophanes had his first comedy produced when he was about nineteen or twenty, and wrote forty plays in all. The eleven surviving plays of Aristophanes are published in the Penguin Classics series as *The Birds and Other Plays, Lysistrata and Other Plays* and *The Wasps/The Poet and the Women/The Frogs*.

DAVID BARRETT studied Classics at Cambridge. After the war he was a lecturer in English at Helsinki University for thirteen years. In 1965 he joined the staff of the Bodleian Library in Oxford, where he specialized in Georgian and Armenian books, retiring from full-time work in 1981. He has translated many works from Finnish, as well as Aristophanes' *The Wasps, The Poet and the Women* and *The Frogs* for Penguin Classics.

ALAN SOMMERSTEIN has been Professor of Greek at the University of Nottingham since 1988. He has written or edited several books on Ancient Greek language and literature, especially tragic and comic drama, and is currently engaged on a complete edition of the comedies of Aristophanes with translation and commentary. For the Penguin Classics he has also translated Aristophanes' *Lysistrata, The Acharnians* and *The Clouds*. He is currently editor of *Nottingham Classical Literature Studies* and joint editor of the international journal *Drama*.

ARISTOPHANES

The Birds
and other plays
The Knights · Peace · Wealth
The Assembly Women

Translated with Introductory matter by
DAVID BARRETT
and
ALAN H. SOMMERSTEIN

PENGUIN BOOKS

PENGUIN BOOKS

Published by the Penguin Group
Penguin Books Ltd, 80 Strand, London WC2R ORL, England
Penguin Putnam Inc., 375 Hudson Street, New York, New York 10014, USA
Penguin Books Australia Ltd, 250 Camberwell Road, Camberwell, Victoria 3124, Australia
Penguin Books Canada Ltd, 10 Alcorn Avenue, Toronto, Ontario, Canada M4V 3B2
Penguin Books India (P) Ltd, 11 Community Centre, Panchsheel Park, New Delhi – 110 017, India
Penguin Books (NZ) Ltd, Cnr Rosedale and Airborne Roads, Albany, Auckland, New Zealand
Penguin Books (South Africa) (Pty) Ltd, 24 Sturdee Avenue, Rosebank 2196, South Africa

Penguin Books Ltd, Registered Offices: 80 Strand, London WC2R ORL, England

www.penguin.com

This translation first published 1978
Reprinted with a Select Bibliography 2003
3

Copyright © David Barrett and Alan H. Sommerstein, 1978
All rights reserved

Application for permission to perform these translations should be addressed to the
Society of Authors, 84 Drayton Gardens, London SW10 9SD

Printed in England by Clays Ltd, St Ives plc
Set in Monotype Bembo

CONTENTS

ABOUT THE AUTHOR

Aristophanes was active as a writer of comedies at Athens from 427 to about 386 B.C.; forty of his plays were known to ancient scholars, and eleven of these have come down to us: *The Acharnians* (425), *The Knights* (424), *The Clouds* (a partly revised version of a play produced in 423), *The Wasps* (422), *Peace* (421), *The Birds* (414), *Lysistrata* and *The Poet and the Women* (*Thesmophoriazusae*) (411), *The Frogs* (405), *The Assemblywomen* (*Ecclesiazusae*) (probably 391), and *Wealth* (*Plutus*) (388).

We know very little of the man except through his work. He does not seem to have taken any direct part in politics: he was probably one of the 500 Councillors for a year in the 390s, but this was an office it was hard to avoid. His comedies, though, were highly political, as comedy was then expected to be, and twice landed him in court (see the Introduction to *The Knights*). From Plato's *Symposium*, written not long after Aristophanes' death, we get an impression of him as a pleasure-loving man, frivolous on the surface but serious underneath – a little like some of his heroes.

Comedies were produced once only, competitively, at two annual festivals, before an open-air audience of some 14,000 (of all ages, but predominantly male); thereafter (apart from occasional re-productions at theatres in outlying parts of Attica) they existed only as written texts. The stage directions in this translation are our own; we hope they are a fair approximation to Aristophanes' or his producer's instructions to actors and chorus, but in many cases anything like certainty is impossible.

With trivial exceptions, Aristophanes' comedies are written wholly in verse. This is of three main types: the six-foot iambic metre of ordinary spoken dialogue; various eight-foot metres (iambic, trochaic, anapaestic), delivered in a more strictly rhythmical manner to musical accompaniment, which predominate in two types of scene of capital importance in Aristophanic drama – the scene of physical

7

and/or verbal conflict (*agon*) in which the main issue of the play is often decided, and the address by the chorus to the audience (*parabasis*); and sung lyrics, performed (with dancing) mainly by the chorus but also by some of the principals. We have followed the pattern of our previous translations, presenting the spoken scenes as prose, the lyrics generally as verse (and in production they certainly ought to be sung), and the 'recitative' passages of the original as one or the other depending on the character of the scene.

A.H.S.

ARISTOPHANES IN ANTIQUITY

In Aristophanes' time literary criticism was in its infancy; indeed, his own *Frogs* ranks among its earliest monuments. It is not therefore surprising that we have very little in the way of contemporary critical appraisal of Aristophanes, most of what usually passes under that name being either the small change of comic insult, or later romance about Plato.

From an older contemporary of Aristophanes, the comic poet Cratinus (*c.* 490–*c.* 420 B.C.), we have one precious word. Cratinus characterized a certain type of poet as 'a hair-splitting master of niceties, a Euripidaristophanist'. In other words, he asserted that Aristophanes resembled Euripides in his concern for verbal precision and dexterity (*dexiotēs*, in Aristophanes always a term of praise) in preference to the bolder, rougher strokes typical of those who, like Cratinus himself, had grown up under the spell of Aeschylus. Aristophanes himself was quite aware of this, but he drew a sharp distinction between Euripidean technique and Euripidean thought; or, as he put it in his lost play *The Pitch-Grabbers* (*Skenas Katalambanousai*) with his unmatchable *chutzpah*,

> I use the rounded polish of his style,
> But make my heroes' minds somewhat less ... vulgar.

The only other judgement on Aristophanes we have from a person who had seen his work performed is that of Plato (427–347 B.C.). Plato could not help being somewhat equivocal. Socrates' trial and condemnation had, as he believed, been in part due to the misleading picture of Socrates' activities and interests that had gained currency as a result of the portrayals of him in comedy, above all in *The Clouds*. (Before dismissing this as an absurd overrating of the power of comedy to influence popular views, consider what in our time might be the effect of a series of satirical shows on television, regularly attacking the same person, if that person, like Socrates, did not regard himself as in public life and never in a quarter of a century troubled to respond to the attacks.) On the other hand, as the *Symposium* makes clear, Plato recognized and admired Aristophanes' powers of imagination and fantasy, and even felt a kinship between the comedian's mind and his own; for the myth he makes Aristophanes relate on the origin of sexual love is not unlike the myths with which Plato himself regularly crowns the dialogues of his middle period (*Gorgias*, *Phaedo*, *Republic*, *Phaedrus*), which called for the same powers, applied (as Plato would claim) to a higher end. What he objected to was the way in which, quite generally, comedy (at least Old Comedy) held everyone and everything up to ridicule – and in particular, philosophers and philosophy. Even the complaint about *The Clouds* in Plato's *Apology* is coupled with the observation that the allegations there made are 'regularly used against all philosophers'.

I have left out of account the epitaph on Aristophanes supposed to have been composed by Plato:

> The Graces sought to occupy a shrine that ne'er would cease:
> They found that shrine within the soul of Aristophanes,

because I find it very difficult to believe that Plato could have written it. The author of the epitaph used the word *temenos* to mean 'temple'; in Plato's time it meant 'area of ground which was sacred'. The syntax is also clumsier than I would have expected from Plato. And as I have already mentioned, there was much late romancing about the relationships between Socrates, Plato and Aristophanes.

Old Comedy quickly went out of fashion. Fifth-century tragedies were regularly revived from 386 onwards at the City Dionysia (quite apart from the many performances known to have taken place in other parts of Attica), but never fifth-century comedies. And already for Aristotle (384–322 B.C.) Old Comedy was so antiquated that he can define comedy in a way that altogether excludes it. Part of the definition of poetry given in the *Poetics*, which distinguishes it from history, is that poetry deals with universal rather than individual matters. 'This is already clear,' he goes on, 'from a consideration of comedy; for they construct their plot from probable events and assign random names to their characters, and unlike the writers of invective they do not discuss particular individuals.' Thus on this definition Old Comedy is not only not comedy but not even poetry!

However, the plays of Aristophanes (and those of the other Old Comedians) continued to circulate as literary texts, though with no stage directions and inadequate indication of who was speaking they must often have been extraordinarily hard to understand; and eventually thirty-nine plays* found their way to the great library of Alexandria, where during the third, second and first centuries B.C. their texts were as far as possible purged of the corruptions that had arisen in a century of uncontrolled copying, and extensive commentaries were written. All this, however – or at least what we can trace of it – was scholarship rather than criticism.

Alexandrian scholarship established the viewpoint that the outstanding representatives of Old Comedy were Aristophanes, Cratinus and Eupolis, though they never attained the same exclusive degree of supremacy as the tragic trinity of Aeschylus, Sophocles and Euripides; and Aristophanes is universally regarded as the greatest of the three. But most ancient discussion of his work runs in predictable channels: the insolence and indecency of his satire, the turpitude of his attack on Socrates ... in short, Aristophanes is discussed in entire isolation from the occasions and the society for which he wrote, and with no reference to literary or dramatic criteria. There are exceptions, to which we will come.

One of these exceptions is Horace (65–8 B.C.), who is particularly interested in Old Comedy because he regards it (somewhat inaccurately) as the remote ancestor of one of his own genres, the chatty verse-essays known as *saturae* or satires (Horace himself preferred the term *sermones* or chats). As a poet himself he is able to appreciate Aristophanes' ability in the manipulation of language and style. The fullest treatment is in the concluding (tenth) satire of his first book, which is a reply to criticisms of Horace's views on satire and particularly on his great Roman predecessor Lucilius:

Yes, I did say that Lucilius' verse is incompetently
composed. Who is so besotted an admirer of Lucilius
as not to admit this? But I also, and on the same page,
praised him for vigorously massaging the City with his wit.

＿＿＿＿＿＿＿＿

*Alexandria missed one play, called *Peace* (not the same as the *Peace* which has survived), which was apparently to be found in at least one other library in the second century B.C., and from which some quotations have been preserved.

In conceding the latter, though, I would not withdraw the former: if
I did,
I might just as well praise the poetic beauty of Laberius' variety shows.
It is therefore not enough to make one's audience open-mouthed
with laughter (not that that isn't desirable too);
brevity is needed, so that the thought runs smoothly and is not
obstructed by words that are a burden on tired ears;
and language now grave, now gay,
playing the part now of an orator and poet,
now of a man of culture who spares or spends
his strength with due deliberation. Laughter is in general
stronger and better at cutting down great objects than is acidity.
Those men by whom Old Comedy was written
were strong in this, and in this should be imitated: they have never been
read by that beauty-king Hermogenes, nor by that ape-critic
whose 'learning' consists only in being able to sing
        (sorry, recite) the works of Calvus and Catullus.

Aristophanes would have agreed with much of that. Perhaps, after
The Knights had entirely failed to affect the political standing
of Cleon, he might have agreed with the remark about laughter
being better than acidity. And it is certainly the case that pungent
brevity and enormous variety of language are among the salient
characteristics of Old Comedy, particularly in comparison with
New.

Horace discusses Old Comedy briefly in two other passages (*Serm.*
i. 4, 1–5, *Ars Poetica* 281–4), but mainly in reference to the freedom
with which the Old Comedians assailed everything and everyone they
considered dangerous. He even asserts that the disappearance of Old
Comedy is to be explained by an alleged law which by abolishing this
freedom deprived the genre of its *raison d'être*. (In point of fact, the
evidence is that no such law or decree was more than temporarily
effective.)

Another rare gem of insight comes in a brief reference by the
unknown author (first century A.D.?) of the treatise *On the Sublime*,
whom we habitually if incorrectly call Longinus. For him Aristophanes, with Euripides and the historian Philistus of Syracuse, was a
prime example of the 'many poets and prose writers who have not
sublimity by nature, or may even be entirely without stature, and use
for the most part common, familiar, unevocative words, [but]

nevertheless through the mere matching and combination of these words clothe their work with dignity, class and elevation'.

For a thoroughly negative judgement on Aristophanes we may turn to Plutarch (*c.* 45 – *c.* 125 A.D.), into whose literary categories Old Comedy simply did not fit. I translate the relevant passages from his *Comparison of Aristophanes and Menander*:

> In Aristophanes there is vulgar diction, vulgar action and general lack of culture ... Ordinary, uneducated people are attracted by Aristophanes' language, but the educated man will wince. I am thinking of antitheses, jingles and puns ... Aristophanes uses them with a frequency and inappropriateness which are nauseating. The sort of thing that is usually praised is:
>
> (1) He gave the Treasurers a dip that day –
>   Not *Treasurers*, but *Treacherous*, I should say.
> (2) Nor'-easterly gale getting up, blowing straight from Informer-land!
> (3)   Let's see you launch
>   Punishing punches at his paunch!
> (4) I'm laughing so much, before I know where I am I'll be in Giggleswick!
> (5) Where shall I chuck you, you rotten pot, when you've given me the chuck?*
> (6) He's that wild, the way he treats us. Comes of being brought up on the wild-vegetable stall, I suppose.
> (7) Don't say the moths have eaten my crests!
> (8)   Now bring the circle of my Gorgon shield.
>   – Now bring the circle of a cheesy cake.†

And there are many others of the same kind. His use of words combines the tragic and the comic, the grandiose and the prosaic, the obscure and the commonplace, bombast and elevation, verbal diarrhoea and plain sickening rubbish. But despite all these variations and incongruities, he does not even allot to each style its suitable and appropriate place, such as dignity to a king, ingenuity to an orator, simplicity to a woman, prosiness to a man of the people, vulgarity to a layabout; rather he distributes to his characters, as if by lot, whatever words happen to be

---

*The speaker appears to be threatened with exile by ostracism; in votes on this issue potsherds were used as ballots.

†Of these quotations, 2 and 3 come from *The Knights*, 6 from *The Poet and the Women*, and 7 and 8 from *The Acharnians*; the others are known only from the present passage.

lying around, and one cannot tell if the person speaking is supposed to
be son or father, rustic or god, hag or hero . . .

  Some dramatists write for the vulgar mob, others for the few, and it
is not easy to say which of all of them had the ability to adapt himself
to both. Aristophanes, however, is neither pleasing to the many nor
tolerable to the discerning; his poetry is like a superannuated *cocotte*
pretending to be a respectable married woman . . .

  Aristophanes' wit is briny and bitter, rough and sharp, and apt to
wound and to bite. Nor do I know where to find his much-discussed
'dexterity' in language or characterization. Why, even what he imitates loses by the portrayal. Roguery is not a civilized prank but really
malicious; rusticity is not simple but stupid; jokes are not playful but
absurd, and joyous love is replaced by sheer unbridled lust. The fellow
seems not to have written for respectable people at all; rather his
indecent and licentious scenes were designed for the immoral spectator,
and his stinging libels for those possessed by the sin of malicious envy.

It will be seen that Plutarch's sense of outrage has not been restrained within the bounds of consistency; at the beginning and end
Aristophanes is a poet of the vulgar to be abhorred by the respectable,
in the middle he is intolerable even to the vulgar. Apart from this
point, Aristophanes would probably have accepted most of Plutarch's remarks (off the record) with the comment that in the inter-
vening five centuries people must have forgotten how to laugh.

But he would wryly have had to admit at least the last count in the
briefer indictment presented by one Diogenianus in Plutarch's
dialogue 'What should one listen to over dinner?' (Book VII, No. 8
of his *Dinner-table Discussions*):

As for comedy, the Old variety is unsuitable as an accompaniment
to drinking, because it is so uneven. The *parabasis*, as it is called, has a
seriousness and outspokenness that makes it too potent and intense;
while the licence given to jesting and buffoonery is so open as to be
nauseating and full of words and expressions of shameless obscenity.
What is more, just as at the banquets of great men every guest has his
personal wine waiter, so we would each need our personal commentator to explain all the allusions to individuals, like the identity of
Laespodias in Eupolis' play, or Cinesias in Plato's,* or Lampon in
Cratinus', or anyone else that was mentioned, and either we'd have to

*Plato the comic poet, of course, not the philosopher. Cinesias is no doubt
the dithyrambic poet we meet in *The Birds*.

turn our dining-room into a classroom or all the jokes would fly meaninglessly and unintelligibly past us.

For all this, Aristophanes (and indeed some of the other Old Comedians) went on being read. Some of the reasons may be gathered from the brief but warm remarks of Quintilian (c. 38 – c. 100 A.D.), who is discussing, in *The Orator's Training* (10. 1. 65–6), the utility, in this major field of upper-class education in the imperial age, of the study of various types of literature:

Old Comedy, almost alone, retains the pristine charm of the Attic dialect, and is also distinguished by a most eloquent freedom of expression. If it is at its best in the reprobation of vice, it nevertheless has great power in other respects also. It possesses grandeur, elegance and attractiveness, and perhaps no kind of poetry, after Homer (who like Achilles must always be excepted from generalizations of this kind*), is either more similar to oratory or more suitable for the training of an orator. There are numerous authors, of whom Aristophanes, Eupolis and Cratinus are the most outstanding.

A lucky break for Aristophanes was the revival in the second century, both in Greek and in Roman literary circles, of interest in the archaic and out-of-the-way. It became fashionable to write in the long-dead dialect and style of the great Athenian writers of the fifth and fourth century B.C.; and among these it was recognized that the comic poets, particularly Aristophanes, and the orators, particularly Lysias, represented that dialect and style in its purest form. So Aristophanes became a school text in the language class as well as the oratorical class, and from this time an upsurge of interest in him can be deduced from the preserved ancient manuscripts (customarily but rather inaccurately called papyri); for Aristophanes these are rare before the second century A.D. and rise to their highest frequency in the fifth, whereas papyri of Menander, for example, are most frequent in the third century and fall off fairly rapidly thereafter, suggesting that Menander (who lived at a time when Attic was already losing some of its distinctive features, and whose style is rich in naturalness but poor in vigour and elevation) was less used in the schools. It was during this long period that interest in Aristophanes gradually concentrated upon the eleven plays we now possess; and when in the

*Homer describes Ajax as 'second to none of the Greeks – after Achilles'.

ninth century the scholars of Constantinople, eager to salvage what they could of ancient literature after two centuries during which it had been largely neglected, hunted out the surviving Aristophanic manuscripts, these eleven were all that they contained.

Near the beginning of the Attic revival, to which, in all probability, we owe the fact that we can read Aristophanes today, stands the prose satirist Lucian (c. 120 – c. 190 A.D.). Discussion of Lucian's debt to Old Comedy is not made easier by the fact that he very rarely makes explicit reference to it, and then usually in connection with the treatment of Socrates in *The Clouds*. But time and again he can be detected using a familiar Aristophanic turn of phrase, so much so that it is occasionally possible to use him as evidence for correcting the text of Aristophanes;* and he also pays Aristophanes the compliment of imitation. It will be fitting to conclude this survey with a specimen. A discussion is being held in heaven on what to do about the misanthropic Athenian, Timon, and it is decided to send him Wealth. Wealth himself objects. Asked why by Zeus, he replies:

Because Timon used to assault me and dig me out of the ground and divide me into little pieces, and me an old family friend of his! He practically drove me out of his house with a pitchfork, as if I'd caught fire in his hands. Am I to go back to him to be handed over to parasites and toadies and women of pleasure? Please, Zeus, send me to someone who'll appreciate the gift and treat me well, do me honour and long for me. Let these cormorants live with Poverty; they prefer her to us. Let them get a leather smock and a fork from her and enjoy making their four obols, poor things, if they're careless enough to throw away a gift of sixty thousand drachmas.

Zeus assures him that Timon is now quite a changed person, and continues:

But really, Wealth, you never seem to be satisfied! You object to Timon because he opened his doors and let you free to wander where you would instead of jealously shutting you up. At one time you'd say just the opposite. You said the rich shut you up with keys and bolts and seals so you never got a peep at the light. At least that's what you com-

*Thus in line 1309 of *The Wasps* a nineteenth-century emendation, *Phrygi* ('a Phrygian') for *trygi* ('new wine'), gets confirmation from Lucian's *How to Write History* (section 20).

plained about to me; you said the darkness was suffocating you. And you looked pale and careworn, with your fingers bent from long years of counting on them, and you always said you'd run away if you got half a chance. And you thought the whole thing was an absolute scandal, that you should have to live a celibate life in a bronze or iron chamber, like my old flame Danae, under two appallingly strict tutors called Interest and Bookkeeping. Why, you said your jailers were acting quite incredibly, because they loved you to distraction but didn't dare enjoy you though you were in their power and they could indulge themselves with impunity; instead they stood wakeful guard, staring at seal and bolt, thinking apparently that the only real enjoyment was not to enjoy you themselves but to ensure that nobody else did, dog-in-the-manger-fashion. And you laughed at them, pinching and scraping, keeping watch over you, and ending up jealous of themselves, never thinking that some contemptible slave or fettered steward would sneak in and play merry hell with you, leaving his miserable and unloved master to burn the midnight oil (feeble little lamp but thirsty little wick) over his compound interest tables.

Wealth defends himself against the charge of inconsistency by appealing to the doctrine of the golden mean:

I mean, Zeus, look at it this way, in Zeus's name! If someone marries an attractive young woman and then shows no possessiveness or jealousy at all, but on the contrary lets her roam where she will night and day and go with anyone who takes a fancy to her, or to be more precise takes her round himself to commit adultery, opening doors and inviting all comers like a pimp, would you say that he loved her? I'm sure *you* wouldn't, Zeus, with your vast experience of love. On the other hand, if someone legally takes a free woman into his house, 'legitimate children for the procreation of', a beautiful virgin in her prime, and then doesn't touch her himself and won't let anyone else even look at her, but locks her up, sterile and barren, like a single girl, and all the time says he's in love with her, and his pale skin, wasted flesh and sunken eyes prove he's telling the truth – wouldn't you say he was insane? When he ought to be reproducing himself and enjoying his marital rights, he lets this radiant, lovely girl wither all her days like a priestess of Demeter Thesmophoros! And that's what I object to. One lot of people care so little for me that they kick me around, gulp me down and drain me to the dregs, while another lot put me in fetters like a branded runaway.

But on receiving further assurances, Wealth agrees to go with Hermes to enrich Timon ('Oh, and Hermes,' adds Zeus, 'on your way back fetch a Cyclops or two from Etna; I need my thunderbolt sharpening'). They descend to Attica, Wealth on his way explaining some of his habits to Hermes; but as they reach Timon's fields, Hermes sees Poverty and Labour there, along with Endurance, Wisdom, Courage and 'all that crowd that march under the banner of Hunger'. Wealth displays his proverbial cowardice (cf. *Wealth*, p. 278), but Hermes with stiff upper lip replies 'We must do the will of Zeus.' Now, however, Poverty intervenes:

POVERTY: Where are you leading that god by the hand, noble Slayer of Argus?

HERMES: We have been sent by Zeus to Timon there.

POVERTY: Wealth sent to Timon! After the state I found him in when I took him over from Luxury! I handed him over to my friends here, Wisdom and Labour, and made him an upright and worthy man. Do you think that Poverty is so contemptible, or that she takes injustice lying down? To deprive me of my sole possession, which I have toiled and toiled to bring to virtue, so that Wealth can take him over, entrust him to Arrogance and Conceit, and make him soft, ignoble and stupid as before, preparatory to returning him to me no better than a rag!

HERMES [*doggedly*]: That is Zeus's decision.

POVERTY: Then I'm off. Come on, Labour, Wisdom and the rest of you, follow me. He'll know soon enough what a treasure he's abandoned, a good fellow-labourer and a teacher of virtue, with whom he could lead a healthy life in body and mind, the life of a man, thinking of himself, and regarding all these superfluities – for that is what they are – as having nothing to do with him. [*Exit.*]

Hermes and Wealth approach Timon and persuade him, rather against his will, to accept the presence in his soil of Wealth's servant Treasure. And before long we find ourselves transferred from *Wealth* to *The Birds*, as a variety of parasites swoop on the newly-enriched Timon like vultures (his word) and are driven off with blows. One of these is a politician, Demeas, for whom Timon had once paid a fine of 96,000 drachmas to secure his release from prison, but who more recently, when Timon, now a poor man, applied to him for the statutory allowance to enable him to attend the state festivals, said he was not aware that Timon was a citizen. Demeas enters, holding an official document.

DEMEAS: Greetings, Timon, great benefactor of your family, stay of Athens, bulwark of Hellas! The assembled People and both the Councils have long been awaiting you. But first hear the decree which I have carried on your behalf. 'Whereas Timon, son of Echecratides, of Collytus, a man not only virtuous but wise beyond all other Greeks, has continually acted to the utmost for the welfare of the City and has won the boxing, wrestling and foot-race at Olympia on the same day and has also won the major chariot-race and the chariot-and-pair race for two-year-olds—'

TIMON: But I've never even *seen* the Olympics.

DEMEAS: So what? You will one day. It's as well to include a lot of that kind of thing. 'And fought heroically for the City last year at Acharnae, cutting two Spartan divisions to pieces—'

TIMON: What do you mean? I'm not even on the Army List; I can't afford the equipment.

DEMEAS: You're very modest, but we would be most ungrateful if we forgot your services. 'And whereas the said Timon has greatly benefited the City by the resolutions he has proposed, the advice he has given, and his service as General: Be it therefore resolved by the Council and the People and the High Court tribe by tribe and by all and singular the Demes of this state, That a golden statue of the said Timon be erected next to Athena on the Acropolis, having a thunder-bolt in his right hand and rays of glory over his head: And that he be crowned with seven golden crowns, and that the crowns be proclaimed today at the Dionysia when the new tragedies are performed (for he is to be responsible for holding the Dionysia today). Proposed by the orator Demeas, being the closest kinsman and disciple of the said Timon, who is himself outstanding in oratory and in every other art to which he cares to apply himself.' That's the decree. I also wanted to bring you my son; I've named him Timon after you.

TIMON: But you're not even married – not that I've heard of anyway.

DEMEAS: I shall marry next year, God willing, and have a child, and I now in advance name the child Timon, since it will of course be a boy.

TIMON [*striking him*]: *Now* are you still so keen on getting married?

DEMEAS: Help! What's the idea? Are you attempting to set up a dictatorship, striking free citizens, and that when you are neither properly free nor a citizen? I will see that you will quickly pay the penalty for your crimes, in particular for the offence of setting fire to the Acropolis!

TIMON: There hasn't *been* a fire on the Acropolis, you villainous trumper-up!

DEMEAS: Do you not owe your wealth to the burglary of Athena's Sacred Treasury?

TIMON: There's been no burglary there; you'll have to think of a better one than that.

DEMEAS: I don't care if you've burgled it already or you'll burgle it later – you've got the money from it.

TIMON [*striking him again*]: Then take that!

DEMEAS: Ooooh, my back!

TIMON: Don't shout or I may give you another. It would be absurd if I could cut two Spartan divisions to pieces unarmed and not be able to beat up one miserable little nobody like you – especially with my Olympic crowns for boxing and wrestling as well. [*Exit* DEMEAS, *rapidly.*]

That scene is Aristophanic through and through; not for many centuries was the great comedian again to be appreciated as a comedian.

A.H.S.

ARISTOPHANES, COMEDIAN
AND POET

I don't know whether ancient Athenian audiences were in the habit of groaning at feeble puns, but they certainly appreciated good ones. Aristophanes gave them a good many of both kinds, little realizing the groans of despair they would elicit from his translators some 2,380 years later. Only very occasionally, by some amazing linguistic fluke, will some piece of Aristophanic word-play slip straight into English: as when, in *The Birds*, a prudent soothsayer is reported as swearing 'by Goose' instead of 'by Zeus' (*nê ton Khêna* instead of *nê ton Zêna*); or when the slave in *The Frogs* describes the occupations of a true gentleman as 'soaking and poking' (*pinein* and *binein*). What is the poor translator to do about the speech defect which makes Alcibiades, in *The Wasps*, say *kolax* (a toady) when he means *korax* (a raven), thus demolishing a well-known political figure with a single letter of the alphabet? How can he convey the comic overtones, so gleefully exploited in the comedies, of so many innocent place-names – the Chipping Sodburies and Steeple Bumpsteads of ancient Attica?

Double meanings abound on every page; there may be even more of them than the scholars have yet discovered. Many have perforce to be ignored, when there seems to be no way at all of reproducing the effect in English. Sometimes a whole scene is built upon them, as when in *The Acharnians*, a Megarian disguises his two little daughters as piglets, and tries to barter them for garlic and salt. The word-play on the two meanings of the Greek word for 'pig' is kept up for thirty solid lines: it is a very funny scene indeed – in Greek. Then there is the scene in *Lysistrata* where the sex-starved Athenian and Spartan delegates, gesturing over a map of Greece, discuss the naval and military implications of an armistice. Between them, perhaps holding the map, stands the nubile (if allegorical) figure of 'Reconciliation'. In this situation, everything they say manages to sound like a reference to some part of her anatomy. It is very cleverly done – but the devil to translate.

Then there are the stock jokes associated with particular people and places, many of which are hard to put across without recourse to footnotes or ponderous insertions in the text ('So-and-so, *that tiresome fellow who, as you know, always* . . .'; 'Such-and-such a place, *which as you know, is famous for the export of* . . .'). Any mention of Salamis, for example, is liable to imply a joke about sex. Why? Because, to get to Athens, the Salaminians had to *row* across to the mainland, and *rowing* has a double meaning, see? Just a piece of everyday un-intellectual Athenian humour; just enough to get a laugh in passing and keep things lively. But by the time the translator has written his eighth footnote to this effect, the joke (both for him and for the reader) has begun to wear a bit thin. Often, of course, the stock jokes about people can be guessed from the context. This, in fact, is often all the ancient commentators have been able to do: their learned notes on many individuals turn out to be nothing more than deductions from the passage they are commenting on. In the case of well-known people like Euripides, Socrates and Cleon, and others who are less well known historically but who appear frequently in the plays (like Cleonymus and Cleisthenes), the stock jokes soon become familiar through repetition, or because they are developed in extended scenes. But what of the scores of others whose names occur perhaps once or twice, and of whom (to quote our most frequent footnote) 'nothing is known'? Who on earth was Smicythion, and why should it have been easier for his wife than anyone else's to get out of the house unseen? How far is one justified in guessing what the joke might have been, and slanting the translation so as to imply it?

Fortunately the comedies of Aristophanes do not live by wit alone. Gilbert Norwood, in his admirable book on *Greek Comedy*, maintained that Aristophanes, though endowed with 'superb wit, splendid poetical genius, immense vitality', lacked humour. But then Norwood's conception of humour is a somewhat idealized one, implying something more like what we would now call compassion. If a sense of fun, a sense of proportion, a delight in the unexpected, and an eye for the eccentricities, the appetites, the stupidities, the pretensions and the basic simplicity of human beings, add up to a sense of humour, it is hard to think of anyone who had it in more abundance than

Aristophanes. It may be true that he was 'without pity or reverence', as Norwood maintains; but whether he had these qualities or not, they are not the ones most needed by a man whose job is to make people laugh. The audience want to see the pompous man made ridiculous, the braggart forced to eat his words, the cheater cheated; for this is right, this is what *should* happen to them; these characters are allegorical, this is what they exist for; they are facets of ourselves, isolated expressly to be ridiculed, not to be pitied or revered. This kind of humour is the essence of comedy and wit is the salt wherewith it is salted. Whatever else has changed over the centuries, the deeper springs of laughter have not. 'How modern it all seems!' is a comment frequently overheard after an Aristophanes performance. 'How ancient all our jokes are!' would be a better way of putting it.

Lovers of Aristophanes all have their favourite funny bits. There is the scene in *The Frogs*, for instance, where Dionysus and his slave have changed costumes for the third time, and each is claiming to be the god. If he is a god, says the slave, he will feel no pain when beaten. So Aeacus has each beaten in turn, and their efforts to disguise their yelps of pain become progressively more extravagant. In the end Aeacus professes himself baffled and suggests going inside Pluto's palace to ask Persephone: she is a goddess herself, she'll know at once. 'I wish you'd thought of that a bit sooner,' Dionysus groans. Or there is the hilarious scene in *The Poet and the Women*, where Mnesilochus, attending a women's festival in disguise, is detected and disrobed by the sexually ambiguous Cleisthenes (who has gained admission without difficulty: 'you're one of us, really'). Most famous of all, perhaps, is the episode in *Lysistrata* where Cinesias, in a state of acute priapism, is led on by his wife Myrrhine to believe that she is about to let him make love to her (in full view of the audience). Delay follows delay, increasing his impatience, as she dashes off to fetch additional comforts – a mattress, a pillow, a blanket, a flask of perfume – until, when everything is at last ready, she eludes his grasp yet again and rejoins her fellow-strikers on the Rock.

The humour of these scenes is basic – physical indignities, embarrassment, sexual frustration: these have been the stock-in-trade of clowns and comedians throughout the ages. Yet, as presented by Aristophanes, they retain a perpetual freshness. This is not only because of the witty lines, but also because of the craftsmanship and stage-sense which he brought to their composition. The wit – which is continually present to give an intellectual edge to the audience's enjoyment – is a kind of counterpoint to the comic situation itself, which is gradually intensified, line by line, until the climax is reached and the bubble pricked.

The timing is usually perfect: occasionally a joke seems to be strung out for just a little too long for our taste, but as a rule Aristophanes knows just how many lines an idea is worth. He will sometimes bring in a character for a tiny scene, make him immortal with a single line (like Sir Oliver Martext in *As You Like It*), and get rid of him at once. My favourite is the Corpse in *The Frogs*. Dionysus asks him to carry the luggage down to Hades for him. 'Two drachmas,' says the Corpse, jerking upright on his bier. The god rummages in his purse: 'Sorry, I can only offer you one and a half.' 'I'd sooner live,' replies the Corpse, and lies down again. That is all. The core of the scene lies in its wit, but its effect derives from the humour: a verbal fancy is turned into a visual one. The plays are full of effective little vignettes, some of them only slightly longer than this one. Almost all the 'unwanted visitors' who tend to turn up in the latter halves of the comedies remain very memorable. *The Birds* is particularly rich in them: whether they represent real people, like the airy-fairy poet Cinesias and the astronomer Meton, or are merely types, like the Inspector and the Oracle-man, these tiny parts are a joy to act and to watch.

With only the written text before us, we are apt to forget that Old Comedy was primarily a visual experience. The dramatic competitions formed part of a great civic and religious festival, and the comedies were performed out of doors, before an enormous assembly. One did not speak of an 'audience', but of 'the spectators'. The central feature was the Chorus; and when the prize was awarded, it was the chorus-trainer, not the author, whose name was cited. Far from being a mere troupe of extras, introduced to provide interludes in the unfolding of a connected narrative, they were the essential part of the pageant: twenty-four proud citizens of Athens, trained and drilled with military precision, however comic their costumes and however energetic their evolutions. To see the Chorus of *The Knights* (which won first prize) in action must have been rather like watching Trooping the Colour, executed on hobby-horses.

The choric structure of comedy was rooted in tradition: though flexibly treated, some of its main elements can be seen in all the surviving works of Aristophanes except *The Assemblywomen* and *Wealth* (see the introductory notes to these two plays). There seem to have been four 'set pieces' which were more or less expected in every comedy: a formal entry, a battle scene or at least a conflict of some kind, a *parabasis* or address to the audience (spoken by the Chorus Leader), and a finale. Sometimes there is no battle scene, sometimes the *parabasis* is in a shorter form than usual, or even omitted; occasionally there is a second *parabasis*. But the general pattern is clear. The addition of 'episodes', consisting of comic dialogue and performed by actors, was a convention of much more recent origin. It was more or less inevitable that these should develop into episodes in some kind of 'plot' or story-line, if only to provide some sort of motivation for the battle scene and a situation for the Chorus to comment on. The burlesquing of tragedy was an obvious source of entertainment, and this again demanded a dramatic 'situation', if only a temporary one. It is quite possible that many writers of Old Comedy went further than Aristophanes did in the direction of firm plot construction; but it was by no means a necessary ingredient, and he himself appears to have been something of a traditionalist. His strength lies, not in his plots but in the whimsicality of his comic ideas and in the crazy logic with which he works them out.

Nor should we look to Aristophanes for anything so alien to Old Comedy as the delineation of character. His actors were clowns masked and grotesquely padded, with dangling leather phalluses: the characters they represented were necessarily caricatures. Like animated drawings, or creatures in strip cartoons, these unreal figures are manipulated against a realistic background of everyday problems and situations, achieving a personality in the process. One is amazed by the vitality that he manages to breathe into them. Among his most successful characters are his gods, who provide ideal subjects for this kind of manipulation, since a personality of some kind is already implicit in the legends about them (which endow them with plenty of human failings, plus the right to indulge them with impunity). Least successful are those in which the allegorical element is too strong, or cannot be sustained convincingly. In *The Knights*, for example, 'The People' has to represent far too much (and cannot safely

be caricatured or made to look ridiculous): the result is an embarrass-
ing failure. Similarly, the difficulty of sustaining an allegory against a
moving narrative is clearly seen in *Wealth* – a more attractive play
than *The Knights*, but one which ultimately fails for this very reason.

One detailed character portrait which he can and does give us,
however, is that of the ordinary Athenian citizen of his day. We are
lucky to know as much as we do about these fifth-century Athenians
and their astonishing civilization. From Thucydides, Plato, Xenophon
and many other writers we have a great deal of information about
their institutions, their political life, the ideas of their intellectuals;
we know in fair detail the events of the Peloponnesian War, which
lasted the greater part of Aristophanes' working lifetime; we have a
great deal of their poetry and many splendid examples of their work
in architecture, sculpture and other visual arts. As far as concrete
facts are concerned, one could probably give a reasonably sound
lecture on Athenian social and political life without any reference to
Aristophanes at all. But if we really want to acquire the *feel* of ancient
Athens, the sense of having actually been there oneself, of knowing
exactly how they talked and what they talked about and what they
liked to eat and what they thought about sex and clothes and money
and democracy and what it felt like to be a woman or a slave and how
much anchovies cost and how fed up they got with a war that went
on for years and years – then Aristophanes is our man. He makes us
so interested in these people that we start asking more and more
questions about them, we even look up the footnotes or consult our
next-door-neighbour's small nephew, who is actually doing Greek
at school.

There is no doubt, then, about the 'superb wit' and the 'immense
vitality'; what about the 'splendid poetical genius'? This is a matter
which the reader of a translation (unless the translator be himself a
splendid poetical genius, which is rarely the case) cannot hope to
judge for himself. It is easy enough to fling a phrase like this at him
and assume that he will swallow it whole, like a sea-lion at feeding-
time. But, to be honest, it is much, much harder to know what it is
supposed to mean, and whether it can be justified.

On the technical side it is not all that easy to make a confident
judgement. Apart from a few fragments, mostly very short, we do
not have the works of his contemporaries in the same *genre*, and thus

we cannot measure his achievement against theirs. Secondly, in spite of all that has been written on the subject, nobody really knows what Attic Greek sounded like. We can make guesses as to the acoustic effect of the various 'tones' and the contrast between long and short vowels, but we know very little about word and sentence stress or the degree to which underlying rhythms (as opposed to the pattern of long and short syllables) would have made themselves felt. It is obvious enough that Aristophanes was a skilful versifier. The iambic dialogue runs smoothly and seems amazingly close to natural speech. In the longer metres used for addresses by the Chorus Leader, or passages of dialogue in which he is involved, emotion can be intensified and greater rhythmical variation is possible, but the verse still bowls along fluently and unobtrusively so that the content, rather than the medium, holds most of our attention. When we come to the lyric passages, however, things are different. Greek lyric metres, apart from the simple stanza forms like Alcaics and Sapphics, are quite unlike anything to which modern ears are accustomed: Greek poetry, moreover, is utterly unromantic, and makes little use of metaphor for its own sake. Such images as are present are there because they mean exactly what they say. If translated literally, most Greek lyrics sound to us spare and unpoetical. As for their form, the irregular metrical patterns, which often change from line to line, are worked out over a whole 'strophe' (a longish stanza) in such a way that I doubt whether many people in modern times have ever managed to develop a real feeling for the underlying rhythms, which were probably brought out by the musical accompaniment. I, for one, would not care to have to pronounce on Aristophanes' technical achievement in this field. In content, his lyrics are often witty, but would hardly seem so in translation unless pointed by rhyme and other modern devices. Sometimes they are scurrilous lampoons, riddles, or anecdotes with a sting in the tail. Some accompany a dance or choreographic manoeuvre, and describe the movements to be executed. Others are hymns, sometimes straightforward, sometimes with a touch of mockery or parody. The lyrics that seem to have appealed most to the last few generations, and that have earned Aristophanes his reputation for 'charm', are those that make mention of the countryside or any feature thereof. *The Birds* and *Peace*, in particular, contain attractive songs and lyrical passages on such themes. But even the

splendidly vulgar 'Frog Chorus', with its flatulent refrain, has been
elevated into this category, because it happens to mention marshes
and reeds: Victorian translations of it have a cloying prettiness, and
not only the farting, but also the drunkenness of the worshippers and
the frogs' marvellous joke about diving into the water to get out of
the rain, are tactfully ignored.

I hope that our own translations, in these three Penguin Classics*
volumes, will not be felt to have gone too far in the opposite direction,
and even that some idea of Aristophanes' qualities as a poet, in the full
Greek sense of the word, will have come through to the reader. For
to the Greeks, a poet was not simply a man who could compose in
metre – almost anybody could do that. (Indeed, until fairly recent
years there were quite large numbers of schoolchildren in this country
who could turn out a passable page of Greek iambics at the age of
fifteen or so.) A poet was a *maker*, a *creator*: but he was also a man who
– to quote Aristophanes himself – 'had a lesson to teach, made people
into better citizens'. Scholars have debated whether Aristophanes was
a die-hard conservative or an enthusiast for new ideas, whether he
favoured democracy or oligarchy, whether he was pro-Spartan; they
have pointed out all kinds of inconsistencies in the 'views' expressed
in his plays. They forget that he was a great Greek as well as a great
Athenian: his lesson for us is the central lesson of ancient Greek
civilization – *mêden agan*, the virtue of moderation. Pray Heaven we
may learn it.

D.B.

*The other two volumes contain *The Wasps, The Poet and the Women, The
Frogs* (translated by David Barrett) and *Lysistrata, The Acharnians, The Clouds*
(translated by Alan H. Sommerstein).

The Knights

Translated by Alan H. Sommerstein

Introductory Note to *The Knights*

The Knights was produced at the Lenaea early in 424 B.C., in the seventh year of the war against Sparta. The previous summer the war had taken what appeared to be a decisive turn in favour of Athens, and the manner in which this had happened had a marked effect on internal Athenian politics as well.

An Athenian force under Demosthenes had occupied the promontory of Pylos on the west coast of the Peloponnese. They had beaten off an attack, and with the help of naval reinforcements besieged their former Spartan besiegers on the neighbouring island of Sphacteria. Sparta, afraid of the possible loss of several hundred of their small citizen body, immediately made a truce and sent representatives to Athens to sue for peace; this mission is mentioned in *The Knights* (p. 66). Cleon, however, who was at this time the dominant personality in the Assembly, persuaded his fellow-citizens to impose pre-conditions that were and were meant to be unacceptable, and the peace mission came to nothing.

The siege of Sphacteria was resumed, but as the weeks passed with no news of its capture public opinion at Athens became restive and inclined to criticize Demosthenes. Cleon, seeking to take advantage of this feeling, proposed that extra troops should be sent, and implicitly called Nicias, the senior general then in Athens, a coward for not already having sailed to Pylos. Nicias promptly resigned his command in Cleon's favour, and Cleon, who is not known to have previously had any experience of military leadership whatever, sailed to Pylos with a small additional force. Before he left he promised to bring back the Spartans, dead or alive, within twenty days. It was afterwards believed that this promise was not as irresponsible as it sounded, because (it was said) Cleon had private information that Demosthenes intended shortly to storm the island in any case. This was done shortly after Cleon's arrival, and he returned with three hundred prisoners (over a hundred of them Spartan citizens) within the promised time.

This victory changed the whole course of the war. Ever since 431 the Spartans had invaded Attica annually and ravaged the country-side, so that the whole population had had to live within the fortified zone of the city and the Peiraeus. Now Athens held three hundred hostages, whom they announced they would put to death if Attica was again invaded. For the rest of 425 Athens took the offensive; and the whole credit for the transformation was given to Cleon. Honours were showered upon him, and his political influence, already great, became overwhelming. It was in this situation that Aristophanes for the first time produced a comedy in his own name.

The play is more than just an attack on Cleon, though the sheer venom of Aristophanes' hatred is unmatched in any of his works. It is a satire on the whole nature of politics and political leadership in Athens. As is repeatedly pointed out by the Chorus, the Sausage-Seller defeats his rival by outdoing him in those very qualities which make Cleon loathsome: the implication is that there is no other way to win influence over the sovereign People. Only at the end of the play does the Sausage-Seller reveal himself in his true colours as restorer of the 'good old days' for which Aristophanes' more sympathetic characters so often yearn. But can one in the real world expect a politician who has risen to the top by means of bribery, flattery and slander to become a paragon of virtue when he attains power? So the audience might well ask themselves. In the play it takes a miracle to give Thepeople his wits back. In life there are no miracles, and if the Athenians do not want all their politicians to become corrupt, even those who are honest by nature, then, Aristophanes suggests, they had better get their own wits about them and learn to distinguish between true and fraudulent merit, instead of awarding men like Cleon 'dining rights in the Town Hall for doing absolutely nothing'.

Aristophanes' hostility to Cleon was personal as well as political. In 426 Cleon had prosecuted him for 'slandering the City in the presence of foreigners' with his play *The Babylonians*, and he had been convicted. Aristophanes had dropped broad hints in *The Acharnians* (425) that he would shortly take his revenge, and he now does so. Cleon, it would seem, was again infuriated beyond measure by *The Knights*, and since the previous charge would not stick this time (no foreigners being present at the Lenaea), he threatened to prosecute

Aristophanes for falsely pretending to be an Athenian citizen. This accusation probably never came to trial; a passage in *The Wasps* seems to suggest that Aristophanes, perhaps fearing Cleon's influence over the juries ('the Comrades of the Order of the Three Obols', p. 46), offered some sort of apology. In any case, he continued to attack Cleon in play after play until Cleon's death in 422.*

In *The Knights* Cleon appears in the thin disguise of a slave from Paphlagonia in Asia Minor. This origin is chosen because of the similarity of the name to *paphlazein* 'to bubble' (cf. 'The pot is boiling over', p. 70). The character is called 'Cleon' in the manuscripts' indications of speakers and in their list of *dramatis personae*; but since in the text itself the character (as distinct from the real-life politician) is always called 'the Paphlagonian', I have so designated him in this translation. For the other two slaves, on the other hand, I have retained the manuscripts' names 'Nicias' and 'Demosthenes'; there seems to me no doubt that they are intended to represent these two generals, and if, as seems likely, the names were introduced into the *dramatis personae* by the conjecture of an ancient critic, that is not in itself a reason for inconveniencing the reader by removing them.

The Chorus consists of twenty-four *hippēs*, conventionally translated 'Knights', though 'cavalrymen' would be more accurate. The Athenian cavalry consisted of a thousand young men of rich and mostly aristocratic families (they were required to provide their own horses), who were naturally opposed to Cleon, the populist who had 'been in trade'. Indeed, it appears from a passage in *The Acharnians* that on one occasion they had forced him to 'cough up' a large sum of money, perhaps in order to avoid prosecution for bribery. They are thus ideal allies for the Sausage-Seller in this play.

It was believed in antiquity that Aristophanes' contemporary and rival Eupolis had had some hand in the composition of *The Knights*. Eupolis himself claimed to have 'collaborated with that baldhead in *The Knights* and made a gift of it to him', but that was after he had been stung by an accusation of plagiarism. Suspicion has chiefly

---

*This view of Cleon's prosecutions of Aristophanes is based on the opinions of J. van Leeuwen and D. M. MacDowell. An ancient biographer says that both prosecutions were brought directly after the production of *The Babylonians*, but it is then hard to see what the *Wasps* passage (lines 1284–91) refers to.

centred on the second *parabasis* (pp. 83–5); the reader may make up his own mind whether the tone of it is Aristophanic.

Although *The Knights* won first prize, Cleon's popularity was unaffected. Many of the poorer citizens who were his chief supporters may not have been present at the performance. At any rate, not many weeks later he was elected one of the board of ten generals, a position which he appears to have retained for the remaining two years of his life.

CHARACTERS

DEMOSTHENES | *slaves of Thepeople*
NICIAS |
A SAUSAGE-SELLER
PAPHLAGONIAN (*Cleon*) *steward to Thepeople*
THEPEOPLE *an elderly Athenian*
CHORUS OF KNIGHTS
TWO GIRLS (*The Peacetreaties*)
SEVERAL SLAVES

ACT ONE

SCENE: *Before the house of* THEPEOPLE *in Athens. Sounds of beating and cries of pain are heard within.*
[*Presently* DEMOSTHENES *and* NICIAS *burst out of the house, doubled up and screaming.*]

DEMOSTHENES: YOWWW! Help! Murder! It's that blasted Paphlagonian again – that horror master's gone and bought! Why don't the gods blast him to hell, him and his tricks? Well, why don't they? Ever since he infected the house, we've not had a day without a flogging!

NICIAS: Hear, hear! To hell with the Arch-Paphlagonian and all his lying tales – and quickly too!

DEMOSTHENES: How are you feeling now, poor thing?

NICIAS: Red and raw, like you.

DEMOSTHENES: Come on, then, why don't we sob a duet to an old Olympian melody?[1] [*They half hum, half sob a few bars together.*] Dammit, what are we standing here moaning for? We need to find a way out of this – a way to stop getting carved up.

NICIAS: What way, though?

DEMOSTHENES: You tell me.

NICIAS: No, you tell *me*.

[DEMOSTHENES *gives him a very black look.*]
Ah – ah – no need for a punch-up, now.

DEMOSTHENES: I *won't* tell you. Tell you what, though. *You* go ahead and say what we should do, and *then* I'll tell you.

NICIAS: I've not got the guts for that. What's the posh way of putting it – what does Euripides say? – oh yes! [*Falling suppliant at* DEMOSTHENES' *feet*] Oh, couldst thou now but speak my words for me![2]

DEMOSTHENES [*dragging him to his feet*]: Enough of that parsley sauce!³ What we've got to do is find a way to trip the light fantastic away from our master.

NICIAS: Away, away! that's an idea. Listen, old chap. Say the word 'way', like this, short and sharp, 'way'.

DEMOSTHENES: All right. Way.

NICIAS: Very good. Now say 'runner'.

DEMOSTHENES: Runner.

NICIAS: That's right. Now do like you were fucking yourself. Starting slowly, like this, 'way', then 'runner', speeding up a little, you see, and then keep repeating faster and faster.

DEMOSTHENES [*following instructions*]: Way, runner, way-runner-way-*run away*!

NICIAS: There! Isn't it absolute ecstasy?

DEMOSTHENES: Well, yes and no. You see, there's a word you used that's sort of making my back tingle. It's a bad omen.

NICIAS: What do you mean?

DEMOSTHENES: They say too much fucking yourself is bad for the skin. And running away, if you're caught, that can be bad for the skin too! [*He points to his whip-scarred back.*]

NICIAS: Well, if that's how you feel, there's only one thing for it. We must g-go and p-p-prostrate ourselves as s-s-suppliants at one of the holy st-t-tatues of the gods.

DEMOSTHENES: What do you mean, st-t-tatues? You don't even believe in the gods.

NICIAS: I didn't use to, but I do now.

DEMOSTHENES: Why?

NICIAS: Because if there weren't any gods, I wouldn't be so bloody god-forsaken. Right or wrong?

DEMOSTHENES: Mm, you have a point there. But we're still looking for our brilliant idea. Here, for heaven's sake, hadn't I better tell these people here [*indicating the audience*] what this is all about?

NICIAS: All right. Just one thing, though, people. We'd like you to let us know: are you enjoying the play?

DEMOSTHENES [*after a pause; apparently satisfied with the audience's response*]: All right, here goes. Our master is a real case. He's a countryman and bad-tempered to match, he's got a morbid craving for beans,⁴ and he flies into a fiery rage in no time. His name's Thepeople, that's right, Thepeople, and he lives on the Pnyx,⁵ and he's as dyspeptic a deaf old man as you ever met. Well last New Moon's day he went and bought a new slave, a tanner from Paphlagonia, and a greater swine of a stool-pigeon never walked this earth. This tanner-fellow soon got to know master's ways, and then he fell at his feet, licked his boots, wheedled, flattered, sucked up, everything to take him in, with all the trimmings – in real leather. 'Thepeople,' he'd say, 'why don't you just try one case today and then have a good bath and get stuck into a slap-up supper on your three obols?⁶ Shall I serve the first course now?' Whereupon he grabs something one of *us* has been cooking, this Paphlagonian does, and gives it to master so master will think *he* cooked it and love him even more. Why, only the other day I'd baked a lovely Spartan cake down in Pylos,⁷ and round he sneaks and grabs it and serves up *my* cake as if it was all his work! And he won't let anyone but himself wait on master. If we try, he chases us away. All through dinner he stands behind master with his fly-whisk (also real leather) and flicks away all the other politicians. And his oracles! He's for ever trotting them out, throwing Sibylline dust⁸ in master's eyes, and when he thinks he's got master sufficiently ga-ga, he starts in with his lies. He'll say anything if it'll get one of us a flogging. And then he makes the round of the whole household, taking bribes, blackmailing people, making everyone's teeth chatter. 'Look at Hylas,' he says. 'Master gave him the works yesterday. All my doing. Best get on the right side of me, that's my advice, else it'll be your turn next.' And we pay up. What else can we do? If we say no, we'll only find ourselves shitting eight times as hard when he spins his yarn to master. [*To* NICIAS] We've got to think hard, old chap. What can we do? Who is there for us to turn to?

NICIAS: I still favour my runner plan. Old chap.

DEMOSTHENES: But how can we do that without that Paphlagonian seeing us? There's nothing he doesn't see. He bestrides the world, one foot in Pylos and the other here on the Pnyx. He's the All-Present – he can have his arse in Bigholia,⁹ his hands in the public purse, and his mind in Robbers' Vale, all at one and the same moment! No, there's nothing left for us to do but lie down and die. Or – what do you think would be the noblest, the manliest kind of death?

NICIAS: Noblest ... manliest ... I know! Let's do what Themistocles did,[10] drink a cup of bull's blood! What could be a nobler death than that?

DEMOSTHENES: I've got a better idea than that. If we're going to drink, why don't we have some good neat wine from the cup of Good Fortune? Maybe that'll help us figure out a good plan.

NICIAS: Neat wine indeed! Trust you to find an excuse for a drink! Liquor never helped anyone to plan anything.

DEMOSTHENES: You watch out, you old water-bibber-babbler! Don't you laugh at wine. Wine's got great creative potential, I'd have you know. There is nothing in the world that has produced so many great inventions as wine has. Use a bit of observation. When is it men get rich? When do they bring off their business deals, win their lawsuits, feel happy, do good to their friends? When they drink, that's when! Come on now, bring me out a jugful. I want to oil my brain and get a few ideas.

NICIAS: I don't know what's going to become of us with all your boozing, I really don't.

DEMOSTHENES: Never you mind. Let's have the stuff. I'll lie down for a bit.

[NICIAS *goes into the house;* DEMOSTHENES *lies on the ground in a luxuriating pose.*]

Just a drink or two, and the whole street will be awash with my brilliant ideas and plans and policies.

NICIAS [*returning with jug*]: Whew, that was lucky that I didn't get caught!

DEMOSTHENES: What's our Paphlagonian up to?

NICIAS: Oh, he's been guzzling a haul of gorgeous cakes, the bastard, confiscated from convicts, and now he's snoring, dead drunk, lying on his back among his hides.

DEMOSTHENES: Come on then, open up, let's have a libation. A real good big one.

NICIAS [*pouring out a cup*]: Here you are. Let the libation be to Good Fortune. [*He hands the cup to* DEMOSTHENES.]

DEMOSTHENES: This cup to Good Fortune, vintage Pramnian![11]

[*Pours a little of the wine on the ground.*] Good Fortune, over to you, let's have an idea! [*He drinks the cup off.*]

NICIAS: What does she say?

DEMOSTHENES: *He*'s asleep, right? Creep inside and pinch those oracles that he keeps and bring them out here.

NICIAS: Okay. You are sure that was *Good* Fortune, not her ugly sister? [*He goes inside again.*]

DEMOSTHENES [*drawing the jug towards him*]: Let's get this a bit closer, so I can oil my brain again. [*He downs another cup.*]

NICIAS [*re-emerging with a scroll*]: Gosh, you should hear him snoring and farting in there, that Paphlagonian. So sound asleep he was, I got hold of his most closely guarded secrets and he never knew I was there. Look, here's the oracle.

DEMOSTHENES: Good man! Here, let's have a look at it.

   [NICIAS *gives him the scroll.*]
And pour me out another cup while you're about it, could you? [*As he opens up the scroll*] Now let's see what's in here ... Good gracious! Quick, give me the cup!

NICIAS [*doing so*]: There. What's the oracle say?

DEMOSTHENES [*who has finished the cup he was given a moment ago*]: Pour me another.

NICIAS: 'Pour me another'? That's an odd thing for an oracle to say. [*Nevertheless he does refill* DEMOSTHENES' *cup.*]

DEMOSTHENES [*after a moment's further reading*]: Holy Bakis![12]

NICIAS: What is it?

DEMOSTHENES: Let's have the cup again, d'you mind?

NICIAS: This Bakis is certainly some drinker!

DEMOSTHENES [*who has been reading more*]: What?! You villainous swine! No wonder you were guarding this oracle so fiercely – it's about Your Paphlagonianship itself, and you didn't dare let it be seen!

NICIAS: What's all this, what's all this?

DEMOSTHENES: It's all in here. *He*'s finished. *He*'s had it.

NICIAS: How, how?

DEMOSTHENES: It's here in the oracle, in black and white. First of all, it says, there will come a hemp-seller, who will direct all the City's affairs.[13]

NICIAS: Seller number one. Yes, what's next?

DEMOSTHENES: Then after him, a sheep-seller.[14]

NICIAS: Seller number two. And what becomes of him?

DEMOSTHENES: He shall hold power until another man appears who is even more loathsome than he is, and then he shall fall. For on his heels will appear a leather-seller, our Paphlagonian, a robber and a shrieker, with a voice like an overloaded sewer.

NICIAS: The sheep-seller was to be overthrown by a leather-seller?

DEMOSTHENES: That's right.

NICIAS: We're in the soup, then, aren't we? Isn't there just one more seller to follow?

DEMOSTHENES: Don't worry, there is – but you'll never guess what he sells.

NICIAS: Tell me, tell me, who is he?

DEMOSTHENES: You'd like to know?

NICIAS: Please!

DEMOSTHENES: The man destined to evict our Paphlagonian is a *sausage-seller*.

NICIAS: A sausage-seller! Poseidon, what a profession! But where are we supposed to find him?

DEMOSTHENES: Well, we can look.

[*They begin to scan the audience; but at this moment the* SAUSAGE-SELLER *himself enters by a side passage. He is extremely rough and dirty, and carries on his back a cooking-table, knives and other implements, and long strings of sausages.*]

NICIAS: Look, look! The gods be praised! Here comes one now, going to the market!

DEMOSTHENES [*to* SAUSAGE-SELLER]: Hey, you! You there with the blessing of heaven on you! Come over here, beloved sausage-seller! Become our saviour and the City's too!

SAUSAGE-SELLER: Wot is it? Woddaya want me for?

DEMOSTHENES: Come here and let us tell you how fortunate and happy the gods have made you!

[*The* SAUSAGE-SELLER, *scratching his head, goes over to them.*]

NICIAS: You take off that table of his and tell him all about the holy oracle. I'd better go and keep an eye on our Paphlagonian. [*He goes into the house.*]

DEMOSTHENES: Come on now, put down all your stuff, and then kiss the earth and make obeisance to the gods.

SAUSAGE-SELLER [*after complying with these instructions*]: A' right. Nah wot's all this abaht?

DEMOSTHENES: Blessings and riches are showered upon you! Today you are nothing, tomorrow you will be everything! You are the destined lord and master of Athens, the most blest of cities!

SAUSAGE-SELLER: Look 'ere, mate, can't yer see I got to wash aht these blinking guts and sell me sausages? I ain't got time to waste with you making a fool of me.

DEMOSTHENES: You blind fool, talking about guts! Look over there [*indicating the audience*]! Do you see all those rows and rows of people?

SAUSAGE-SELLER: Yerss.

DEMOSTHENES: Of all these you shall be the absolute ruler. You will be monarch of all you survey – the Market Square, the harbours, the Pnyx, everywhere. You will plant your foot on the Council's neck and compel the Generals to toe the line. You will have the right to throw whom you will into prison, and to screw whom you will in the Town Hall![15]

SAUSAGE-SELLER: Wot me?

DEMOSTHENES: Yes, you – and you haven't seen the tenth part of it yet. Come on, stand on this table and look round the horizon. Can't you see all our subject islands?

SAUSAGE-SELLER: Yerss, I see them.

DEMOSTHENES: And our trading posts, and all the ships plying to and fro?

SAUSAGE-SELLER: Yerss.

DEMOSTHENES: Don't you see how the gods have blessed you? Now try and look even further. Look out of the corner of your right eye, and you'll see Caria; and out of the left, right away to Carthage.[16]

SAUSAGE-SELLER [*trying to comply*]: Ouch! Bless me if I ain't pulled a neck muscle! [*He overbalances and falls off the table.*]

DEMOSTHENES [*picking him up*]: What I mean is that all these countries will be your stock in trade, I mean your empire. This oracle which I have predicts that you will become a Great Man.

SAUSAGE-SELLER: A sausage-seller be a great man? Ha! ha! Come on, tell me another.

DEMOSTHENES: No, I'm serious. That's precisely your qualification to be a Great Man – that you're born and bred in the Market Square, and that you're a brazen-faced rogue.

SAUSAGE-SELLER: But look 'ere – I don't think I deserve to be great.

DEMOSTHENES: What's all this about not deserving to be great? You've not got any secret virtues on your conscience, have you?

[*The* SAUSAGE-SELLER *shakes his head.*]

You're not of good birth, by any chance?

SAUSAGE-SELLER: The worst birth you could think of.

DEMOSTHENES: Thank heaven! That's just what's wanted for a politician.

SAUSAGE-SELLER: But look 'ere – I 'ardly went to school, I got no learning. Why, I can only just read an' write.

DEMOSTHENES. What a shame you can only just! If only you couldn't at all! Come off it, you don't think politics is for the educated, do you, or the honest? It's for illiterate scum like you now! I beg you, don't let slip the marvellous opportunity the holy oracle has revealed.

SAUSAGE-SELLER: Why, what's the oracle say?

DEMOSTHENES: It's full of blessings, cleverly concealed in riddling words. [*Unrolls the scroll and recites.*]

When that within the great jaws of the crook-talon'd Eagle of
                                                           Leather
Shall be entrappèd the serpent Stupidity, drinker of swine's blood,
Then shall the tannery-brine of the Paphlagonians perish,
Then to the sellers of guts (unless they prefer to continue
Flogging their sausages still) shall the god give the power and the
                                                           glory.

SAUSAGE-SELLER: 'Ere, 'ow's that got ter do with me?

DEMOSTHENES: Well, the Eagle of Leather is our Paphlagonian here. [*Pointing at Cleon in the front row of the audience.*]

SAUSAGE-SELLER: But wot's 'crook-taloned' mean?

DEMOSTHENES: Why, that he's a crook and a thief, of course.

SAUSAGE-SELLER: I see. And the serpint?

DEMOSTHENES: That's most obvious of all. A serpent's long and thin, right? and so's a sausage. Then a serpent drinks blood, okay? and so does a sausage. So it means that the serpent, that means you, will vanquish the Eagle of Leather, so long as it doesn't let it talk it out of it.

43

SAUSAGE-SELLER: So long as wot doesn't let wot – never mind. I like that oracle. But I still don't know how you expect me ter manage all the People's business.

DEMOSTHENES: Dead easy. Just carry on doing what you've always done, Mix all the City's policies into a complete hash, butter the People up a bit,[17] throw in a pinch of rhetoric as a sweetener, and there you are. All the other essentials of a good politician you've got already. You've a voice to scare a Gorgon, you were brought up in the Market Square, oh yes and born in the gutter – what more do you need? And all the oracles and Pythian Apollo himself point the way to greatness. Here, put on this wreath and pour libation to Stupidity.

[*The* SAUSAGE-SELLER *does as he is told, using the wine brought out earlier.*]

There you are; now for the fray!

SAUSAGE-SELLER: But 'oo will there be to 'elp me? That there Paphlagonian frightens the rich aht of their wits, and the poor, when 'e's arahnd, they can't even keep their arses shut.

DEMOSTHENES: Have no fear, the Knights will be here, a thousand of them, all hating his guts – I beg your pardon, all hating him. They'll be on your side. So will all honest and decent citizens, and all our audience here – well, all those that have any brains; and so will I, and the god of Delphi too. Oh, and by the way, you needn't be afraid to look at his face. It won't look like the real one. You see, our sponsor was a bit worried in case you-know-who might – you know what.[18] Ah, but he'll be recognized all right; as I say, we've a brainy audience!

NICIAS [*shouting from within*]: Look out! Look out! It's the Paphlagonian! He's going to come out!

[*And indeed out of the house comes the* PAPHLAGONIAN, *a tall, blond, powerful and exceedingly ugly slave. In manner he is slightly, but only slightly, more polished than the* SAUSAGE-SELLER.]

PAPHLAGONIAN [*thunderously*]: By the Twelve Gods, I'll not let you get away with this! Conspiring against the People again, I'll be bound. [*Seizing from the* SAUSAGE-SELLER *the cup used for the libation*] Ha! what have we here? A Chalcidian cup, indeed! So the two of you are plotting to stir up a revolt in Chalcidice![19] This cup is irrefutable proof, I say, irrefutable proof. Villains, you

shall perish! The just rage of the People will annihilate you!
[*The* SAUSAGE-SELLER *takes to his heels.*]

DEMOSTHENES: Hey! Sausage-seller! Noble sausage-seller! Come
back! Why are you running away? Don't give up the ship! –
Knights! Knights! Come to the rescue! [*Breaks into song.*][20]

> Come on here, come on here, come on every Knight,
> Come and charge, come and charge upon the right!
> Here they come, here they come, wheel around and fight,
>> And put the hated foe to flight!
>
> See the dust, see the dust, as it rises from the ground – the Knights
>> are close at hand!
> They are near, they are near, and Panaetius and Simon come at my
>> command!
>
> Come on here, come on here, come on every Knight,
> Come and charge, come and charge upon the right!
> Here they come, here they come, wheel around and fight,
>> And put the hated foe to flight!

[*The* CHORUS OF KNIGHTS *charge in, long-haired, fastidiously
dressed young men, and make straight for the* PAPHLAGONIAN.]

CHORUS:
> Strike, strike and never cease
> The wrecker of our peace –
> He's the whirlpool who sucks all the Revenue away;
> The cheat, the cheat, the cheat!
> This word we now repeat,
> 'Cos he repeats all his cheating tricks several times a day.
>
> Now chase him and catch him and beat him, bash him, mash him,
>> smash him, just like us.
> Set upon him, scout him, flout him, shout and call him names and
>> swear and cuss!
>
> Now take care that he don't escape from you,
> 'Cos he knows all the back ways to get through,
> Like Eucrates[21] once to his warehouse ran
>> And hid himself among the bran!

[*Music continues as the* CHORUS, *aided by* DEMOSTHENES *and the*

SAUSAGE-SELLER, *who has returned with new heart, surround the* PAPHLAGONIAN *and rain blows upon him.*]

PAPHLAGONIAN [*through music*]: Help! Members of the jury! Comrades of the Order of the Three Obols![22] Remember how I've fed you all these years with my prosecutions – right or wrong, I never gave a damn, I just shouted as hard as I could! Come quickly and help! I'm being assaulted by a gang of conspirators!

LEADER: And you deserve it too. Haven't you had your finger in the public pie for years? Don't you size up all the ex-magistrates when they render their accounts,[23] feeling them like figs to see if they're dry or just ripening or really juicy? And if you find one of them's a bit of a novice at political infighting, don't you drag him all the way home from the Chersonese,[24] floor him with a speech miles below the belt, get a hold on him, twist his arm half off and then devour him? And anyone in the City who's a bit of an innocent lamb, rich and honest and not caring for squabbles, you've got your eye on him too. No one's safe.

PAPHLAGONIAN: What, so you Knights are in this too? Don't you realize that the indignities I'm suffering are all on your account? I was just about to propose that in honour of your gallantry a public monument ought to be set up on the Acropolis! [*He ducks, and, protecting his head with his arms, tries to force a way through the* CHORUS, *but they block him by weight of numbers and relentlessly continue hitting him.*]

CHORUS:
>The twister and the liar!
>He thinks we've lost our fire,
And he flatters us as though we were old and had no brain!
>Don't try and take to flight,
>For, go you left or right,
We will bash you so hard you will never walk again!

PAPHLAGONIAN:
Let the People and the City witness how these swine are winding me!

LEADER:
So you think you'll cow the City with your shouts again? Well, we shall see!

SAUSAGE-SELLER:
>No he won't, for I'll outdo him,
>And beat him, and shout him down!

CHORUS:
>If you really can outdo him,
>>We'll give you the victor's crown!
>So we'll now have a battle of impudence,
>See if yours or if his is more immense;
>And if you can defeat him in every way,
>>Then we will take the cake[25] today!

[*Music continues as the* PAPHLAGONIAN, *held helpless by the* CHORUS, *and the* SAUSAGE-SELLER, *restrained from assaulting him by* DEMOSTHENES, *shout at each other at the top of their unpleasant voices.*]

PAPHLAGONIAN: I indict this man for high treason! I charge him with supplying strings of sausages to undergird warships in the Peloponnesian fleet!

SAUSAGE-SELLER: I indict this man for 'igh gluttony! 'E rushes into the Tahn 'All every day wiv a hempty stomach, and a moment later rushes aht wiv a full one![26]

DEMOSTHENES: And with a bag stuffed full of public bread and meat and fish into the bargain, which it's strictly forbidden to consume off the premises! Not even Pericles was allowed to do that!

PAPHLAGONIAN: I'll sentence you to death, that's what I'll do!

SAUSAGE-SELLER: I bet I shaht three times as lahd as you.

PAPHLAGONIAN: I'll beat you hollow with my raucous yell!

SAUSAGE-SELLER: I'll scream yer dahn and send yer strite to 'ell!

PAPHLAGONIAN: When you're a General, I'll accuse and try you!

SAUSAGE-SELLER: I'll chop yer back in tiny bits and fry you!

PAPHLAGONIAN: My lying talk will catch you by the heels.

SAUSAGE-SELLER: I'll cut yer footsies up for 'igh-class meals.

PAPHLAGONIAN: Just look me in the eye now, if you dare!

SAUSAGE-SELLER: I'm also a son of Athens' Market Square!

PAPHLAGONIAN: Another word and I'll cut up your hide!

SAUSAGE-SELLER: Come on, you shit, I gotter chuck you ahtside!

PAPHLAGONIAN: What impudence! I'm a *real* thief – are you?

SAUSAGE-SELLER: Yerss, and if caught, a first-rate liar too!

PAPHLAGONIAN [*breaking free*]: That's trespassing on my territory!

Members of the Executive Committee![27] I hereby indict this man for being in unlawful and sacrilegious possession of consecrated guts on which no tithe has been paid!

[*During the succeeding chorus the* PAPHLAGONIAN *and the* SAUSAGE-SELLER *continue to glower and shake their fists at each other.*]

CHORUS:

> O villain and monster and screamer so base,
> The whole of the City is full of your face
> > (In both of its senses);
> O'er all the Assembly and all of the Courts,
> Indictments and taxes and tolls at the ports,
> > Are spread your offences.
>
> You stir up the mud and you muddy the stream,
> You've made all of Athens stone deaf with your scream,
> > And drained her of money;
> You take up your stand on the top of a cliff
> To spy the approach of the tribute,[28] as if
> > The tribute were tunny [29] –
> > And don't think that's funny!

PAPHLAGONIAN: I know just how and where this conspiracy was stitched together!

SAUSAGE-SELLER: Well, you bloody well oughter know abaht stitching. 'S yer trade, innit? Like I sell sausages, you stitch shoes together. Or wot you *call* shoes. I remember the time you pulled a fast one on those farmers with cutting up yer leather so it looked thicker than wot it was – *and* yer chose a bad animal to take the 'ide off as well. They all thought it was good solid stuff, and a day later they fahnd they 'ad shoes six inches wider than wot their feet were!

DEMOSTHENES: That's just what he did to me. Just the same thing. Made me the laughing-stock of all my friends and neighbours. I hadn't got two miles out of town, and my shoes were so big I was swimming in them!

CHORUS:

> > The leopard keeps his spots
> > The same from start to end;

48

He's full of shamelessness,
　　The politician's friend.

All foreigners of wealth
　　You milk to earn your keep;
And at the sorry sight
　　All honest statesmen[30] weep.

But now – O joy, O bliss! –
　　Appears a champion new,
Who's manifestly much
　　More villainous than you.

For he'll surpass you far,
　　It's obvious to see,
In trickery and crime
　　And sheer audacity.

LEADER:
Now, you who come whence all men come who reach the top
　　　　　　　　　　　　　　　　　　　　　　today,
Prove once for all that decent education doesn't pay.

SAUSAGE-SELLER: I'll tell yer first of all wot kind of a cit'zen 'e is.

PAPHLAGONIAN: Look here, I should speak first.

SAUSAGE-SELLER: Why? I'm as big a crook as you are *or* bigger.

LEADER: If that doesn't shut him up, trot out your ignoble ancestry
as well.

PAPHLAGONIAN: I say I should speak first.

SAUSAGE-SELLER: No, by Zeus!

PAPHLAGONIAN: By Zeus, yes!

SAUSAGE-SELLER: By Poseidon, no! I'll fight yer for it first.

PAPHLAGONIAN: I shall burst in a moment!

SAUSAGE-SELLER: I won't never let yer –

LEADER: Oh, please do! Please do let him burst!

PAPHLAGONIAN: Where did you get the audacity to speak in oppo-
sition to me?

SAUSAGE-SELLER: 'Cos I can talk as well as you, and garnish my
speech with the best sauces too.

PAPHLAGONIAN: You can talk, eh? I suppose you can take a case all
red and raw, dress it up beautifully and serve it to the jury, yes?

You know what? I think you've got swelled head. A lot of people get that way. You had some simple little case against a resident foreigner. You burnt the midnight oil over it, you repeated your speech to yourself walking down the street, you took the pledge, you bored your friends stiff with reciting extracts. When the day came you managed to win the case, and now you think you're an orator. [*Shakes his head.*] I pity your simplicity.

SAUSAGE-SELLER: Taken the pledge, 'ave I? Wot's your liquor, then, that makes you able to paralyse every tongue in Athens with one wag of your own?

PAPHLAGONIAN: Who is there that can compare to me? When I've had my pickled tunny fish, topped by a gallon of neat wine, I can screw the Generals in Pylos to the wall!

SAUSAGE-SELLER: Well, when I've gulped dahn a cow's stomach and a pig's guts, drunk orf the gravy and not washed me 'ands, I can throttle every politician in tahn, and Nicias too!

LEADER: We're delighted with your performance so far, but we do hope you don't intend to slurp down *all* the national gravy yourself.

PAPHLAGONIAN: Did you ever eat the Milesians' bass and then put the wind up their arse?[31]

SAUSAGE-SELLER: No, but I'll 'ave pleasure in eating a few ribs o' beef and then buying some juicy mining concessions!

PAPHLAGONIAN: I'll pounce on the Council and shake them out of their little wits!

SAUSAGE-SELLER: I'll stuff up your arsehole like a sausage-skin!

PAPHLAGONIAN: I'll grab you by the backside and throw you out of town!

DEMOSTHENES: If you do, you'll have me to reckon with as well!

PAPHLAGONIAN: I'll shove you in the stocks unless you yield!

SAUSAGE-SELLER: I'll charge you with desertion in the field!

PAPHLAGONIAN: I'll stretch your hide, I'll give you no relief!

SAUSAGE-SELLER: I'll make your skin a wallet for a thief!

PAPHLAGONIAN: I'll pin you to the ground with iron pegs!

SAUSAGE-SELLER: I'll make bad mincemeat of your arms and legs!

PAPHLAGONIAN: I'll pluck your eyelashes from out each eye!

SAUSAGE-SELLER: I'll slit your crop, and like a fowl you'll die!

[They wrestle with each other. Soon the SAUSAGE-SELLER *has the* PAPHLAGONIAN *on the ground.]*

DEMOSTHENES [*to* SAUSAGE-SELLER]:

> Yes, prop his cakehole open wide,
>   His reeking tongue pull out,
> And then look very carefully
>   Beneath his swinish snout,
> And while his mouth gapes large and broad
>   (His arsehole gapes thus ever)
> Examine him for little spots
>   In case he's got swine-fever.

CHORUS [*to* SAUSAGE-SELLER]:

> O heat than fire yet more intense!
>   Your speech all speech surpasses
> In brazen, barefaced impudence!
>   Your arrogance first-class is.
> Now nothing common do or mean,
>   But get a throttling grip
> And wring his neck; for now you're seen
>   To have him on the hip.

LEADER:

> Now get in close and smash him up – you'll find his face turns
>   yellow;
> I know him coward through and through, this Paphlagonian
>   fellow.

SAUSAGE-SELLER: 'E's been the same all 'is life. Look wot 'appened when 'e pretended to be a big tough man and went and reaped someone else's 'arvest.[32] Look wot 'e's done with the ears o' Spartan corn 'e brought back. 'E's chained 'em all up and letting 'em parch away till 'e sees an opportunity to make a killing by selling them.

PAPHLAGONIAN: I'm not afraid of you, not while the Council Chamber stands and the People sits in assembly! [*Aside*] With open mouth and empty brainbox.

CHORUS:

> How shameless the colour that stays in his face!
> Of remorse or repentance there isn't a trace!

If I do not hate you and wish you were dead,
Then a sheet may I be on Cratinus's bed![33]
And when he's finished weeing, that very same day
May I sing in the chorus in Morsimus' play![34]
O bee that so often in search of more honey
Alights upon flowers all teeming with money,
I wish that as fast as you suck the cash up
You would puke it all out so the People could sup.
For then would I raise old Simonides' song,
'Let's drink to the triumph' – of right over wrong![35]

And the man that tests the bread,
    Who comes of noble line,
Will quickly lose his head
    (With the help of potent wine)
And sing 'Now joy will follow!
    No more will *he* attack us!
All glory to Apollo
    And Bacchi-Bacchi-Bacchus!'

PAPHLAGONIAN: I vow that your shamelessness will never surpass mine. If I fail, may I never taste the sacrifices to the God of Public Meetings again!

SAUSAGE-SELLER: And I swear, by all the fists that 'ave pummelled me right since I was a boy, and by all the carving-knives that have ever been brandished at me, overcome you I will. Not for nuffing did I eat gutter scraps for twenty years to grow big and strong like wot I am nah.

PAPHLAGONIAN: Gutter scraps? Huh! Dog's food! And you dare fight, you fool, with a deadly dog-eating monkey like me?

SAUSAGE-SELLER: Yeah! Monkey business' been my trade since I was so 'igh. Know 'ow I useter diddle the cooks? I sang out, 'Look, the spring's 'ere,' says I, 'the swallow's come, don't yer see 'im?' and they all gawped up at the sky, and then I whipped some o' their meat.

LEADER: I must congratulate you on your foresight about that meat. It's as true of stolen meat as of stinging nettles – you can only eat 'em before the swallow comes.[36]

SAUSAGE-SELLER: And o' course, none on 'em ever saw a thing. Or if they did, I'd just tuck it behind my bollocks and swear by all the gods I knew that I'd never stolen it, not never. Fact I remember there was some politician feller, saw me at it and 'e said, 'This lad will go far,' 'e said, ''e'll be the People's watchdog one day.'

LEADER: Well predicted! And you can see how he knew. Pinch the meat, stuff it up your arse and act the little innocent – how could such an infant prodigy fail to make his mark?

PAPHLAGONIAN: I'll stop your tongue yet, and yours too, What's-your-name. I'll sweep down upon you like a rushing mighty wind, and throw land, sea and sky into confusion.

SAUSAGE-SELLER: Well, in that case I'll take in sausage and run before the storm, and you can do what you something well like.

DEMOSTHENES: And if there's a leak, I'll be there to man the pumps.

PAPHLAGONIAN [drawing a deep breath]: You have embezzled a sum from the Treasury that runs into five figures, and I swear you shall pay for your villainy!

LEADER [to SAUSAGE-SELLER]: Ahoy there, slacken sail! Nor'-easterly gale getting up, blowing straight from Informerland!

SAUSAGE-SELLER: You got sixty thousand drachmas from the Potidaeans, and don't deny it![37]

PAPHLAGONIAN: Would you be prepared to take six thousand to keep quiet about it?

LEADER: I'm sure he would, with pleasure. [To SAUSAGE-SELLER] You can let out a bit more sail now, I think the wind's dropping.

PAPHLAGONIAN:
　　　　I'll have you fined for bribery
　　　　A million drachs, for sure!
　　　　No, wait a minute, that's too light.
　　　　One million? Make it four!

SAUSAGE-SELLER:
　　　　I'll 'ave you fined for cowardice
　　　　Not less 'n twenny times,
　　　　And thahsandfold for robbery
　　　　And all yer other crimes!

PAPHLAGONIAN:
　　　　Your ancestors were of the race
　　　　That bears Athena's carse![38]

SAUSAGE-SELLER: Your grandad was a bodyguard –

PAPHLAGONIAN: Of whom?

SAUSAGE-SELLER: King Happy-arse!³⁹

PAPHLAGONIAN: Monkey!

SAUSAGE-SELLER: Villain!

LEADER: Get him now!

[*The* SAUSAGE-SELLER *and* DEMOSTHENES, *supported by the* CHORUS, *give the* PAPHLAGONIAN *a pasting.*]

PAPHLAGONIAN: Help! Conspirators! Eeow!

CHORUS: Hit him hard! Let's see you launch
    Punishing punches at his paunch!

[*Eventually, the* PAPHLAGONIAN *being quite black and blue, his attackers desist.*]

LEADER:

    O choicest meat, O soul of souls the best,
    Of Athens and her People saviour blest,
    So well you used each skilful verbal ploy
    To beat your foe, we scarce can voice our joy.

PAPHLAGONIAN: Don't think I'm unaware how this conspiracy was built up. I know exactly how it was fixed and who oiled the wheels of it.

LEADER [*to* SAUSAGE-SELLER]: Quick! Think of some good workshop expressions, or we're sunk.

SAUSAGE-SELLER: And you needn't think *I'm* unaware wot you're up to with the Argives. You know wot all those little trips of 'is to Argos are abaht? 'E *says* 'e's trying to bring 'em into the war on our side, but all the time 'e's busy there intriguing with the Spartans. And I know where 'is plot gets its rivets from. The steel will be tempered with them Spartan prisoners we've got.

LEADER: Bravo! Tempered steel to match his oily wheels. That's the stuff!

SAUSAGE-SELLER: Yerss, and there are Spartans 'elping to 'ammer it aht as well. And not all your silver and gold nor all the threats of those pals of yours is gonna stop me telling the 'ole story to the People.

PAPHLAGONIAN: I've had enough of this. I'm going straight to the Council. I'll tell them about the whole lot of you and all your anti-Athenian conspiracies. How you hold secret meetings on the Acropolis at night. How you've made a deal with the King of

Persia. How you've been and cooked up a great big Boeotian cheese
of a plot[40] with the Thebans.

SAUSAGE-SELLER [*innocently*]: Oh, you know the price of Boeotian
cheese, do you? I wonder if you could tell me how much it is?

PAPHLAGONIAN: I'll have you flat on my tanning-board yet, I swear.
[*He storms out.*]

LEADER: Now what's your plan? What do you think you'll do? Now
we'll see if that story of yours is true, how you stole that meat and
hid it behind your bollocks. You'd better dash off to the Council
Chamber right away now. You know what *he's* going to do – rush
in there, scream himself hoarse, and make the most dreadful
accusations against all of us.

SAUSAGE-SELLER: Yerss, I'd best be off. But first of all p'r'aps I
ought to get rid of my guts and my carving-knives. [*He gives these
to some* SLAVES *who carry them away.*]

DEMOSTHENES [*who has fetched a bottle of ointment*]: Come on now,
rub this on your neck, so you'll be able to slip out of his grip when
he tries to throttle you with a lie.

SAUSAGE-SELLER: Good idea. Thanks a lot, coach.

DEMOSTHENES: And now, if you'd just eat this piece of garlic.

SAUSAGE-SELLER: What for?

DEMOSTHENES: To make you a real fighting-cock.[41]

[*The* SAUSAGE-SELLER *eats the garlic.*]

On your way, then!

SAUSAGE-SELLER: Okay, I'm off.

DEMOSTHENES: Don't forget, use your teeth and your tongue well,
and grab his comb in your beak and gobble up the feathers. See
you soon!

[*The* SAUSAGE-SELLER *goes out, and* DEMOSTHENES *goes into the
house.*]

CHORUS:
> Go your way, and may fortune go with you!
> May you fare as I dearly desire!
> May the Orators' Patron protect you,
> May Zeus all your speeches inspire!
> May you conquer, and then to your followers
> A hero triumphant return;
> And may your linguistic persuasion

A garland of victory earn!
– And now, dear spectators, attend us;
We'll adopt a professional tone,
For we know that you civilized people
Have courted each Muse on your own.

LEADER [*advancing to address the audience*]:
No poet of the older generation
Would win from us such keen cooperation
In speaking for him in a comic play
As the young man for whom we speak today.
Our poet's worthy of this honour great:
He speaks the truth, he hates the men we hate,
He does not shy from danger like a child
But dares the storm and braves the whirlwind wild.
He says that he's been asked on every side
The reason why he's not till now applied
To have a Chorus of his own[42] and seek
Crowns for himself; on this he's bid us speak.
He says he wasn't stupid, but he thought
This job was with more difficulties fraught
Than any other job that mortals do:
Though many court the Muse, she yields to few.
He knew your favour was a fickle jade
And ditched old poets when it saw them fade:
Just look at what old Magnes had to bear
When streaks of white appeared among his hair!
Year after year, till then, he took the crown;
He had no equal, not in all the town.
But though he spoke to you in every voice,
Lute, Lydian, Bird, Fly, Frog[43] to suit your choice,
Though in his prime you loved him, when with age
His jokes grew stale, you chucked him off the stage.
Then there's Cratinus, who in his great days
Flowed o'er the plains in a great flood of praise,
And in his might uprooting every tree,
Oak, plane, competitor, swirled out to sea.
At drinking-parties you would ne'er go wrong
If you could sing his 'Architects of Song'

56

Or 'Bribery-Goddess of the Figwood Shoe'.[44]
Such was he when he bloomed. Now, shame on you!
He in his dotage babbles round the City,
But on his misery you take no pity.
He's like a lyre that's lost its pristine tone:
His pegs have fallen out, his strings are gone;
He's just like Connas[45] with his withered crown;
Half dead, he yearns to gulp a neat draught down.
His former victories would seem to call
At least for drinking rights in the Town Hall,[46]
And at dramatic feasts it's only fit
That he should next his Dionysus[47] sit.

What wrathful buffets Crates had to bear
For feasting you on inexpensive fare!
But with his clever wit in driest vein
He satisfied you – well, now and again.
He apprehended well your angry side,
And said this proverb to the stage applied:
'Before you take the helm, first ply the oar;
Then for'ard stand, and study weather-lore;
Then you may steer.'
                              And this, our poet claims,
Is why he didn't leap from childish games
Straight to a premature and silly play,
But waited till his moment came today.

        So raise every oar
        And let's have a real roar,
A cheer this occasion beseeming;
        Let our poet depart
        With delight in his heart
And his forehead with victory gleaming.[48]

CHORUS:

            Poseidon, lord of horses,
                Thou lov'st the clip–clop beat
            Of hooves in war's encounters,
                And neighs to thee are sweet;
            And when our black-beaked warships

57

Remuneration gain,[49]
Their swiftness cheers the Ruler
  Of all the foaming main.
When in the chariot-races
  The victory's in doubt,
Thou joyest (in particular
  If someone tumbles out):
Now, Sovereign of the Dolphins,
  Thou God of Sunium great,[50]
Lord of the Golden Trident,
  Thy Chorus thee await.
Thou art the Son of Cronos
  Throned on Geraestus high,
And Phormio[51] loved thee dearly
  Whose end makes good folk sigh;
And as things are at present,
  All Athens' people pray:
Poseidon, lord of horses,
  Remember us today.

LEADER:

Our fathers that begat us let us with our praises crown,
Men worthy of this land and of Athena's sacred gown.[52]
They manned the naval ramparts and the armies of your state,
And, everywhere victorious, they made the City great.
Not one of them would ever count the numbers of the foe,
But breathing fire and brimstone, he would up and at 'em go.
And if in any fight he chanced upon his arm to fall,
He'd just wipe off the dirt and swear he never fell at all,
Then grapple with the foe once more. And generals were too proud
To beg of Cleon's father to be dining rights[53] allowed;
While *now*, if they don't get the grub *and* the front seats they like
At all the big occasions, why, they warn they'll go on strike!
But we will freely fight for Athens and her gods: no pay
Do we demand, but only grant us this one boon, we pray:
If peace shall come again and we from toil shall be released,
Don't grudge us our long flowing hair and skin so sleekly greased.

CHORUS:

Pallas our Protectress, guardian

Of the holiest land on earth,
Home of power and home of valour,
Home of poets of true worth:

Come thou hither with our ally
In the chorus and the field,
Victory, who ever with us
Fights our foes and makes them yield.

Come, Athena, now if ever!
Let us now thy glory see!
Now, O Maid and Queen, we pray thee,
Give thy Chorus victory!

LEADER:
We wish to praise (for praise is due) the many valiant deeds
Of derring-do we know about, done by our noble steeds.
Invasions they've been through with us and battles by the score;
Yet at their prowess nautical we marvel even more.[54]
They got their garlic, onions too and drinking-vessels, then
They leaped aboard their transport-ships just like so many men.
They took their oars as we do and they hollered 'Yo-neigh-ho!
Lay to! Pull harder! What's all this? Gee up there, make her go!'
They disembarked at Corinth, where the young ones by and by
Went hunting for some fodder when they'd dug a place to lie.
They couldn't get the grass they like, so crabs they ate instead,
Not just on land – they fished them out right from the water's bed.
And so a source reliable (Theorus is his name)[55]
Declares he heard a crab from Corinth to his god exclaim:
'Poseidon, it's disgraceful, I'm denied my natural rights!
On land or in the depths of sea, I can't escape the Knights.'

ACT TWO

SCENE ONE: *The same.*

[*The* CHORUS *are present as before. Enter* SAUSAGE-SELLER, *garlanded.*]

LEADER: Back safe and sound! My dear impetuous friend! How we worried while you were away! Now tell us, tell us, how did the battle in the Council Chamber go?

SAUSAGE-SELLER: Why, I'm the All-comers' Champion of the Council Chamber!

CHORUS [*dancing round him*]:[56]
> Let's give three cheers for the man who brings
> Such wonderful news and has done great things!
> I long to hear your tale unfurled –
> To hear it I'd go right round the world!
> Take courage, friend, and tell us all
> Of everything that did befall –
> > We're all excited
> > And so delighted
> > That on you we thus can call:

Hail to the champion, hail to the champion ... *etc.*

SAUSAGE-SELLER: 'S worth 'earing an' all. I rushed orf there right be'ind 'im. When I got there, I fahnd 'im 'urling great big thunderbolts o' words and crushing them dahn monstrous 'ard on the 'eads of the Knights. Gigan'ic rocks o' words 'e was throwing, specially 'conspirators', over an' over again, and they was swallowing it all, listening all intently, you could see the liesweed[57] sprahting aht o' their ears, and they looked 'ot mustard and contracted their brahs like Zeus 'isself. And when I saw 'ow they was being all taken in by 'is lies and trickery, I said, 'Gods of Worthlessness,' I said, 'Gods of Wool-pulling and Folly and Monkey-business, Protector of the Drunk and Disorderly, and you, O Market

Square, wot brought me up from a baby, please give me a nimble tongue, loads of imperdence, an' a voice to put all men to shame, 'cept meself'. An' as I was saying that to meself, some pansy bloke or other let orf an enormous fart on my right side, and I bowed low in acceptance of the omen. Then I burst open the swinging gate wiv me backside, opened me mahth wide, took a deep breath and howled, 'Members of the Cahncil! I got lovely noos for you! Ever since the war broke out, I've never known sardines be as cheap as wot they are today!' That took the storm signals orf their faces all right, and they put this crahn on me in token of the good noos I'd brought. Then I said I'd got a secret to tell 'em. 'Know 'ow to get them sardines really dirt cheap? You want to go aht and grab all the bowls in all the shops so no one else'll be able to take 'em 'ome.' Oh, such applause yer never 'eard, and they was all looking enraptured at me. But the Paphlagonian, yer see, soon as 'e realized wot was going on, 'e thought quickly wot kind of thing the Cahncil would like best, an' 'e proposed a motion. 'Gentlemen,' 'e said, 'it is *may* opinion that in honour of the good *tay*dings we have just received we should forthwith sacri*fayce* one hundred oxen to Athena.' An' 'ey presto, the Cahncil was all 'is again. Well, I could see this bullshit was going to smother me, so I overbid 'im with *two* 'undred oxen, and 'wot's more,' I said, 'if by tomorrer sardines is an 'undred for an obol, I think as 'ow we should offer one thahsand she-goats to Artemis, the 'Untress.³⁸' And the 'ole Cahncil did an eyes right and looked 'ungrily at me. An' 'im, 'e was struck dumb; 'e could do nothing but babble, until the Executive Committee ordered the constables to remove 'im. By nah the Cahncil were all on their feet, shahting 'Sardines! Sardines!' an 'e, while they was trying to drag 'im away, 'e was begging them to stay and listen a moment. 'Won't you give audience to the Spartan Ambassador? He is here with peace proposals.' And with one voice they cried, 'Wot? Peace nah? They must've 'eard abaht our cheap sardines. Trying to get their 'ands on 'em, eh? No peace nah, thank you, let the war go on!' And they shahted to the Executive Committee to close the meeting, and then they rushed orf as fast as they could, jumping over all the bars of the 'ouse. Meantime I slipped orf to the Market Square and bought up all the leeks and coriander leaves they 'ad; so when the Cahncillors came and couldn't find anything to season their sardines with, I 'ad seasoning to give 'em for nothing. And they was all over me, fussing over me, congratulating me, in fact for an obol's worth of coriander I've got the 'ole Cahncil in me pocket. An' 'ere I am back.

CHORUS [*dancing round him*]:
        Success, success in every point!
        The villain's nose is out of joint!
        We've found a villain even deeper,
        A crook, a wheedler and a creeper,
        Full of every crafty wile,
        A man of truly perfect guile!
The contest isn't over yet; consider means and ends,
But never let yourself forget that we're your loyal friends!

SAUSAGE-SELLER: Yer right it's norrover. I see that Paphlagonian coming. You can feel the groundswell – it's going to blow a hurricane. 'E looks like 'e wants to swaller me 'ole. [*To the* PAPHLAGONIAN, *who now enters*] Boo! That's all I care for you and your threats!

PAPHLAGONIAN: If there's one lie left in my armoury, then if I don't destroy you may I fall to pieces!

SAUSAGE-SELLER [*laughing uproariously*]: Oh, I just love that! Ha! ha! ha! Wot marvellous bombast! Fa la la la! [*He dances a little jig.*] Cuckoo! Cuckoo!

PAPHLAGONIAN: I swear, if I don't devour you and exterminate you from this land of ours, I shall di-i-ie!

SAUSAGE-SELLER: Devour me, will you? May I die if I don't drink you up, belch you out and burst in the process!

PAPHLAGONIAN: I swear by the front seat I won at Pylos[59] –

SAUSAGE-SELLER: Front seat is it now? Oh, I'm looking forward to seeing you very soon sitting in the very back row!

PAPHLAGONIAN: By heaven, I'll have you in the stocks yet.

SAUSAGE-SELLER: Hah very bad-tempered! Wot shall I give diddums to eat? Wot does baby like best? Real stuffed leather purses?

PAPHLAGONIAN: I'll tear your guts out!

SAUSAGE-SELLER: I'll scratch your name off the Town Hall Dining Rights list!

PAPHLAGONIAN: I'll haul you before Thepeople! Thepeople will see you pay for this!

SAUSAGE-SELLER: I'll 'aul *you* before Thepeople, and then we'll see 'oo can throw the most mud!

PAPHLAGONIAN: Thepeople never takes any notice of no-goods like you. Whereas I can spin him round my little finger.

SAUSAGE-SELLER: How convinced you are Thepeople belongs to you!

PAPHLAGONIAN: He does. I'm the only one that knows all his favourite goodies.

SAUSAGE-SELLER: Yerss, and then 'ow do you feed 'im? Like a bloody baby-farmer. You chew the stuff up yourself, give 'im a tiny tiny little bit, and pop three times as much dahn yer own throat!

PAPHLAGONIAN: Why, I'm such an expert, I can inflate and deflate Thepeople at will.

SAUSAGE-SELLER: That's nothing – even my prick knows how to do that.

PAPHLAGONIAN: Don't think, my man, you can get away with your insolence this time like you did in the Council. I shall appeal to Thepeople!

SAUSAGE-SELLER [*marching off towards the audience*]: Awright. 'Ere, come on, wot's stopping you? [*He realizes that the* PAPHLAGONIAN *is making for the door of* THEPEOPLE'S *house, and runs back to the door himself.*]

PAPHLAGONIAN [*knocking violently on the door*]: Thepeople! Thepeople! Come outside! Come here!

SAUSAGE-SELLER [*pushing him out of the way and knocking himself*]: Here, Thepeople! My darling Thepeoplekins! Daddy!

PAPHLAGONIAN: Thepeoplekins! Come here! Thepeople, my one true love! Come outside and see how terribly I've been maltreated!
[THEPEOPLE *comes out of the house, an old man, scantily and meanly clothed, and in none too good a mood.*]

THEPEOPLE: Who's doing all this shouting? Get away from the door!
[*The* PAPHLAGONIAN *and the* SAUSAGE-SELLER *retreat a little way.*]
Look, you've ruined this wreath!¹⁶⁰ Ah, my dear Paphlagonian! Who's been ill-treating you?

PAPHLAGONIAN: I've been beaten up – by this fellow and these young men here [*indicating the* CHORUS] – and all because of you.

THEPEOPLE: How come?

PAPHLAGONIAN: Because, Thepeople, I love you, I truly do.

THEPEOPLE [*to* SAUSAGE-SELLER]: And who are *you*?

SAUSAGE-SELLER: I am also your lover. I've loved you for a long time and wanted to 'elp you, and so 'ave many other honest folk too, but this one won't let us. Come to think of it, sir, you treat your lovers just like the young boys do. You turn away all the fine upstanding men and give yourself to the lamp merchants⁶¹ and shoemakers and cobblers and most of all the *tanners*.

PAPHLAGONIAN: That's because I do good to Thepeople.

SAUSAGE-SELLER: Like 'ow?

PAPHLAGONIAN: Like when I sailed round to Pylos, crept up on the General there and brought the Spartans home myself.

SAUSAGE-SELLER: I can do that sorter thing just as well. Like the time I went rahnd to the back of a shop and pinched a pot of soup someone else had cooked.

PAPHLAGONIAN: I propose, Thepeople, that you should immediately call an Assembly and decide which of us more truly loves you, and then you can love, honour *and* obey the winner for ever!

SAUSAGE-SELLER: Good idea! Good idea! Only don't hold it on the Pnyx.

THEPEOPLE: I will sit nowhere else. Forward to the Pnyx, everyone! [*All come forward. Slaves bring in two or three long benches, on one of which* THEPEOPLE *takes his seat.*]

SAUSAGE-SELLER [*aside*]: Help, I'm lost! At 'ome the old man's perfectly intelligent, but just put 'im on top of that 'ill an' 'e gawps as if 'e was trying to catch a fig in 'is mahth!

CHORUS:

> Your sails must all be set,
>   Your spirit must be bold,
> Your words must all strike home
>   And lay your rival cold.
> But since from any jam
>   He's apt to tunnel out,
> You'd better gird your loins
>   For battle long and stout.

LEADER:

Watch, and before his onslaught comes prepare to strike your foe;
Your leaden dolphin hoist on high,[62] then close and let it go!

PAPHLAGONIAN: First I pray to Lady Athena who watches over our
City, that if I perform of all men the most valuable services for the
People of Athens – of all men, that is, except Lysicles,[63] and all
women except Cynna and Salabaccho – then may I continue to
enjoy my dining rights in the Town Hall for doing absolutely
nothing. But if I hate you, Thepeople, and am not your sole champion and defender, then may I perish and be chopped into pieces
to be used as yokestraps!

SAUSAGE-SELLER: And I, Thepeople, if I don't love and cherish you,
may I be cut up into mincemeat for boiling. And if that's not good
enough for you, may I be grated into a cheese salad on my own
table, and dragged by the bollocks on my own meathook all the
way to the Potters' Quarter!

PAPHLAGONIAN: How could anybody love you more, Thepeople,
than I do? Remember when I was on the Council? Didn't I fill your
Treasury full? I'd rack and throttle and extort – I didn't care a fig for
the rights of the individual, so long as I pleased you.

SAUSAGE-SELLER: Nothing so marvellous abaht that, Thepeople; I
can do just the same. I can pinch any number o' loaves of bread and
serve them up to you on a plate. Meantime I'd just like to prove to
you that 'e don't really love you or care for you at all, 'cept that 'e
likes sitting in front of your fire. You defended yer country against
the Medes at Marathon, and you was victorious, and every year
since we've been minting new speeches abaht yer courage and yer
glory. But does 'e take pity on you sitting there on them hard
benches? Not a bit of it! Whereas I [*he takes a cushion from a* SLAVE
who has unobtrusively brought it in] 'ave made this specially for you.
If you'd just get up for a moment [THEPEOPLE *does so*] and then sit
dahn gently. You mustn't rub yer Salamis battle-scars,[64] yer know.

THEPEOPLE [*settling gently into the cushion*]: Mmm! Who are you, my
man? Not a descendant of Harmodius the Liberator,[65] by any
chance? That was a truly noble act of yours. You are indeed a lover
of Thepeople.

PAPHLAGONIAN: Is that your way of showing you love him, these
petty little suckings up?

SAUSAGE-SELLER: Norralf as petty as the baits you've dangled for 'im *an'* 'ooked 'im with.

PAPHLAGONIAN: I tell you – if there's ever been a greater friend or defender of Thepeople than I am – I'm willing to eat my head!

SAUSAGE-SELLER: Friend of the People, indeed! You wot's seen 'ow they've lived these last seven years in tubs and turrets and birds' nests,[66] an' 'ad no pity on them, but kept the 'ive locked so you could pinch the 'oney? What 'appened when Archeptolemus came with noos of a peace offer? You threw it to the winds, and the Spartan envoys, wot 'ad come begging on their knees for peace, you kicked 'em clean out of the City!

PAPHLAGONIAN: So that you, Thepeople, could fulfil your manifest destiny and rule over all Greece. There is an oracle that if Thepeople does not flag or fail, he will one day try cases in Arcadia at five obols a time.[67] But be that as it may, I will nourish you and protect you, and ensure, by fair means or foul, that you get your jury pay.

SAUSAGE-SELLER: Huh! Rule over Arcadia! That's all balls; wot 'e wants is to be able to plunder and peculate every city in Greece, while you, Thepeople, with all the mud the war throws in yer eyes, can't see wot 'e's getting up to, so's you just go on gawping at 'im, 'alf because you can't 'elp it an' 'alf because 'e's your pay-master. If ever you go 'ome to live in peace in the country and get back to munching your toasties and negotiating your pressed olives, then you'll realize just 'ow much 'e's been cheating you aht of while 'e's been fobbing you off with that three obols of jury pay. Then you'll be a furious 'ound 'ot on 'is trail, clutching yer 'guilty' vote between yer teeth. That's why 'e keeps deceiving you and making up all these dreams and oracles and wotnot abaht 'isself.

PAPHLAGONIAN: It is nothing short of outrageous for you to utter these disgraceful slanders against me in the presence of the entire People! I have done more good for the City than the great Themistocles, by Demeter, ever did![68]

SAUSAGE-SELLER: O Argive city, hear'st these words?[69] What? you set yerself up against Themistocles? 'E fahnd the City 'alf full, and filled her to overflowing, and wot's more coupled on the Peiraeus as well. 'E didn't take anything away from the City, 'e added more to it. But you, with your blessed oracles and your internal walls,[70] you've been trying to make us all into parish-pump citizens, you

great rival of Themistocles. An' 'e ended up in exile, while you
wipe yer fingers on top-grade Tahn 'All bread!

PAPHLAGONIAN: I repeat, Thepeople, is it not outrageous that
this fellow should speak of me in this way simply because I love
you?

THEPEOPLE [to PAPHLAGONIAN]: Quiet, you! no more slanging.
How long have you been carrying on your fiddles without my
knowing?

SAUSAGE-SELLER:

> Yes, while you gawp, Thepeople sweet,
> He shows himself a first-class cheat;
> On magistrates' accounting-day[71]
> He whips the juiciest stalks away
> And wolfs the whole lot down himself;
> What's more, he swipes Thepeople's pelf.

PAPHLAGONIAN: You'll not get away with this, I vow! I'll nail you
yet, and convict you of stealing thirty thousand drachmas'

SAUSAGE-SELLER:

> Why beat the sea with futile blade?
> You chose to ply the robber's trade.
> Now may the gods my death prescribe
> If I don't prove you've had a bribe
> From Mytilene to the east
> Of *forty* thousand drachs at least.

CHORUS:

> Oh saviour of mankind,
> My tongue of yours shall sing.
> If you press on this way,
>   Of Greece you'll be the king.
> The City you will rule,
>   You'll make our allies quake,
> And with your trident's power
>   A pile of cash you'll make.

LEADER:

Now that you've got a hold on him, make sure he don't slip free;
Your muscles are so strong, you'll win an easy victory!

PAPHLAGONIAN: Not so, by Poseidon, not yet! I have wrought an
exploit that will shut the mouth of each and every one of my

enemies till the end of time, so long as one of the captured shields from Pylos remains.

SAUSAGE-SELLER: Whoa! The shields! That's your weak spot. If you really love Thepeople, would yer be so good as to explain why you 'ave wilfully and maliciously arranged for them to be 'ung up *with their 'andles on*? It's a plot, Thepeople, a plot, to make sure that if you ever want to punish this blighter for 'is wicked deeds, yer won't be able to. 'E's got an 'ole battalion of young tanners at 'is beck and call, *an'* the honey and cheese merchants in the next street; and they've put their 'eads together and decided that if you should ever start getting stroppy with 'im and itching to play a little game of ostracizing,[72] all they'll do is run dahn to the Painted Portico, grab all those shields and occupy your lifeline[73] till they've starved you aht!

THEPEOPLE: Bless me, I never knew they had handles! You swine! You deceiver of Thepeople! All that time you've been gulling me!

PAPHLAGONIAN: Now, my dear Thepeople, do beware of being the slave of the last word! Don't imagine you'll ever find a more faithful friend and watchdog than me. All on my own I've foiled every plot and conspiracy against you, and nothing that's hatched in the City ever escapes me; I bark instantly.

SAUSAGE-SELLER: Yerss, you're just like an eel-fisher, you are. When the lake's smooth and clear, they never catch nothing; but when they stir up the mud a bit, up come the eels. An' it's the same with you – you can only make a killing by stirring up confusion in the City. Just tell me this. You sell I don't know how many pairs of shoes every day. 'Ave you ever given Thepeople a single scrap of leather for 'is shoes, you who say you love him so?

THEPEOPLE: I can tell you, he hasn't.

SAUSAGE-SELLER: So nah yer see wot 'e's like. [*Signals to a* SLAVE *who brings him a pair of shoes.*] But I, I've bought you a lovely new pair of shoes to wear, and 'ere they are.

THEPEOPLE [*putting the shoes on*]: I really must say you're the best friend I can ever remember Thepeople having. Such loving care for the City and for my poor cold little tootsies!

PAPHLAGONIAN: Disgraceful! That you should be swayed by a mere pair of shoes and forget all the services I've performed for you!

Didn't I put a stop to buggery by striking Grypus off the roll of citizens?

SAUSAGE-SELLER: Nah, it was disgraceful of *you* to 'ave such an un'ealthy interest in people's arses and buggery and that. Anyway, you only put a stop to it because you was frightened the boys would all become politicians like you did. But you didn't do nothing for Thepeople here. At 'is age, without even a tunic! You never gave 'im one, not even in winter. But now I 'ave come, and I nah give you this. [*Takes a sleeved tunic from a slave, and gives it to* THEPEOPLE.]

THEPEOPLE [*fingering the tunic*]: Even Themistocles never thought of that. That Peiraeus idea was a clever one, I admit, but really, for my money, this tunic is the greatest boon that's ever been conferred on Thepeople of Athens!

PAPHLAGONIAN: More bloody monkey tricks!

SAUSAGE-SELLER: Not a bit of it. If a man can put on someone else's slippers at a party when 'e wants to go and crap, why can't I use your methods?

PAPHLAGONIAN: You'll never outdo me in the toadying line. [*A* SLAVE *hands him a leather jacket.*] I'm going to put this on him with my own hands and you can go and eat coke!

THEPEOPLE [*Trying to wriggle out of the jacket*]: Yecch! This leather stinks to high heaven. Take it to hell and stay there!

SAUSAGE-SELLER [*rescuing him from the jacket and discarding it*]: Yer see, 'e did that deliberately to suffocate you. 'E's tried it on before. Remember when the price of silphium came dahn?

THEPEOPLE: Yes.

SAUSAGE-SELLER: That was a trick of 'is too. 'E wanted you to buy lots of it and eat it, then start farting when you were sitting on the jury and kill each other with the fumes!

THEPEOPLE: Ah yes, I remember, I heard about that from old Dephaecatus.[74]

SAUSAGE-SELLER: Turned yer all blond at the wrong end, di'n' it?

THEPEOPLE: Just the sort of trick Blondie here [*meaning the* PAPHLAGONIAN] would get up to.

PAPHLAGONIAN: Any more of your stupid buffoonery and I'll –

SAUSAGE-SELLER: It's Athena's will that I'm to ahtmatch you in talking balls!

PAPHLAGONIAN: You'll never outmatch me! Thepeople, I promise
to provide you with a whole bowlful of jury pay to guzzle every
day, and you needn't do anything for it at all!

SAUSAGE-SELLER: I'll give you a little box with ointment in, so you
can soothe the sores on your legs!

PAPHLAGONIAN: I'll pluck out your grey hairs and make you young
again!

SAUSAGE-SELLER: Look, take this hare's tail to wipe your eyes with!

PAPHLAGONIAN: Blow your nose, Thepeople, and use my head to
wipe your hands! [*He kneels in front of* THEPEOPLE, *who begins to
blow his nose.*]

SAUSAGE-SELLER [*elbowing the* PAPHLAGONIAN *out of the way*]: No,
use mine!

PAPHLAGONIAN [*vice versa*]: No, mine!

[THEPEOPLE, *who has been somewhat inconvenienced by this alter-
cation, eventually grabs the* PAPHLAGONIAN *by one ear and rubs
the products of his nose-blowing into his eyes.*]

PAPHLAGONIAN [*half blind*]: Blast your eyes!
    I'll make you captain of an old
        And leaky man-o'-war,
    On mending and rebuilding which
        You'll fork out more and more.
    And when she's fit (if e'er she is)
        To put to sea at last,
    I'll see the sail's so rotten that
        It falls right off the mast! [75

CHORUS:
        The pot is boiling over! Quick,
            Some faggots take away!
        And from the cauldron let's fish out
            The threats in what you say!
[*The* LEADER *lifts the* SAUSAGE-SELLER's *meathook threateningly
towards the* PAPHLAGONIAN.]

PAPHLAGONIAN:
        I'll see the weight of tax on you
            Split open wide your arse –
        I'll make damn sure you're registered
            Within the surtax class!

SAUSAGE-SELLER:[76]

No threats I make, but I
Call down this imprecation:
When cuttlefish you have
In sizzling preparation,
O may the Milesians that day
Preparing be to pay
     Six thousand drachs
     All free of tax
Which you will pocket away.

(Miletus had said, you see,
'This sum your reward will be,
     If you can in
     The Assembly win
     The vote on this decree.')[77]
So may you eager be
The cuttlefish to swallow,
And dashing to the Pnyx
Ensure success will follow;
Then may a political mate
Come warning that you're late,
     So that in panic mood
     You gulp down the food
And thus you suffocate!

CHORUS:

It simply could not be worse!
Oh, what a marvellous curse!
To choke him of air!
By Zeus I swear
I ne'er heard such a curse!

THEPEOPLE: Neither did I. And in every other way too he seems to me to be a truly good citizen, a man of unmatched goodwill towards the bought masses of the people. I mean the broad masses of the people. And you [to the PAPHLAGONIAN], you always claimed to love me, and all the time you were treating me no better than a fighting cock. Give me back my ring; you will no longer be my steward.

PAPHLAGONIAN [*handing over the ring*]: Here it is. But I warn you, if you won't have me as your steward, you'll find my successor a far greater villain.

THEPEOPLE: Here, this isn't my ring! At least the seal looks different. Or is it just my eyesight? Here, have a look. [*He gives the ring to the* SAUSAGE-SELLER.]

SAUSAGE-SELLER: Lessee ... Wot did yer 'ave on yours?

THEPEOPLE: A baked election bean sandwich.[78]

SAUSAGE-SELLER: Can't see that 'ere.

THEPEOPLE: What's there, then?

SAUSAGE-SELLER: An open-mahthed shark[79] on a platform, making a speech.

THEPEOPLE: Ugh!

SAUSAGE-SELLER: Woss wrong?

THEPEOPLE: Get rid of it! Take it away! It's not mine, it's Cleonymus's![80] [*Taking another ring from his finger*] No, this is my real ring. Take it, and be my steward.

PAPHLAGONIAN [*flinging himself at* THEPEOPLE'*s feet*]: Not yet dear master, I beg of you! Don't take such a step before you've heard my oracles!

SAUSAGE-SELLER: Wot abaht mine?

PAPHLAGONIAN: Huh! If you listen to *him* you'll end up turned into a bottle![81]

SAUSAGE-SELLER: Well, if yer listen to '*im*, 'e'll make you the biggest, reddest cock-up that ever said 'excuse me'!

PAPHLAGONIAN: My oracles say, master, that you are destined to rule the whole earth and be crowned with roses!

SAUSAGE-SELLER: And mine say as 'ow you'll 'ave a golden crahn *an*' a jewelled purple robe, and ride in a golden chariot to court to prosecute Smicythes' – husband![82]

PAPHLAGONIAN: All right then, go and get your oracles, so master can hear them.

SAUSAGE-SELLER: Sure. And you do the same.

PAPHLAGONIAN: Right.

SAUSAGE-SELLER: Right.

   [*Both rush into the house; they collide at the door.*]
'Ere, wot's stopping you?

72

[*The* PAPHLAGONIAN *replies only with a furious gesture; both go into the house.*]

CHORUS:[83]

How joyful is the day
When we are saved from danger,
    From him who traps for prey
Both citizens and stranger!
For everyone that's here,
One thing they'll all agree on:
    They'll greet with cheer on cheer
The overthrow of Cleon!
    They'll greet with cheer on cheer
The overthrow of Cleon!

Down where the suits are sold
(The 'suits' they sell are legal)
    I heard a juror old
Defend that tanner regal:
    'If e'er the Knightly band
Should burst the Cleon bubble,
    'Twould ruin all the land –
The damage would be double –
    We'd lose our pestle and
Our stirrer-up of trouble!'

His musical training's a marvellous tale,
    For at school all his comrades aver,
As a lyre-player always in majors he'd fail
    And the minor modes ever prefer.
At length from the school-house the master irate
    Expelled that ineffable swine:
'Only thieves love the *minors*,' that teacher would state,
    ''Cos they think "I'll make everything *mine*"!'[84]

[*The door bursts open; stuck in the doorway are the* PAPHLAGONIAN *and the* SAUSAGE-SELLER, *each carrying a vast load of scrolls containing oracles. Eventually they disentangle themselves and rush to take their places before* THEPEOPLE. *The* PAPHLAGONIAN *wins by a short head.*]

PAPHLAGONIAN: Look, look, here they are! And this isn't the lot by a long chalk.

SAUSAGE-SELLER: This load's bursting me bowels, and *it's* not all by a long chalk eiver.

THEPEOPLE: What is all this stuff?

PAPHLAGONIAN: Why, oracles.

THEPEOPLE: What, all that lot?

PAPHLAGONIAN: Surprised? Let me tell you, I've a wardrobe full of them inside.

SAUSAGE-SELLER: Thass nothing. *I've* got a loft and two cellars crammed full of 'em.

THEPEOPLE: Tell me, from whom do these oracles come?

PAPHLAGONIAN: Mine are from Bakis.[85]

THEPEOPLE [*to* SAUSAGE-SELLER]: And yours?

SAUSAGE-SELLER: Were given by Frontis, wot's Bakis's elder bruvver.

THEPEOPLE [*to* PAPHLAGONIAN]: Your oracles, what are they about?

PAPHLAGONIAN: All sorts of things: Athens, Pylos, you, me, everything.

THEPEOPLE: And yours?

SAUSAGE-SELLER: All sorts o' things: Athens, lentil soup, Sparta, fresh mackerel, dealers wot give short measure of barley, you, me –
[*The* PAPHLAGONIAN *is showing signs of restiveness.*]
Oh, go and suck yourself!

THEPEOPLE: Now please read them to me. And don't forget that one I really love about myself, that I'm going to become an eagle in the clouds.[86]

PAPHLAGONIAN: Now listen to me. [*Clears his throat and recites*]
Son of Erechtheus, mark you the path of the words that Apollo
Spoke from his inaccessible shrine through his glorious Tripods:
Never abandon The Dog,[87] the jag-toothed and holy, but keep
him;
He 'tis that barketh before you and for you so fearfully howleth;
He 'tis that getteth your pay (if he getteth it not, then he's done for,
Since that full many a jackdaw is croaking in hatred against him).

THEPEOPLE: I'm sorry, but I can't make head or tail of that. What on earth have Erechtheus, jackdaws and dogs got to do with each other?

PAPHLAGONIAN: The Dog, that's me, because I always bark on
your behalf. And Apollo says that you're to keep me and never
abandon me.

SAUSAGE-SELLER: Thass not wot it means at all. This Dog, as 'e
calls 'isself, is just nibbling orf a bit of the oracles like it was a door.
'E's taking it aht of context. I've got the right oracle 'ere abaht that
dog.

THEPEOPLE: All right, you tell me yours. But I'd better get a stone,
in case the oracle bites me.

SAUSAGE-SELLER [unrolling his oracle]:
Son of Erechtheus, mark you this canine Cerberus-pirate,
Who when you dine stands fawning and wagging his tail, watching
closely,
Till, when you gawp to the right or the left, he snaps up your
entrée;
Then in the darkness of night he goes doglike, unseen, to the
kitchen,
Then he licks clean every plate, and then he licks clean every
island.[88]

THEPEOPLE: Give me Frontis every time!

PAPHLACONIAN: Listen to this before you make up your mind.
There is a woman shall bring forth a lion in Athens' fair city,
Lion who'll fight for Thepeople with myrmidon hordes of
mosquitoes,
Just as if you were his cubs. This lion protect thou and cherish,
Building a great wooden wall and raising great towers of iron.
Get that?

THEPEOPLE: Can't say I do.

PAPHLAGONIAN: The god says you must protect and cherish me.
Don't I have a truly leonine nature?

THEPEOPLE: Well, I must admit you're more than a bit like Leon.[89]

SAUSAGE-SELLER: One thing 'e's not explained. 'E don't say wot
that wooden wall the oracle mentioned, that you should protect
'im with, wot it is.

THEPEOPLE: Well, what did the god mean by it?

SAUSAGE-SELLER: 'E meant you should keep 'im in a wooden wall
with five 'oles in it – two for 'is feet, two for 'is 'ands and one for
'is 'ead![90]

THEPEOPLE: I've a good mind to get that one fulfilled!

PAPHLAGONIAN:
Do not believe him; the crows all around me are jealously croaking.
Love and remember your Hawk, who brought you the rāvenous
Spartans
Bound in fetters –

SAUSAGE-SELLER: A risk that he'd never have taken if sober.
Foolish son of old Cecrops, why think that a mighty achievement?
Even a woman a burden can bear, if a man puts it on her,
But she can't fight; when the spears start hittin', she promptly starts
shittin'.

PAPHLAGONIAN: Heed what the god once declared:
'There is Pylos on Pylos in plenty, Pylos on Pylos on Pylos'⁹¹ –

THEPEOPLE [*interrupting*]: What the hell is this 'Pylos on Pylos'?

SAUSAGE-SELLER: 'E's thinking of 'ow 'e's going to make 'is pile
by stealing all the tubs in the public baths.⁹²

THEPEOPLE: You mean he's going to force me to just stay dirty?

SAUSAGE-SELLER: Yerss, 'e's cheating Thepeople so's 'e can make
'is pile. But listen, I've got a very important oracle 'ere abaht the
Navy. Nah pay very close attention.

THEPEOPLE: I will. And start off by telling me when the sailors are
going to get their back pay.

SAUSAGE-SELLER:
Son of Aegeus, beware of the Dog (or the Fox) who deceives thee,
Swift-footed sneaker, the sly and resourceful and cunning embezzler.
Know what that means?

THEPEOPLE: 'The Dog or the Fox ...' That's Philostratus, ain't
it?⁹³

SAUSAGE-SELLER: No, no, no – it's '*im* again! 'E's always askin' for
more warships to go rahnd collecting tribute, and wot Apollo is
saying is, don't give 'im them.

THEPEOPLE: But what has a warship got to do with a dog or a fox?

SAUSAGE-SELLER: Well, a dog runs fast, so does a warship, right?

THEPEOPLE: Yes, but where does the fox come into it?

SAUSAGE-SELLER: The foxes are our soldiers. Yer know how they
both eat all the grapes in everyone's vineyard?

THEPEOPLE: Ah, I get it! But as I said a moment ago, where's these
foxes' pay going to come from?

SAUSAGE-SELLER: Leave that to me; I'll do it in three days, see if I don't!

Listen again to the oracle wherein Apollo commands thee
Shun Cyllene,⁹⁴ the Harbour of Palms, for fear it beguile thee.

THEPEOPLE: What is this Harbour of Palms?

SAUSAGE-SELLER:

             He speaks of this fellow, and rightly;
Does he not always say 'Cross my palm with a purseful of silver'?

PAPHLAGONIAN: No, that's not what it means; any palm mentioned in an oracle can only refer to Diopeithes.⁹⁵ But listen to what I've got here! This oracle has wings! 'Know that an eagle you'll be and the whole earth govern unchallenged!'

SAUSAGE-SELLER: I've got one too. 'Know that you'll govern the earth, and the Red Sea into the bargain; and in Ecbatana cases you'll try, munching cakes as you try them!'

PAPHLAGONIAN [casting his oracles aside]: I have had a dream! I saw Athena herself holding a cornucopia, and ladling out health and wealth in profusion upon Thepeople!

SAUSAGE-SELLER: I've 'ad a dream as well! I saw Athena coming aht from the Acropolis, with 'er owl on 'er shoulder an' 'er bucket in 'er 'and, and from that she poured ambrosia on yer 'ead and tanner's brine on 'is!

THEPEOPLE: Bravo! I vote Frontis the wisest seer who ever lived! [To SAUSAGE-SELLER] I commit myself to your care. Be my guardian and guide. Re-educate me.

PAPHLAGONIAN: Not yet, not yet, please! Just wait a moment and I'll give your your daily barley bread.

THEPEOPLE: I've had enough of your barley. You and Thuphanes⁹⁶ have done me too often over those so-called free distributions.

PAPHLAGONIAN: But I'll give you the flour all finely milled!

SAUSAGE-SELLER: I'll give you the cakes ready made, with baked savouries to taste. All you need to do is eat 'em.

THEPEOPLE: All right, be off and get on with it. And whichever of you makes me the best meal, I'll make him King of the Pnyx!

PAPHLAGONIAN [running off towards the house]: I'll be the first inside, then.

SAUSAGE-SELLER [running after him]: That's what you think! [He *catches up with him at the door, shoves him aside and goes in; the* PAPHLAGONIAN *follows.*]

CHORUS:

> Thepeople's power's a glorious thing;
> All nations fear him like a king.
> Yet he's an easy one to cheat,
> A prey to flattery and deceit.
> He sides agawp with every speaker;
> There's none who has convictions weaker.
> If he has got a brain, I'd say
> It always is on holiday.

THEPEOPLE:

> My brain's all right; it's *your* long hair
> That hides a mind that isn't there!
> I just *affect* simplicity;
> I *like* to suck my thumb, you see.
> I make a politician fat –
> I let him cheat and steal and that –
> And when he's full, I cease to clown
> And get me up and strike him down.

CHORUS:

> Ah, now I see your cunning ways!
> Your cleverness deserves all praise.
> Of purpose set you feed the beasts
> Like victims for the public feasts,
> And then whene'er you're shot of meat
> You choose the one you want to eat,
> You kill the fatted calf or swine
> And on a politician dine!

THEPEOPLE:

> Those crafty chaps that think they're clever,
> Be sure that they outwit me never.
> I watch them closer than they know
> While on their thieving way they go;
> And then I make them all in pain
> Regurgitate their ill-won gain!
> I stick a funnel down their throats –
> The funnel where we cast our votes![97]

[*The* PAPHLAGONIAN *and the* SAUSAGE-SELLER *come out at the same moment, and collide in the doorway.*]

PAPHLAGONIAN: Get the hell out of my way!

SAUSAGE-SELLER: You get aht of *my* way, you carcass!

PAPHLAGONIAN [*rushing to where* THEPEOPLE *is sitting*]: Oh, Thepeople, I've been sitting here ready and waiting to minister to all your needs for *ever* so long.

SAUSAGE-SELLER [*rushing to his place*]: I've been waiting ever-ever-ever so long-long-long-long-long! I couldn't *tell* you how long!

THEPEOPLE: Well, I've been waiting too, ever-ever-ever-ever so long-long-long-long-long-long, and I'm bloody fed up with the both of you.

SAUSAGE-SELLER: Know wot you oughter do?

THEPEOPLE: I will if you tell me.

SAUSAGE-SELLER: Look, 'ere's our starting line, right? You be the starter and give us the signal, together, so we can minister to you on level terms, see?

THEPEOPLE: Good idea. Are you ready?

PAPHLAGONIAN }
SAUSAGE-SELLER } [*crouching as at the start of a race*]: Yes!

THEPEOPLE: Go!

[*They run towards the house.*]

SAUSAGE-SELLER: Here, you, stop cutting in on me!

[*He and the* PAPHLAGONIAN *disappear into the house.*]

THEPEOPLE: Well, I must say, if having two lovers like this isn't going to make me happy, I don't know what is.

PAPHLAGONIAN [*returning with a chair*]: Look, I'm first. I've got this for you.

SAUSAGE-SELLER [*entering with a table*]: He hasn't brought you this, though; I win this round.

[*Both rush back into the house and return with enormous hampers.*]

PAPHLAGONIAN: I bring you here a beautiful little cake made of sacred barley from Pylos.

SAUSAGE-SELLER: And *I* bring you these pieces of bread soaked in soup by Athena 'erself with 'er ivory 'and.[98]

THEPEOPLE: Oh, Athena, what a big finger you've got!

PAPHLAGONIAN: What about this? Lovely green pea soup, and Athena stirred it, Athena the Conqueror of Pylos.

SAUSAGE-SELLER: Oh, Thepeople, 'ow true it is that the 'Oly Maid watches over you! Look 'ow she stretches forth 'er 'and to protect you, with a bowl full o' soup in it!

THEPEOPLE: Yes, if Athena didn't pour her soup over us, there'd be no Athens today. [*He begins to tuck into the soup.*]

PAPHLAGONIAN: Here is a slice of fish, given you by the Striker of Terror.

SAUSAGE-SELLER: And here's the meat boiled with the soup, from the Daughter of the Almighty Father. And a special cut of tripe, second, third and fourth stomach all in one!

THEPEOPLE [*indistinctly*]: Good for her, to remember all the tripods we dedicate.⁹⁹

PAPHLAGONIAN: The Lady of the Dreaded Crest bids you make good use of this gravy boat. She says if you do, she'll bless the real Navy.

SAUSAGE-SELLER: Ah, but take *these*!

THEPEOPLE: Ribs of beef? What am I supposed to do with them?

SAUSAGE-SELLER: For the ribs of yer warships, of course. That's why Athena sent you them. Don't you see 'ow lovingly she watches over the Navy? Look, 'ere's wine. [*Pours.*] Special mixture, forty per cent strength.

THEPEOPLE [*drinking*]: Marvellous! How sweet – you'd never know it was sixty per cent water. Who made this wine?

SAUSAGE-SELLER: It was made by the Maid herself.

PAPHLAGONIAN: Here, take a slice of this lovely rich cake.

SAUSAGE-SELLER: A slice, eh? 'Ere's an *'ole* cake.

PAPHLAGONIAN: But I bet you haven't got any hare's meat you can give Thepeople; I have. Look! [*He brings a dish of jugged hare out of his hamper.*]

SAUSAGE-SELLER [*to himself*]: 'Elp! Where can I get some 'are from? [*Scratches his head.*] Come on, brain, think of something to fool 'im.

PAPHLAGONIAN [*displaying the dish*]: Ha, ha, poor fellow, what do you think of *this*?

SAUSAGE-SELLER: I couldn't care less. [*Suddenly pointing off.*] Look, I can see somebody coming!

PAPHLAGONIAN: Who, who?

SAUSAGE-SELLER: Ambassadors from somewhere – with enormous purses full of money.

PAPHLAGONIAN: Where, where? Quick! [*He puts down the dish and runs in the direction indicated by the* SAUSAGE-SELLER.]

SAUSAGE-SELLER: What business is that of yours? Leave the men alone. Look, Thepeoplekins, 'ere's lovely jugged 'are for you.

PAPHLAGONIAN [*returning empty-handed*]: Swine! You've stolen my hare!

SAUSAGE-SELLER: Look 'oo's talking. 'Oo stole the credit for Pylos?

THEPEOPLE [*who is thoroughly enjoying the hare*]: Tell me, I would like to know, how did you get the idea of pinching it like that?

SAUSAGE-SELLER: 'The idea was Pallas', but the pinching mine.'¹⁰⁰

PAPHLAGONIAN: And I took all the risks of catching the beast! And I cooked it! [*Stamps in impotent rage, and bursts into tears.*]

THEPEOPLE: Away with you! To the waiter belongs the tip.

PAPHLAGONIAN: I can't believe it! I've been outdone in shamelessness! [*He retires to lick his wounds.*]

SAUSAGE-SELLER: Well, Thepeople, isn't it time nah to give judgement, like, on which of·us two is more devoted to you, or should I say to yer tum-tum?

THEPEOPLE: Yes, but what evidence should I use? I've got to prove to the audience that I judged sensibly.

SAUSAGE-SELLER: I'll tell you. Go and take a quiet look at my 'amper, and see wot's in it, and then do the same with 'is. Then you'll be able to give the right verdict all right.

THEPEOPLE [*opening the* SAUSAGE-SELLER's *hamper*]: Let's see now, what have we here?

SAUSAGE-SELLER: Doncher see, daddy? It's empty. I gave everything in it to you.

THEPEOPLE: This basket is on the side of Thepeople all right!

SAUSAGE-SELLER: Nah come over 'ere and look at 'is. Wot do you see?

THEPEOPLE [*opening the* PAPHLAGONIAN's *hamper*]: Good heavens, it's chock full of goodies! Look at all those cakes he's stashed away, and he just gave me a tiny tiny slice, no bigger than this! [*Demonstrates with his fingers.*]

SAUSAGE-SELLER: 'At's wot 'e's always done to you, Thepeople. Gives you a tiny slice of 'is takings, and puts by all the rest for 'isself.

THEPEOPLE [*seizing the* PAPHLAGONIAN *and shaking him almost senseless*]: You unutterable villain! So you've been hoodwinking me all the time! And 'twas I that did croon ye and gift ye sae mickle![101]

PAPHLAGONIAN: Whatever I stole was for the good of the City.

THEPEOPLE: Come on, off with your crown. This man deserves it better.

SAUSAGE-SELLER: You 'eard 'im, no-good. Off with it.

PAPHLAGONIAN [*shaking himself free*]: No, I won't! There is a Delphic oracle about me that declares there is but one man in the world that can oust me.

SAUSAGE-SELLER: It'll be me, you'll see.

PAPHLAGONIAN: Evidence. I'll cross-examine you and see if you match up with the oracle's requirements. First of all, then, answer me this. [*Clears his throat*] When you were a boy, where did you go to school?

SAUSAGE-SELLER: The singeing-'ouse, 'cept they only taught with their fists.

PAPHLAGONIAN: What did you say? [*Aside*] The oracle's very words! [*To* SAUSAGE-SELLER] Well, then: your gymnastic lessons, what did they consist in?

SAUSAGE-SELLER: 'Ow to look someone straight in the eye and say I 'adn't never stolen a thing.

PAPHLAGONIAN [*aside*]: Phoebus Apollo, what dost thou to me? [*To* SAUSAGE-SELLER] When you grew up, what was your profession?

SAUSAGE-SELLER: Selling sausages – oh yes, and a little male prostitution on the side.

PAPHLAGONIAN [*aside*]: Oh, woe is me, I'm finished, I'm no more! Ah, but there's still one ray of hope that's left. [*To* SAUSAGE-SELLER] Tell me just this: where did you sell your sausages? In the Market Square, or at the City gates?

SAUSAGE-SELLER: At the gates, next to the salt-fish stalls.

PAPHLAGONIAN: Aaah! It's all fulfilled! 'Take me within, most wretched as I am!'[102] [*Removes his garland.*] Farewell, my crown. I don't want to part from you, but I must. Now another must possess you – never a greater thief, but just more lucky.[103] Aaah! [*He falls insensible.*]

SAUSAGE-SELLER: Zeus, Lord of Greece, thou 'ast conquered! [*He takes the garland from the ground and sets it on his head.*]

DEMOSTHENES [*appearing at the window of the house*]: Congratulations, my friend and saviour! Don't forget, will you, that it was me that made you great. I don't ask for a great reward: only to be allowed to sign your writs, like Phanus did your rival's.[104] [*The* SAUSAGE-SELLER *nods and waves his agreement, and* DEMOSTHENES *disappears.*]

THEPEOPLE: And now I think it's time you told me your name.

SAUSAGE-SELLER: My name's Agoracritus, 'The Market 'Aggler'. Since boy'ood I've lived by 'aggling in the Market Square.

THEPEOPLE: Well, then, Agoracritus, I entrust myself to you, and I commit this Paphlagonian also [*kicking the* PAPHLAGONIAN] to your loving care.

SAUSAGE-SELLER: I'll cherish you and nourish you, Thepeople, so well you'll swear you've never known a man who was a greater benefactor to the City of Gawpers. [*Leads* THEPEOPLE *into his house; the* PAPHLAGONIAN *remains on the ground.*]

CHORUS:

> What fairer way to start a song,
>   What fairer way to end,
> Than when the Knights from horses swift
>   In harmony descend
> And sing *not* of Lysistratus[105]
>   Nor persecute Thumantis,
> Who never eats, Apollo knows,
>   Whose raiment very scant is?
> At Delphi he grasps the sacred quiver
> With many a tear and many a shiver
> And begs the god for milk and honey
> Or at any rate for a little money!

LEADER:

If we upbraid the wicked, it should be begrudged by none;
If reasonably you look at it, it's just what should be done.
Now if the man who of my words must feel the pointed end

Himself were quite well known, then never would I name a friend
In company with him; but as it is, I must. You all
Know Arignotus, if you know true men from lyres[106] at all.
A brother Arignotus has, in morals unrelated:
Ariphrades the wicked he, with evil never sated.
He isn't just a villain, for that's common nowadays,
Nor yet a super-villain – he has new unheard-of ways.
He prostitutes his tongue: in black and white to put it down,
He cunnilingus practises on all the whores in town
(Soiling his chin) and pokes their fires in unapproved-of style;
He acts just like Oeonichus or Polymnestus vile.
Whoever loathes not such a man or holds he doesn't stink
Shall never from one cup with me at any party drink.

CHORUS:

When in the night my thoughts roam free,
There's one thing always beats
My comprehension, viz. to wit,
Just how Cleonymus[107] eats.
He grazes on the rich men's boards
And never lets them be,
So when they see their larders bare
They beg on bended knee:
'We pray thee, Lord, depart this place!
Oh, show thy mercy, show thy grace!
We beg thee, beg thee, go away,
And spare our table now, we pray!'

LEADER:

Not long ago the warships held a meeting, as we're told,
And first to speak rose up a ship most dignified and old:
'Girls, have you heard the rumour? That a hundred ships or so
Against the Carthaginians are being urged to go?
Hyperbolus[108] proposes this, an evil man and sour.'
'We must oppose this outrage to the utmost of our power!'
The meeting cried; and one young ship, who man had never
known,
Said, 'Gods, but I will never be Hyperbolus's own!
If I could find no other way to escape so foul a lot,
I'd rather just remain in dock until I age and rot!'

Then the *Nauphante* said, 'And me, I vow the same as you,
If I'm a shipwright's daughter, made of pinewood good and true!
If that is what they want, then let us sail to Theseus' shrine
For sanctuary, or where there dwell the Eumenides divine.[109]
But never will Hyperbolus command *us* in his pride,
Though o'er the land his mouth be open fifty fathoms wide.
If he so badly wants to sail, then let him sail to hell
Upon the oil-boats which he once with lanterns used to sell!'[110]

SCENE TWO: *The same. The house now represents the Acropolis.*
[*The* CHORUS *are present as before. Enter the* SAUSAGE-SELLER *in
resplendent new clothes.*]

SAUSAGE-SELLER:
> Keep silence all!
> Your breath, O save it!
> Let no one file
> An affidavit!
> The Courts, in which
> This land rejoices,
> Must all be closed!
> Now raise your voices,
> Spectators all,
> In gladness singing
> To celebrate
> The news I'm bringing!

LEADER [*recitative*]:
> O light for sacred Athens newly kindled,
> Protector of the Isles that once were swindled,
> What is your good news? Wherefore is it meet
> That we should sacrifice in every street?

SAUSAGE-SELLER:
> I've boiled Thepeople, made him young again![111]

LEADER:
> O marvellous idea! Where is he, then?

SAUSAGE-SELLER:
> In violet-crownèd Athens[112] holds he sway.

LEADER:
> O can we see his form and his array?

SAUSAGE-SELLER:

> He is as when, in the brave days of old,
> Just Aristides and Miltiades bold[113]
> Dined with him once, when all was bright as gold.
> But see, the Propylaean Gates unfold!

[*The doors open wide, and* THEPEOPLE *appears rejuvenated, wearing a linen tunic of the type fashionable at the time of the Persian war, his hair bound up with a golden grasshopper brooch.*]

SAUSAGE-SELLER:

> Behold your City great,
> Old Athens in her glory,
> The poets' favourite state,
> Acclaimed in song and story,
> Where in his power and pride
> Thepeople doth reside!

CHORUS:

> Rich and shining, violet-crowned,
> Athens' envied, holy ground,
> Forth from out thy portals bring
> Him who of all Greece is King!

[THEPEOPLE *comes forward.*]

SAUSAGE-SELLER:

> Thepeople now behold,
> A dish for jaded palates!
> Dressed in the fashion old,
> His smell is not of ballots
> But myrrh and love and peace
> For every part of Greece.

CHORUS:

> Hail, O King, says every voice!
> With you we will now rejoice!
> Just reward for you who won
> Victory at Marathon!

THEPEOPLE: Come here, my dear Agoracritus. I must say that boiling treatment was very effective. Thank you very much indeed.

SAUSAGE-SELLER: Yer thank me nah; but, my dear chap, you dunno wot you useter be like and wot you useter do. If you did, you'd think me a god.

THEPEOPLE: Why, what was I like before? What did I use to do?

SAUSAGE-SELLER: Well, for one thing, whenever anyone in the Assembly talked like this, yer know, 'Thepeople, I love you, I cherish you, I care for you, I am yer only protector', the sorter standard opening, you know, well, you flapped yer wings and bellowed ''Ear, 'ear!' like a bloody bull.

THEPEOPLE: Did I really?

SAUSAGE-SELLER: And then he pulled the wool over yer eyes and left you in the lurch.

THEPEOPLE: What? They did that all the time, and I never realized it?

SAUSAGE-SELLER: That's right. And you'd open and close yer ears like an umbrella – open to *them* and tight shut to everyone else.

THEPEOPLE: Was *I* as stupid and as senile as that?

SAUSAGE-SELLER: Why, if there was two speakers, and it was a question of 'ow to spend some money, and A said we should use it to build warships and B said we should spend it on officials' and jurymen's pay, B would win every time by acclamation. Come on, no need to 'ang yer 'ead like that. 'Ere, where are you off to?

THEPEOPLE: I'm so ashamed of all the wrong things I did.

SAUSAGE-SELLER: Come orf it, it wasn't your fault, it was them that deceived you. Let's test you. Tell me, suppose some layabout of a prosecutor says to you, 'If you don't convict this prisoner, gentlemen of the jury, you won't get your daily bread'114. Wot would you do to 'im?

THEPEOPLE: Up-end him and chuck him into a felon's grave – with Hyperbolus round his neck for good measure.

SAUSAGE-SELLER: *Dead* right! Just the job! Now let's 'ear something abaht a few of yer other policies.

THEPEOPLE: Well, first of all, all the rowers in the fleet, I'd give them their full pay as soon as they came into port.

SAUSAGE-SELLER: Many a worn backside will 'oot its delight at that.

THEPEOPLE: Next, when a soldier's name appears on the list for an expedition, on that list it will stay, with no chopping and changing of any kind for the benefit of the well-connected.

SAUSAGE-SELLER: Cleonymus is going to feel the pinch!

THEPEOPLE: And no beardless youths will be allowed in the Market Square.

SAUSAGE-SELLER: Then 'ow's Cleisthenes and Strato[115] to do their shopping?

THEPEOPLE: No, I don't mean them – I mean those boys who sit in the perfume market and talk fancy talk, you know, 'That Phaeax,[116] isn't he clever? Wasn't it ingenious, the way he got off on that capital charge? He's so logical and rhetorical, so inventively phraseological, so very clear, so dynamical, and so extremely drastical when it comes to countering theatricals.'

SAUSAGE-SELLER: Well, when it comes to cahntering them chatteronicals, you're right blowafartical, I can see that.

THEPEOPLE: Yes, I'll make them abandon all that resolution-moving of theirs and do some good healthy stag hunting.

SAUSAGE-SELLER [presenting a BOY who carries a stool]: Then 'ere's a good old Athenian folding stool for you,[117] and 'ere's a boy to carry it for you, with both 'is balls in place. If you feel like it you can make him your stool too.

THEPEOPLE [who is quite taken by the BOY]: Ah, back to the good old days with a vengeance!

SAUSAGE-SELLER: You'll say that all right when I give you your thirty-year peace treaties. [Calling off] Peacetreaties! come here.
[Two beautiful girls enter and stand one on each side of THEPEOPLE.]

THEPEOPLE: Whee-whew! Holy Zeus, but they're a pair of smashers. Can I give them, you know, a bit of the old thirty years? Tell me, how did you get them?

SAUSAGE-SELLER: Why, that Paphlagonian hid them in the cupboard so you could never get at 'em. But now I 'and them over to you to take 'ome to the country.[118]

THEPEOPLE [kicking the still prostrate PAPHLAGONIAN]: Yes, what about this one? He was responsible for all my miseries. What are you going to do to him?

SAUSAGE-SELLER: Oh, nothing very terrible. Let 'im take over my stall. 'E can 'ave a monopoly of selling sausages at the City gates. 'E can mix dogs' meat with donkey's meat to 'is 'eart's content, get drunk, argue with the tarts, an' 'ave used bathwater to drink!

THEPEOPLE: Good idea. Having shouting contests with the tarts and the bath attendants, that's just about his level. And now, Agoracritus. I invite you to dine with me in the Town Hall, in the very seat formerly occupied by that sub-human swine. [Taking a bright *green robe from a slave and giving it to the* SAUSAGE-SELLER] Here, wear this to match the occasion. Come on, let's go. [*Glancing at the* PAPHLAGONIAN] Oh – him! Here, someone, take him away to his new job. I want all our allies, whom he so grievously wronged, to see him at the City gates selling sausages, or in the vernacular –

ALL: FLOGGING HIS GUTS OUT!!!

[THEPEOPLE *and the* SAUSAGE-SELLER *leave, escorted by the* CHORUS, *while* SLAVES *drag the* PAPHLAGONIAN *off on the other side with a meathook.*][119]

Peace

Translated by Alan H. Sommerstein

Introductory Note to *Peace*

In the summer of 422 an event of great importance for the Greek world occurred at Amphipolis, an Athenian colony in Thrace. This had been captured in 424 by the Spartan general Brasidas, rather to the embarrassment of his home government, which wanted to end the war in order to recover the prisoners taken in the Pylos campaign; and Cleon now sailed to Thrace in an attempt to undo some of the harm Brasidas, exceptional among contemporary Spartans both for his vigour and for his humanity, had been doing to Athenian interests there. All went well for Cleon until, being taunted (somewhat unjustly) with inactivity by his men, he led them to reconnoitre before Amphipolis, unaware that Brasidas had been watching all his movements and had occupied the city with his forces before Cleon reached it. A surprise attack, just as the Athenian army was retreating, put most of them to flight and inflicted heavy casualties on the remainder. But what gave the event its importance was that both Cleon and Brasidas were killed.

There was now no obstacle to peace, as far as Sparta and Athens were concerned. Some of Sparta's allies, indeed, wanted to continue the war – Aristophanes has hard words for Megara and Boeotia on this account – but they were outvoted. Athenian politics, for the time being, were dominated by Nicias, who was strongly in favour of peace because (so Thucydides says) he thought it, in all senses, less dangerous; and in the spring of 421 a peace treaty, to last fifty years, was duly sworn. It took effect on the 25th of Elaphebolion. About a fortnight earlier, in celebration of the great deliverance now almost assured, Aristophanes' *Peace* was performed at the City Dionysia, winning second prize.

The play shows to an extreme degree that dramatic construction in any modern sense was not an essential feature of Old Comedy. The action proper ends when Peace is recovered – but much of the spectacle, and most of the satire and the farce, is still to come, and it does not need dramatic tension to be effective. Still less do the two great prayers (pp. 132, 145), which express the aspirations of characters, poet and audience alike. But in order to appreciate the play fully it is necessary, to some extent, to enter into the feelings of people who had been engaged in a bloody and unwinnable war for ten years – and who had lost more than one golden opportunity to end it. Was it quite certain that the God of War had no more surprises up his sleeve?

The Chorus of *Peace* have been a subject of much discussion. When they first appear, they are 'men of Greece' (in the Greek 'Panhellenes'); and in the hauling scene some of them seem to be addressed as representing Argos, Megara, Sparta and other states. But on p. 115 only 'the farmers' are hauling, and from then on the Chorus is fairly consistently regarded as composed of farmers, and later specifically of Athenian farmers (they can complain about the wiles of Athenian army officers, p. 139). A possible exception is Hermes' remark about 'the cities of Greece' (p. 116); it cannot be regarded as certain, though, that this refers to the Chorus, since if it does it seems to imply that they wore masks with black eyes – and if so it is odd that attention is not drawn to this earlier.

It seems to me that the best solution is to assume that in *Peace*, as in *The Wasps* and *The Frogs*, Aristophanes had a subsidiary Chorus, some of whose members represented various states, others various occupations, and one or two prominent individuals (Lamachus is mentioned by name, p. 114; but it is unlikely that the performer in question wore a portrait-mask). This subsidiary Chorus may leave the scene at p. 115 (though Trygaeus' 'Get out!' is not in the Greek), or they may remain, their dramatic identity being gradually forgotten, until the Chorus address them as 'props-men' on p. 122, whereupon they depart with the Chorus's now superfluous agricultural equipment. (Compare the departure of the boys in *The Wasps* with their fathers' cloaks.)

Peace's two attendants, whom I have named Harvest and Festival, are literally 'the Vintage Season' (*Opora*, corresponding roughly to August and September) and 'Delegation' (*Theoria*), sc. to one of the Panhellenic festivals. (This is the reason for the Slave's reference to the Isthmian Games (p. 128), or at least the respectable reason; and it is also why Festival is presented to the Council, since its members normally manned the delegations.) Unlike Peace, these two appear as very live girls.

I am grateful to David Barrett for allowing me to use his translation of the passage in the *parabasis* (p. 123) which Aristophanes repeats from *The Wasps*.

CHARACTERS

TWO SLAVES *of Trygaeus*

TRYGAEUS *an elderly farmer*

DAUGHTER *to Trygaeus*

HERMES *caretaker of Heaven*

WAR

HAVOC *servant to War*

CHORUS OF FARMERS

HIEROCLES *an oracle-monger*

SICKLE-MAKER

ARMS SALESMAN

FIRST BOY *son to Lamachus*

SECOND BOY *son to Cleonymus*

CHILDREN *to Trygaeus*

SUBSIDIARY CHORUS *of citizens of various Greek states*

HARVEST
FESTIVAL } *Peace's beautiful companions*

JAR-MAKER

SPEAR-POLISHER

HELMET-MAKER

SLAVES, CITIZENS, *etc.*

PEACE (*a statue*)

ACT ONE

SCENE: *The action begins in front of* TRYGAEUS' *house in Athens, and ends in heaven. A building on the left represents the house of* TRYGAEUS; *to this a stable is attached, with a door opening on to the stage. A building on the right will presently represent the palace of the gods. In the centre, well up stage, is a trapdoor.*

[*The* SECOND SLAVE *is outside* TRYGAEUS' *house, apparently engaged in kneading dough, when the* FIRST SLAVE *comes out of the stable door, holding his nose and turning his head away.*]

FIRST SLAVE: Quick, quick, another bun for the beetle!

SECOND SLAVE [*putting something into* FIRST SLAVE's *hand*]: There. He's welcome to it, the bugger. I hope it's the sweetest thing he ever eats!

[*The* FIRST SLAVE *goes into the stable, and almost immediately returns.*]

FIRST SLAVE: Another one. Make it donkey shit this time.

SECOND SLAVE: There you are. What's happened to the one you just gave him? He can't have eaten it!

FIRST SLAVE: He did, though – grabbed it out of my hand, rolled it into a ball with his feet, and just wolfed it down. But come on, quick, he needs them thick and fast. [*Runs into the stable.*]

[SECOND SLAVE *sets feverishly to work making further 'buns'.*]

SECOND SLAVE [*to the audience*]: For heaven's sake, you muckshifters there, can you help me, please? Please – unless you want me to die of air pollution!

FIRST SLAVE [*putting his head out of the door*]: Another, another! From a boy with lots of lovers. He says he likes them friction-treated.

SECOND SLAVE: Here.

[FIRST SLAVE *takes it and disappears.*]

Well, at least there's one thing nobody could accuse me of: they can't say I pinch the dough and eat it!

FIRST SLAVE [*emerging again*]: Pfooh! More, more, we need more! keep on getting them ready!

SECOND SLAVE: Look, I'm finished. I just can't stand the stench any longer.

FIRST SLAVE: All right, then, I'll see to it myself. [*Takes* SECOND SLAVE's *kneading-trough and goes into the stable*.]

SECOND SLAVE: Tell him to go to hell – and go with him if you like! [*To the audience*] I wonder, can anyone tell me if he knows where I can find a nose that doesn't let the air in? This making buns for a beetle to eat is the ghastliest job you can imagine. I mean, a pig, say, or a dog, they just take it as you shit it. But this creature, it's so conceited! It stands there nose in air and refuses to eat the stuff unless I spend the whole day shaping it and rubbing it and kneading it first – you'd think it was a woman! I'd better go and see if it's finished. I'll just open the door a crack, I don't want it to see me. [*Goes to the stable door and peeps in.*] Go on, go on, that's right, keep eating till you burst! Gods, the way the bugger eats! Keeps his head down like a wrestler or something, swings his jaw from side to side, and twists his head and hand round like this [*illustrates*] – as if he was plaiting hawsers for a ship or something!

FIRST SLAVE [*bursting out of the stable*]: The filthy stinking greedy so-and-so! It must be a punishment that some god has brought down on us. Who, though? Not Aphrodite, for sure.

SECOND SLAVE: And certainly not the Graces either.

FIRST SLAVE: Well, who, then?

SECOND SLAVE: There's only one possibility. It must be Zeus himself, shitting enthroned in heaven.[1]

FIRST SLAVE: I expect by now someone out there is asking – some young fellow who always knows all the answers, but not this time – asking 'What's this all about? What's the beetle mean?' and the Ionian visitor sitting next to him is telling him 'Ah think it's all an allego-ry about Cleon, "cahz, you see, *he*'s eatin' shit these days down amerng the dead men, you know!'[2] – But I'd better go and give the beetle a drink. [*He goes into the stable*.]

SECOND SLAVE: Well, I think I'd better explain the plot to you people. To all of you   the kiddies, the teenagers, the grown-ups, the top people, the top-top people, and the top-top-*top* people. My master, he's mad. No, not the way you are – a completely new

kind of madness. What he does is, all day long he stares up at the
sky with his mouth open – like this – and complains and complains
to Zeus. 'Zeus,' he says, 'what is it you're trying to do? Why
don't you put your broom down before you've swept the whole
of Greece clean?' Hey! Quiet a moment, I think I hear something.

TRYGAEUS [*inside*]: Zeus, what are you trying to do to our people?
Any time now you'll have unmanned every city in Greece.

SECOND SLAVE: You see? Just what I said. That's how he goes on
all the time. At the beginning it was like this. He used to mutter
to himself, 'I wonder how I can manage to go up and see Zeus?'
Then he started making little ladders to climb up to heaven on, but
he always fell down and bruised his head. Then yesterday he went
out some damn place, I don't know where, and brought home this
beetle, an enormous one bred on Mount Etna,[3] and told me, if you
please, to keep it here in the stable. And he, he rubbed the creature
down like a thoroughbred colt and he said to it, 'Well, my little
Pegasus, my noble winged steed, soon you'll be flying up to Zeus
with me on your back.' I'll take a look and see what he's doing
now. [*Peeps through the stable door.*] Help! Come here, everybody,
quick! My master's flying up in the sky on beetle-back!

[*A crowd gathers in front of the house. At the same moment a giant
beetle appears above the stable, suspended on the machine normally
used by gods in tragedy, and with* TRYGAEUS *astride it.*]

TRYGAEUS [*singing*]:

> Gently, gently, beetle-chick!
> Mind you don't start off too quick
> Trusting in your strength and fire;
> Wait until your limbs perspire,
> Till the movement of each sinew
> Loosens up the muscles in you.
> (And watch it, let's have no bad breath,
> Or else you'll stay at home till death.)

SECOND SLAVE:

> O lord and master, how you rave!

TRYGAEUS:

> Hold thy tongue, thou meddling slave!

SECOND SLAVE:

> What's this hare-brained thing you've tried,

Through the upper air to ride?

TRYGAEUS:

'Tis a scheme that I contrive,
'Tis for all of Greece I strive.

SECOND SLAVE:

Yes, but tell us, why d'you fly?
What's this madness? Tell us why!

TRYGAEUS:

Watch your words, say naught of madness,
Speak no ill, but shout for gladness.
Let this message all men reach,
They must all refrain from speech.
(They should also put a wall
Round any heap of shit at all,
And if they wish to speed my flight
They all should shut their arses tight.)

SECOND SLAVE: I will not keep quiet – not unless you tell me where
you're trying to fly to.

TRYGAEUS: Why, to Zeus in heaven, of course.

SECOND SLAVE: What for?

TRYGAEUS: I want to ask him about the Greek people, the whole lot
of them, what the hell he thinks he's doing with them.

SECOND SLAVE: And if he doesn't tell you, what will you do?

TRYGAEUS: I'll prosecute him for betraying Greece to the Mede!⁴

SECOND SLAVE [appalled at this blasphemy]: Over my dead body!

TRYGAEUS: Whether you like it or not!

[The beetle rises higher in the air.]

SECOND SLAVE: Help! Help! Children, come out here!

[Three or four CHILDREN come out of TRYGAEUS' house.]

Children, your father has secretly deserted you, left you orphans,
and gone off to heaven. Poor infants! Come, beg him to return.

DAUGHTER [singing]:⁵

Father, oh father, these rumour-borne words
    Portend neither fairly nor well
Is it true, is it true, thou hast flown with the birds
    And sped on the breezes to hell?

[Speaking] Say, is it true, is it true? Speak, father, if ever you loved
me.

TRYGAEUS:

That you must guess, my sweet maiden; what I know is, I really
                                                    can't stand it,
Time after time, when you ask me for bread and call me your
                                                    daddy,
While I know only too well that we haven't an obol between us.
If I succeed in my quest, I promise I quickly will give you
One gigantic roll with a clout on the ear for a filling!

DAUGHTER:

But what can be your transport on this journey?
For sure no ship can travel such a road.

TRYGAEUS:

No ship shall bear me, but a wingèd steed.

DAUGHTER:

But what is in thy heart that thou shouldst ride
Up to the gods upon a beetle, daddy?

TRYGAEUS:

In Aesop's fable will you find it writ
'Tis the sole creature that to heaven has flown.

DAUGHTER:

A tale I cannot credit, O my father,
That such a smelly insect should have done so.

TRYGAEUS:

It went to seek revenge upon the eagle,[6]
And, reaching heaven, smashed the eagle's eggs.

DAUGHTER:

But shouldst thou not have flown on Pegasus,
To make the gods think thee a *tragic* hero?

TRYGAEUS:

But then I would have needed double rations,
Whereas this beetle – everything *I* eat
Will subsequently serve as food for *him*.

DAUGHTER:

But what if into ocean's depths thou fallest?
Winged as thou art, how think'st thou to escape?

TRYGAEUS:

I have a rudder ready to be used, [*indicating his phallus*]
And am I not riding a *beetleship*?[7]

DAUGHTER:
    What harbour though will shelter such a craft?
TRYGAEUS:
    Why, Beetle Harbour, down at the Peiraeus!
DAUGHTER:
        Take care thou fallest not from off thy steed
        And break'st thy leg, and giv'st Euripides
        A plot to write another tragedy.[8]
TRYGAEUS: I'll see to that, don't you bother. Cheerio!
    [*Exeunt all but* TRYGAEUS.]
Please, everybody – I'm doing all this for your sake – could you
possibly abstain from shitting and farting for the next three days?
If Pegasus here gets a whiff, he'll chuck me head over heels and
swoop down for a meal! [*Sings*]:
        Come, Pegasus, go on with joy,
            Behind thee put all fears,
        Let golden-bridled harness sounds
            Assail thy shining ears.
    [*The beetle suddenly stops moving and assumes a descending attitude.*]
        What doest thou? Why thus incline
            Thy nose towards the john?
        Stretch forth thy wings in speedy flight,
            Away from earth! Go on!
    [*He prods the beetle, which resumes its flight.*]
        Now straight towards the halls of Zeus!
            Recall those famous words:
        'From shit refrain thy nostrils, and
            Thy nose from mortal turds.'
    [*The beetle again stops, and* TRYGAEUS *has difficulty holding on.*]
        Hey, you there in Peiraeus, where
            The whores and pimps abound!
        What are you playing at, laying eggs
            Of shit upon the ground?

        The only way to save me, sir,
            Is if you dig a trench
        And cover it with earth and flowers
            And myrrh to stop the stench.

If I should suffer any ill,
    The Chians will be fined
Some thirty thousand drachs, and all
    Because of your behind!⁹

[*The beetle wobbles violently, and* TRYGAEUS *all but falls off.*]

He-e-elp! No, I mean it, this is serious! Here, you down there, the crane-handler, do for heaven's sake be a bit more careful! I've already got breezes blowing in my stomach, and if you don't watch out I'll be giving the beetle a meal!

[*The beetle steadies, and begins to come in to land at the right-hand end of the stage.*]

I think I must be getting near heaven now.

[*The beetle lands in front of the palace of the gods, and* TRYGAEUS *alights.*]

Whew! Ah, this must be Zeus's house. [*Knocks.*] Anyone at home? Here, can't somebody open the door?

HERMES [*coming to the door*]: Whence comes this mortal's – [*Opens the door and gapes at the beetle.*] Heracles save us, what is that monstrosity?

TRYGAEUS: Why, a hippobeetle.

HERMES: Why, you foul, shameless, desperate, good-for-nothing villain!¹⁰ How dare you come here, you villainest of villains? What's your name? [*Shakes him.*] Come on, out with it!

TRYGAEUS: Villain.

HERMES: And where do you come from? Well?

TRYGAEUS: I'm a Villain.

HERMES: And your father's name?

TRYGAEUS: Why, Villain.

HERMES: Let me have your real name, or I swear you will be exterminated!

TRYGAEUS: All right. I'm Trygaeus of Athmonon, an honest farmer with a vineyard. I'm not an informer, and I'm not a busybody.

[*During the following conversation the beetle is unobtrusively removed.*]

HERMES: And why have you come here?

TRYGAEUS [*taking some meat from a bag slung over his shoulder*]: I've brought you a present.

HERMES [*wolfing the meat down*]: What, you mean you came all the way here for that? Poor fellow!

TRYGAEUS: Well, greedyguts, I wasn't a villain for long, was I? Now could you please ask Zeus to come and speak to me?

HERMES: Ha! ha! ha! You mean you thought you'd find the gods here? They're gone! They left home yesterday.

TRYGAEUS: Where on earth did they go?

HERMES: Nowhere on earth, you fool.

TRYGAEUS: Where in heaven, then?

HERMES [with an expansive gesture]: Far, far away, right in the furthest recesses of the sky.

TRYGAEUS: You mean they've left you here alone?

HERMES: Yes, I'm supposed to look after the stuff they've left behind, you know, furniture, pots and pans and what not.

TRYGAEUS: But why did they leave?

HERMES: They were fed up with you Greeks. So here where they used to live, they got War to move in, and said he could do as he pleased with you; and then they set up house as high in heaven as they could get, so they couldn't either see you fighting each other or hear you praying to them.

TRYGAEUS: But what made them want to do that?

HERMES: Because they'd tried to make peace over and over again, and still you insisted on carrying on with the war. If the Spartans had a slight advantage, they'd say to themselves 'Och, by the Twa Gudes,¹¹ the wee Athenians are going to be punished the noo!' While if you wee Athenians got the upper hand, and the Spartans came suing for peace, you'd immediately say 'They're trying to cheat us, by Athena! But by Zeus, we mustn't be taken in. So long as we hold on to Pylos¹² they'll come again sure enough!'

TRYGAEUS: Sounds familiar.

HERMES: And so I don't know if you'll ever see Peace again.

TRYGAEUS: Why, where has she gone?

HERMES: War has taken her and thrown her into a deep dark cave.

TRYGAEUS: A deep dark cave?

HERMES [pointing to the trapdoor]: Yes, down there. You can see the enormous stones he's piled on top so you can never get her out.

TRYGAEUS: And what's he mean to do with us?

HERMES: All I know is, when he came here last night he brought a mortar – a gigantic mortar.

TRYGAEUS: A mortar? What's he going to do with it?

HERMES: Pound every city in Greece to a pulp. But I'd better be off. I think he's coming out. [*A roar is heard.*] Yes, listen, there he is. [HERMES *rushes off.*]

> [*Enter, from the palace,* WAR, *a ferocious monster, carrying a mortar and some foodstuffs.*]

WAR: Aaaah! O miserable, miserable, miserable mankind! Today you will receive the pounding of your lives!

TRYGAEUS [*aside*]: Lord Apollo, what a monstrous mortar! And how vile this War is to look at! No wonder we always tremble at the mention of his name and call him terrible and ferocious and the Emptier of Bowels!

WAR [*putting some leeks into the mortar*]: Aaaah! Ruin to Prasiae,[13] city of leeks, ruin on ruin on ruin! Prasiae, today you shall be destroyed!

TRYGAEUS: Well, that's the Spartans' headache – nothing for *us* to worry about.

WAR [*adding garlic*]: Aaaah! Megara, Megara, city of garlic, I shall pound you to pieces and mix you in my salad!

TRYGAEUS [*tears in his eyes from the garlic*]: Megara will weep today all right! [*Rubs his eyes.*]

WAR [*adding cheese*]: Aaaah! Sicily, Sicily, land of cheese, you will perish too!

TRYGAEUS: Poor island, all grated up!

WAR [*adding honey*]: Now let's just pour a bit of Attic honey on top.

TRYGAEUS [*keeping well out of the way*]: Here, I should use another kind if I were you. The Attic costs four obols. You really should save it, you know!

WAR [*ignoring him*]: Boy! Boy! Havoc!

> [*Enter* HAVOC, *a small edition of* WAR.]

HAVOC: You called, sir?

WAR: What do you mean just standing there like that? I'll teach you to be lazy! Here! [*Boxes his ears.*]

HAVOC: Ow, that stung! Ow! You didn't pack your punch with that garlic, did you?

WAR: Run and fetch a pestle, will you?

HAVOC: But we haven't got one. We only moved in yesterday.

WAR: Well, go to Athens and get one. And get it fast.

HAVOC: Yes, yes, yes, I know what you'll do if I don't. [*He runs off.*]

TRYGAEUS: What are we poor mortals to do now? Look at the terrible danger we're in. If he comes back with that pestle, War will sit down and pound up the whole of Greece with it. Dionysus, please destroy him![14] Or at least make sure he doesn't bring one back!

HAVOC [*returning*]: Sir!

WAR: Well? Haven't you got it?

HAVOC: Um – ah – the – the Athenians have lost their pestle![15]

TRYGAEUS: Great, by Athena! He couldn't have chosen a better time to get lost!

WAR: Well, run off to Sparta and get another, quick!

HAVOC: Yes sir, yes sir. [*Exit.*]

WAR [*shouting after him*]: Hurry up about it!

TRYGAEUS [*to the audience*]:What's going to happen to us all now? This is the crunch. Has anyone been initiated in the Mysteries up in Samothrace?[16] If so, now's the time to pray. Ask the gods to turn aside the danger, or sprain his ankle, or something.

HAVOC [*returning*]: Help! Help! Calamity!

WAR: What's all this? Don't tell me you've come without it again!

HAVOC: The Spartans have lost their pestle too!

WAR [*shaking him furiously*]: What do you mean, damn you?

HAVOC: They lent it to some friends in Thrace, and never got it back.

TRYGAEUS: Good old Twins![17] It may turn out all right after all. Keep your chins up, everyone.

WAR: Take all this stuff inside. I'll go and make a pestle myself. [WAR *and* HAVOC *go into the palace, the latter carrying the salad in the mortar.*]

TRYGAEUS: At last! As Datis[18] said one fine day when he was fucking himself –

[*sings*] 'I'm so happy and delighted,
I'm so pleasant and excited!'

Now's the time, men of Greece! We can get rid of all our troubles and all our wars! We can pull our beloved Peace out of her prison! – before some other pestle comes to stop us. Come here, quickly! Farmers! Merchants! Carpenters! Craftsmen! Immigrants! Visitors! Islanders! Everyone, come here!

Bring shovels, crowbars, ropes and all, to haul the goddess up! Our draught-work here will earn a draught from out Good Fortune's cup![19]

[*The* CHORUS *of farmers come running in, followed by a secondary Chorus of Athenians, Spartans, Argives, Boeotians and citizens of other states. In the following scene all dance, but only the main* CHORUS *sings. Both Choruses carry the implements just mentioned.*]

CHORUS:

> Come, quickly, all!
> I hear salvation call!
> Come, men of Greece,
> And let us rescue Peace!
>
> The call-up's dead and gone –
> See, the redcoats[20] are dismayed!
> Behold the joyous dawn
> That has Lamachus afraid!

[*To* TRYGAEUS]:

> Come, tell us what to do –
> We shall never fail or flag.
> With crowbars strong and true
> We'll wrench, with ropes we'll drag.
>
> We'll bring her to the light –
> Darling Peace for whom we pine!
> A goddess of great might
> And a lover of the vine!

TRYGAEUS: Do be quiet! Not so much euphoria! Do you want your shouting to bring War out here again?

LEADER: It was just that we were delighted with the kind of proclamation you made. For once it wasn't 'Come prepared with rations for three days'.

TRYGAEUS: Don't forget old Cerberus down below![21] If you're not careful he'll start bawling in Paphlagonian like he did when he was alive and stop us pulling Peace out of her cave.

LEADER: This time, if once we get our hands on her, there's no one will ever take her away again!

CHORUS: Hear, hear!

TRYGAEUS: You'll ruin the whole thing with your damn shouting. He'll rush out kicking and screaming and make chaos.

LEADER: Let him! Let him kick, let him rage, let him ruin! Today we're going to be happy!

[*The* CHORUS *burst into a wild dance of joy.*]

TRYGAEUS [*trying to stop them*]: What's wrong? Gentlemen, what's happened to you? In heaven's name I beg you – don't dance away the greatest opportunity you ever had!

LEADER [*the* CHORUS *still dancing as hard as ever*]: We're *not* dancing – it's our legs, they're so happy they're disobeying orders and dancing on their own!

TRYGAEUS: Please, no more. Stop dancing! STOP!

LEADER: There, we've stopped.

TRYGAEUS: No, you haven't.

LEADER [*they are still going strong*]: Just once more, and then we'll stop. [*They perform another evolution.*]

TRYGAEUS: There. Now enough. No more dancing from now on.

LEADER: All right, if that's what you want, we'll stop.

TRYGAEUS: But look, you *haven't* stopped!

LEADER: Look, one more kick of the right leg and we've stopped. All right?

TRYGAEUS: All right, and then stop making a nuisance of yourselves.

LEADER [*who is now, like all the* CHORUS, *standing on one foot*]: Excuse us, our left legs are complaining of discrimination.

[*The* CHORUS *resume their dance.*]

CHORUS:

> I feel I'm young again!
> I sing, I laugh, I fart,
> Rejoicing that at long, long last
> My shield and I can part!

TRYGAEUS [*still desperately trying to restrain them*]:

> Wait till it's certain and then rejoice!
> Wait till we've rescued Peace!
> Then you can dance and shout and laugh,
> Revel and never cease,
> Travel, rest, or screw some dames,
> Go to the Olympic Games,
> Wine and dine till dead of night,
> Be a regular Sybarite!
> Then you can hail the glorious day,
> Then, please, not now, you can shout 'hurray'!

CHORUS [*continuing to dance*]:

Would I could see that day!
I've drunk my fill of woe,
I've had enough of beds of straw
As used by Phormio.[22]

On juries when I sit
No more shall I be stern,
But now I'm free from toil and care
To pity I will turn.

We're sick of those parades
All round Lyceum Field,[23]
March here, march there, from morn till night,
Arrayed with spear and shield.
[*Forming a circle round* TRYGAEUS.]
Your wish is our command!
Come, tell us what to do!
We lacked a leader all these years,
Now Fortune's chosen you!

TRYGAEUS: Now let me see how we can shift these stones – [*He begins to examine the stones around the cave when* HERMES *suddenly re-enters.*]

HERMES: What do you think you're doing, you villain?

TRYGAEUS: As Cillicon[24] said – nothing that's wrong.

HERMES: Miserable mortal, you shall die for this!

TRYGAEUS: Oh, I don't know, Hermes. Being who you are you'll naturally select the victims by lot,[25] and how can you be sure my number will come up?

HERMES: You shall die, you shall die!

TRYGAEUS [*nonchalantly*]: Could you tell me the date when?

HERMES: Right away, this minute!

TRYGAEUS: That's impossible. I haven't bought my barley and cheese, and nobody ever goes off to die without taking their three days' rations![26]

HERMES: You're doomed! You'll be crushed to pieces!

TRYGAEUS: That would be a delightful sensation, but you're lying – I can't feel a thing.

HERMES: Don't you know that Zeus has decreed the death penalty for anyone discovered attempting to take Peace out of her cave?

TRYGAEUS: You mean it's absolutely certain I've got to die?

HERMES: Absolutely.

TRYGAEUS: Could you lend me three drachmas for a piglet, then, so I can see to my initiation?[27] Mustn't risk losing my eternal bliss!

HERMES: O Zeus, wielder of the thunderbolt –

TRYGAEUS [wheedlingly]: Lord Hermes, I beg you, please – for the gods' sake, don't inform on us!

HERMES: I cannot remain silent!

TRYGAEUS: Lord Hermes, I beg you, please – for the meat's sake! Remember I brought it here specially for you.

HERMES: But my dear chap, I'm under orders from Zeus. 'Cry it from the rooftops,' he said, 'shout aloud, let thy voice be piercing; else shall I level thee with the dust.'

TRYGAEUS: Oh, Hermes – my lovable Hermikins – I beseech you, don't! [To the CHORUS] What's happened to you, standing frozen like statues? Say something, blast you! Do you want him to start his rooftop act again?

CHORUS [kneeling around HERMES]:

> Lord, withhold your dreadful threat!
> Think of all that pork you ate,
> All from offerings of mine:
> Have respect to slaughtered swine!

TRYGAEUS:

> Hermes, Lord, accept their plea!
> See their loving care for thee!

LEADER:

> Stay thy wrath and let us save
> Peace from out her gloomy cave!

CHORUS:

O Hermes, lover of all men, most generous of the blest,
    If you hate Peisander's[28] shaggy brows and crests with strange
                                                             devices,
Be gracious to us, and henceforth with never-flagging zest
    We'll honour you with great processions and with sacrifices.

TRYGAEUS: Have mercy, I pray thee, on their piteous cries, inasmuch as they revere thee far more than heretofore –

HERMES: Of course; they *steal* more than ever before.[29]

TRYGAEUS: No, but I've got something absolutely vital to tell you. There's a *conspiracy* afoot against the gods – all of them.

HERMES: Go on. I'm listening.

TRYGAEUS: It's the Moon and that villain the Sun. They've been plotting against you all for years. They mean to betray Greece to the barbarians.

HERMES: And what do they hope to achieve by that?

TRYGAEUS: Don't you see? *We* sacrifice to you – but the barbarians all sacrifice to the Sun and Moon, and so you see they want to get rid of us, so that *they* can take all the gods' perks.

HERMES: Ah, that explains why they've been cutting the calendar short,³⁰ the filthy sods, and robbing us of all those days!

TRYGAEUS: Exactly. So, dear Hermes, be our helper, pull along with us, and we promise to give all the gods' perks to *you*! We'll turn the Great Pan-Athenian Games into a feast to Hermes, we'll make the Mysteries yours and the feasts of Zeus and Adonis yours and *everything* yours! And the other cities of Greece, released from all their sorrows, will all sacrifice to *Hermes* the Defender instead of Apollo! Oh, and lots and lots of other marvellous things. And just to begin with – I'm sure you must have to pour a lot of libations – would you like to accept this? [*He presents* HERMES *with a gold cup.*]

HERMES [*fondling the cup and letting a tear drop*]: Dear me! I always had a soft spot for gold.

TRYGAEUS [*to the* CHORUS]: Now then, everybody! Take your shovels and let's get a move on shifting these stones.

LEADER: We will. [*The remaining members of the* CHORUS *set to work.*]

Hermes, wisest of gods, will you please be our foreman and tell us what to do? We'll follow your instructions fully and faithfully.

[*The stones having rapidly been cleared away, the whole* CHORUS *gathers round* HERMES.]

TRYGAEUS: Lift up the cup, Hermes, and when we've said our prayer, we'll do our share of the lifting up.³¹

HERMES [*raising the cup*]: Libation will be poured. Keep silence all!

LEADER: With this libation we pray that this day be the beginning of abundant blessing to all Greece, and that whosoever pulls with all his might on the ropes may never wear a shield again –

TRYGAEUS: But live in peace all the days of his life with a cuddly little tart, with nothing to consume his energy but poking . . . the fire.

LEADER: But whoever shall prefer there to be war –

TRYGAEUS: May Dionysus see to it that he is for ever taking splinters out of his elbows.

LEADER: And if any, out of a desire to attain the rank of regimental commander, shall begrudge, O holy Lady of Peace, thy return to the light, then in all his battles –

TRYGAEUS: May he drop his shield, like Cleonymus![32]

LEADER: And if any spear-maker or shield-merchant, intent on protecting his profits, wishes for more battles –

TRYGAEUS: May he be captured by robbers and forced to eat the worst barley!

LEADER: And if anyone ambitious to be a general, or any slave eager to run away, shall fail to pull his weight –

TRYGAEUS: May he be whipped and broken on the wheel!

LEADER: But on us may blessing light! Amen! Hail to Apollo, our shield and healer!

TRYGAEUS: Do you *have* to mention shields?

LEADER: All right. Hail to Apollo, our and healer![33]

TRYGAEUS: And to Hermes, the Graces, the Seasons, to Aphrodite and to Desire!

LEADER: But not to Ares.

TRYGAEUS: No.

LEADER: Nor to any other war-god.

TRYGAEUS: Definitely not.

[HERMES *pours a little wine out of the cup and drinks the rest. All cheer. The* CHORUS *form two lines, holding on to ropes which during the preceding scene slaves have been attaching to the statue of Peace down in the 'cave'.*]

HERMES: Now put your shoulders to it, and let's haul her up!

[*The* CHORUS, *with the secondary chorus behind them, begin to pull on the ropes.*]

CHORUS: Heave, ho!

HERMES: Haul away!

CHORUS: Heave, ho!

HERMES: Haul, haul away!

CHORUS: Heave, ho,
                           Here we go!

TRYGAEUS:

                                You at the back,
                                Why do you slack?
                           Why those Boeotian airs and graces?
                                Pull every man
                                Hard as you can,
                           Or I'll wipe that smile right off your faces!

HERMES: Heave, ho!

TRYGAEUS: Haul away!

CHORUS: Don't just shout,
                           Help us out!

TRYGAEUS [as he and HERMES join the straining CHORUS]:
                           Heave, ho,
                           Here we go,
                           Hard and strong!

CHORUS: Then – what's wrong?

TRYGAEUS [extracting himself from the line and running round to the end furthest from the 'cave']: Lamachus,34 it's you! You're just obstructing things. Clear off – we can do without your Gorgon-worgon shield!

HERMES [who has also left the line]: And those Argives35 – they're not hauling at all, just laughing at everyone else's troubles like they've been doing for years, and growing fat at both sides' expense too!

TRYGAEUS: But look, the Spartans are pulling their weight all right.

HERMES: You bet? Only the ones in prison,36 and even they're finding it a bit hard, what with all those chains.

TRYGAEUS: Yes, and the Megarians aren't doing anything either. You can see though it's not for want of trying. Why, they're biting on the ropes like dogs!

HERMES: Of course; it's a long time since they had anything else to eat.37

LEADER: We're getting nowhere, men. Now then, take hold again. All together now –

CHORUS: Heave, ho!

HERMES: Haul away!

CHORUS: Heave, ho!

HERMES: Haul, haul away!
CHORUS: Heave, ho,
               This is bloody slow!
TRYGAEUS:

                   You there, I say,
                   Haul the right way!
               Traitor's the only word to fit you!
                   Argives, don't slack –
                   We have no lack
               Of fists all ready and willing to hit you!
HERMES [rejoining the line]:
                   Heave, ho!
TRYGAEUS: Haul away!
CHORUS: We can see
                   Treachery!
TRYGAEUS: Heart and soul,
               Peace is your goal!
               Haul in hope!
CHORUS: Someone's sitting on the rope!
HERMES [to those at the end of the line]: You, Megarians, damn you,
   get out of here! Peace doesn't like you – she remembers too well
   what you did to her, when you rubbed your garlic in her face![38]
   And you too, Athenians, stop sitting down on the job! This isn't
   the law-courts, you know! If you want Peace to be saved, can't
   you withdraw a bit and stick to the sea in future? Get out!

   [The secondary chorus leave the ropes and run off.]

LEADER:

               Now it's up to us, boys,
                   Now the rest are gone.

HERMES:

               I think you've got it moving –
                   You're better off alone.

LEADER:

               He thinks we've got it moving!
                   Now heave with all your might.

TRYGAEUS:

               The farmers by themselves now
                   Will bring her to the light.

LEADER: Heave away! Haul away!

HERMES: Nearly there! Nearly there!

LEADER: Don't let up! Harder still!

HERMES [*as the head of the statue of* PEACE *begins to appear*]:
            Here she comes! Here she comes!

CHORUS:

            Heave away! Haul away!
            Heave, heave away!
            Haul, haul away!
            Hurrah! Hurrah! Hurrah!

[*Out of the trapdoor comes a gigantic statue of* PEACE *on a large
platform, flanked by two beautiful girls,* HARVEST *and* FESTIVAL.]

TRYGAEUS: My Lady of Bountiful Vineyards, what can I say to you?
Where can I find words rich enough, capacious enough to address
you with? I'd have brought some from home specially for you, but
I didn't have any. Welcome, Harvest! Welcome, Festival! Oh,
Festival, what a beautiful face! And what delicious perfume!
[*Taking a sniff in* FESTIVAL's *bosom*.] Gorgeous! Like incense and
myrrh! The true scent of demobilization!

HERMES: No whiff of a soldier's kit-bag?

TRYGAEUS: No fear! As someone said,[39] 'I spurn a hateful man's
most hateful pack.' A kit-bag! that only smells of onions, vinegar
and bad breath. But this little darling [*sniffs*] – smells of vineyards
and parties and festivals and flutes and dramatic contests and songs
by Sophocles and roast thrush and neat little speeches by Euripides –

HERMES: Watch it! That's slander, that is. Peace only likes real poets,
not that lawcourt quibbler.

TRYGAEUS: – and ivy and wine-strainers and little bleating lambs,
and women running to the oven with dough at their bosoms, and
slave-girls getting drunk and wine-jars getting upset and lots, lots
more marvellous things.

HERMES [*pointing off*]: Look now, look how happy all the cities of
Greece are now! All reconciled, chatting merrily away and laughing –

TRYGAEUS: Yes, even if they *are* all busy draining their black eyes!

HERMES [*pointing to the audience*]: And now look at that lot and see if
you can guess from their faces what they do for a living.

TRYGAEUS: Rubbish, I can't do that.

HERMES: Can't you? Don't you see that crest-maker over there? He's tearing out his hair, isn't he?

TRYGAEUS: Why, yes! And I think that one makes mattocks or something – the one that just farted in the sword-maker's face.

HERMES: And the sickle-maker, isn't he happy?

TRYGAEUS: Nearly nudged the spear-polisher off his feet!

HERMES: Now make the proclamation. Tell the farmers they can go home again.

TRYGAEUS: Oycz! Oyez! Oyez! It is hereby proclaimed that all farmers may return to their farms, taking their implements with them, and *not* taking any spear, sword or javelin. The whole country is now teeming with ripe, juicy Peace. Raise the hymn of thanksgiving and return to your home and your work!

CHORUS:
O day for which all farmers and all righteous men have yearned,
How happily I greet you, day of Peace at least returned!
What joy to see my vines again, what joy to say hello
To the fig-trees that I planted in my youth so long ago!

TRYGAEUS: Now, friends, let us first make reverence to the goddess who has set us free from war, helmet-crests and Lamachus; then let's buy some really *good* salt-fish for a change and zoom off home to our farms!

[*The* CHORUS *kneel silently before* PEACE, *then form a close square. Slaves bring out their agricultural tools.*]

HERMES: Don't they look a picture? Packed tight there with shining faces, like a feastful of cakes!

TRYGAEUS: Yes, indeed, their clod-breakers are all ready and gleaming, and their pitchforks catching the sun. That's the way to keep a vineyard tidy! Why, it makes me want to go home too and shove a mattock into the dear old earth again! [*Sings*]

> Remember now the ancient life
>   Which Peace once gave you all,
> The fruit-cakes, figs and myrtle wreaths,
>   The violets by the wall,
> The sweet new wine, the olive-groves
>   For which we've yearned so long,
> And thanking Peace for all these gifts
>   To her address your song.

CHORUS:

> Hail, O Peace, of the gods the most lovely!
> O how old and how deep is my yearning
> And my hope that once more I could see you
> > And go back to my old farm again!
> Once you poured all your blessings upon us,
> And for you our desire still is burning:
> You alone of the gods were the saviour
> > And the strength of the poor country men.
>
> When you ruled all our lives with your sweetness
> You had groats mixed with happiness for us,
> And our dearest desires found fulfilment,
> > And the joy that you gave us was free;
> Now our plants and our vines and our fig-trees
> Their rejoicing in unison chorus:
> 'Hail, O Peace, of the gods the most lovely!
> > We receive you with laughter and glee.'

LEADER:

> Say, Hermes, kindest of the gods above,
> What was it robbed us of the Peace we love?

HERMES: Listen to me, my poor farming friends, and you will hear what became of her. It all started when Pheidias got into a spot of bother.[40] Because Pericles was afraid he'd share Pheidias' fate – he knew how you liked to get your teeth into people – and so before anything could happen to him, he threw a little firebrand into the City marked 'Megarian Decree'[41] and in a moment it was all ablaze, with him fanning the flames, and the smoke was in the eyes of every Greek, at home or abroad. The vines tried hard to resist, but in the end one of them began crackling, the wine-jars started hitting and kicking one another in rage, and there was nobody could bring the blaze under control and Peace just vanished.

TRYGAEUS: I never heard that before – and I never realized there was a connection between Peace here and Pheidias.

LEADER: Neither did I, but I see now. That's why she's so beautiful–she's a connection of his! The things one doesn't realize!

HERMES: And then your subject allies saw you roaring and baring your teeth at each other, and so being in any case fed up with having to pay tribute they plotted against you and went and bribed the Spartan leaders to go to war. The Spartans were always greedy, and very bad hosts as well,[42] so they chucked Peace into the street and took up with War instead. Their gain, of course, was sheer loss to their own farming community. The Athenian fleet started those reprisal raids, destroying the fig-trees of perfectly innocent country folk.

TRYGAEUS: Not innocent! It was the Spartans chopped down *my* black fig-tree that I'd planted and tended with my own hands.

LEADER: Hear, hear! And I had a six-bushel corn-bin ruined by one of them with a stone.

HERMES: Meanwhile in Athens, all the farmers were packed into the city. They were being sold down the river in just the same way, but they didn't tumble to it. All they could think of was the grapes and figs they'd lost, and they looked to the politicians to help them. *They* knew very well that the ordinary people were poor and short of bread; but they drove Peace out of town with a sharp goad made of bluster – and though she loved the City and kept coming back over and over again, they always chucked her out again. In the allied states they blackmailed all the men of any importance with allegations that they were in league with Brasidas; and every time, like a pack of hounds, you tore the victim to pieces. The City was pale and frightened, and any bit of juicy slander anyone threw at it, it snapped up. When the allies realized what was happening they rushed to stop the politicians' mouths with money. So a few men became richer and richer, while Greece was being bled white under your noses. And you know who was the greatest exponent of all this. It was the Tanner!

TRYGAEUS: Stop, Lord Hermes, please, not a word more! Let sleeping Cleons lie. That man's not our headache any more, he's yours.[43] [*Sings*]

> So even if he was a crook,
> A speaker prone to babble,
> A slanderer of the innocent,
> A rouser of the rabble,
> He's dead, and so if now you say
> Such things as that to me,
> You're injuring your own, because

He's now *your* property
                              (thank God!)
He's now *your* property!
But Peace, why don't you speak? Tell me. Why?

HERMES: You don't think she'd talk to them [*indicating the audience*], do you? After all she suffered at their hands?

TRYGAEUS: Well, at least let her say something to you.

HERMES: All right. [*Puts his ear to* PEACE'*s mouth.*] Beloved Peace, tell me your feelings about these people. [*Pause.*] Come on, dear Remover of Shields. [*Pause.*] Yes, I've got that. [*Pause.*] Is that what you're annoyed about? [*Short pause.*] I see. [*To the audience*] Listen, everybody; this is her complaint. She says she came to you of her own accord after the Pylos campaign, with a basket full of peace treaties for you, and three times, in full Assembly, you voted her down.

TRYGAEUS: We were wrong. But you will pardon us, Peace, won't you? We were suffering from leather on the brain.

HERMES [*after 'listening' to* PEACE *for a few moments*]: Listen what she's just asked me. She wants to know which of the Athenians is most opposed to her, and which of them is fondest of her and most keen on there being no more battles.

TRYGAEUS: Well, her best friend, by a long way, is Cleonymus.

HERMES: Why, what's Cleonymus like as a fighting man?

TRYGAEUS: Oh, extremely brave – except we found out he wasn't really his father's son. Every time he went out to battle it became obvious that he was really a *castaway.*[44]

HERMES: Another thing she wants to know. These days, when the Assembly meets, who's cock of the walk there on the Pnyx?

TRYGAEUS: Oh, Hyperbolus,[45] no doubt about that. [*The statue of* PEACE *suddenly rotates to face away from the audience.*] Here, what are you hiding your face for?

HERMES [*after consulting* PEACE]: She's furious with the People for choosing such a rotten leader.

TRYGAEUS: Oh, she needn't worry, we'll get rid of him. It was just that the People weren't used to fending for themselves without a guardian. They felt naked. So they put him on as a kind of temporary wrap.

HERMES [*after consulting*]: But she still wants to know what earthly good he'll do the City.

TRYGAEUS: Oh, our policy will be much sounder with him around.

HERMES: Why?

TRYGAEUS: Because he's a lamp maker, of course. Before he came we were groping in the dark; now we can make our decisions by lamplight!

[HERMES *is about to consult* PEACE *again when she suddenly turns once more to face the audience and in doing so hits* HERMES *in the face.*]

HERMES: Ow! [*He 'listens' again.*] Do you know what she wants me to ask you now?

TRYGAEUS: No, what?

HERMES: A lot. About the old friends she left behind when she went. First of all, how's Sophocles doing?

TRYGAEUS: Very well; but he's undergone an incredible transformation.

HERMES: What's happened to him?

TRYGAEUS: He's not Sophocles any more, he's Simonides!

HERMES: Simonides? what do you mean?

TRYGAEUS: He may be old and decayed, but these days, if you paid him enough, he'd go to sea in a sieve![46]

HERMES: And good old Cratinus, is he still alive?[47]

TRYGAEUS: No, he died of apoplexy last time we had a Spartan invasion.

HERMES: How come?

TRYGAEUS: He couldn't endure seeing all that lovely wine wasted when they broke the jars. Oh, and so many other horrible things have happened here since you've gone! I promise you, Peace, we'll never let you go again.

HERMES: Well then – on that condition I give you Harvest here to be your wife. Live with her in the country, and may you be the father of innumerable pretty little bunches of grapes!

TRYGAEUS [*to* HARVEST]: Come here, darling, and give us a kiss. [*She does so.*] Er – Hermes, do you think it would do me any harm if I indulged myself in her again after such a long lay-off?

HERMES: Take one cup of pennyroyal mixture directly afterwards.

Don't forget Festival here. She used to belong to the Council.[48]
Take her too, and give her back to them.

TRYGAEUS [*receiving* FESTIVAL *from him*]: Lucky Council! No more
'three days' rations'[49] – now it'll be three days' luscious soup, boiled
beef and tripe! Goodbye, my dear Hermes, and many, many
thanks.

HERMES: Goodbye to you. Remember me.

TRYGAEUS: O beetle, homeward, homeward we must fly. [*It is
nowhere to be seen.*] Here, what's happened to it?

HERMES: Zeus has taken it to draw his lightning-cart.

TRYGAEUS: But poor thing! it won't have anything to eat.

HERMES: It'll have its own ambrosia, specially produced by our
resident human being, Ganymede.[50]

TRYGAEUS: And me, how am I supposed to get home?

HERMES: Just go past the goddess, keep straight on and that'll take
you there.

TRYGAEUS [*to* HARVEST *and* FESTIVAL]: Come on, girls, hurry up,
come with me. There are a great many eager pricks waiting down
there!

[*They pass by the statue of* PEACE *and go into the central door;*
HERMES *goes into the palace of the gods. The* CHORUS *advance.*]

CHORUS [*handing over their agricultural and other implements to* SLAVES
who take them backstage]:

        All good fortune we wish to our hero,
          May he homeward return safe and sound;
        To the props-men we say, Watch this tackle,
        'Cos there's thieves always hanging around.
        Guard it closely and don't let them pinch it
          By sneaking their way round behind;
        For now is the time for the audience
          To hear what we've got on our mind.

LEADER:

        The stewards ought to beat a comic poet
        Who uses speeches like the one I'm making
        To preen himself before the audience.
        But all the same – O Muse, O Child of Zeus,
        If it is meet and right and fitting and due
        To honour him who is the most renowned

And best of all the comic tribe, our poet
Asserts that he alone deserves such honour.

He stopped his rivals poking fun at rags
And waging war on paltry fleas and lice;
He put an end to scenes where Heracles
Kneads dough, or waits and waits and waits for dinner;
He sacked the slaves who used to run away
Or cheat their masters, or get whipped in order
That someone else could get a laugh by asking
'Poor chap, what's happened to you? Has a whip
Invaded you, assailed your ribs in force
And overrun your back with fire and sword?'
Our poet's booted all that rubbish out
And given us works of art, great towering structures
Of words and thoughts, and jokes that are not vulgar.

Nor does he aim his shafts at private men
Or women; no, our Heracles took on
The greatest monster in the land, despite
The loathsome smell of leather it exuded
And all its awful Paphlagonian threats.
Jag-toothed it was, and from its staring eyes
Shot rays more terrible than Cynna's smile;
And in a grisly circle round its head
Flickered the tongues of servile flatterers,
Foredoomed to groan; its voice was like the roar
Of mighty floods descending from the hills,
Bearing destruction; noisome was the scent
That issued from the brute as it slid forth,
With camel's rump and monstrous unwashed balls.[51]
Undaunted by the sight, he stood his ground
And fought for you, and for your subject isles.

Remember then his deeds, requite his kindness;
Remember how, when he came first before,
He didn't hang around the wrestling schools
Hoping to catch a pretty boy or two;
He packed his bags and went, leaving behind

A little pain, much pleasure, and a feeling
That he had given all what they deserved.

So both boys and adults
    Should be glad when I win,
And especially those
    Who have hair that is thin,[52]
Because everyone then,
    When a party gets gay,
When they see that he's bald,
    Will admiringly say,
'Give old Baldy more sweet!
    Let's give honour, and show it,
To one who resembles
    Our noblest poet.'

CHORUS:

O Muse, abandon thoughts of war
And dance with me, thy friend of yore;
Come, sing of bridal rites above,
Of all the joys the immortals love,
And feasts that here on earth we hold;
For these thou lovest from of old.[53]

If Carcinus should come and say
'Come dancing with my sons today',[54]
Ignore him, keep away, disdain
Those neckless dwarfs who dance in vain,
Those mini-cocks with sheepshit spurs,
Those gimmick-hunting wanderers.

Do you remember how their dad
Once wrote a play, or thought he had,
In his opinion very nice,
To which he gave the name *The Mice*?
Alas, he found one evening that
His work was throttled by a cat!

The Graces fair should sing an air
    To hymn our poet wise,

When in the spring the swallows sing
  With joyous vernal cries,⁵⁵
And when (if still 'tis heaven's will
  To heed our prayers sage)
Melanthius and Morsimus
  Are both kept off the stage.

I once did hear (it pained my ear)
  Melanthius declaim,
When in their pride those brothers tried
  To sully Drama's name.
Those Gorgons vile in mythic style
  Both flesh and fish wolf down;
They show their face in the market-place –
  Old women flee from town.

Their armpits smell like goats from hell,
  They hunt for tasty skate;
O Muse most fair, hear now my prayer,
  On them expectorate!
Spit good and hard on that vile bard
  And on his viler brother,
And then at least we'll spend the feast
  Alone with one another.

ACT TWO

SCENE: *In front of* TRYGAEUS' *house.*

[*Enter, by a side passage,* TRYGAEUS *with* HARVEST *and* FESTIVAL.]

TRYGAEUS: Whew! It's a tough journey to heaven all right – and back too. Oooh, my legs! [*To the audience*] You know, from up there you really looked minute, like a lot of very nasty insects. But you didn't look half as nasty as you do from here!

SLAVE [*coming out of the house*]: Master, you're home at last!

TRYGAEUS: So I've been told. [*He is standing very awkwardly.*]

SLAVE: What's wrong with you?

TRYGAEUS: Got a pain in my legs. It's – it's such a long way.

SLAVE: Tell me –

TRYGAEUS: Yes?

SLAVE: When you were up there in the clouds, did you see anyone else flying around there?

TRYGAEUS: No – except there were two or three lyric poets I noticed.

SLAVE: What were they doing?

TRYGAEUS: Flitting about collecting dithyrambs. You know the sort of stuff, 'O-the-fair-air-and-the-breeze-floating-free' and so on and so on.

SLAVE: So it's not true what they say, then, that when we die we become stars in the sky?

TRYGAEUS: On the contrary, it's quite true.

SLAVE: So who's been made a star lately?

TRYGAEUS: Ion of Chios.[56] Remember he wrote *The Morning Star*? Well, as soon as he got to heaven, they appointed *him* Morning Star!

SLAVE: And what about those shooting stars that burn as they fly – who are they?

TRYGAEUS: They're very rich stars who are going home after dinner, carrying portable lamps. Now could you take this lady inside [*presenting* HARVEST], fill the tub with good hot water, and make up the bridal bed for the two of us? When you've done that, come back here. In the meantime I'll hand over the other lady to the Council.

SLAVE: Excuse me, sir, but where did you pick them up?

TRYGAEUS: In heaven, of course.

SLAVE: You mean the gods have whorehouses just like us? What a hypocritical lot! From now on I don't give a damn for the gods.

TRYGAEUS: Don't be unfair. Only *some* of them earn their living that way.

SLAVE [*taking* HARVEST]: Come with me, darling. [*To* TRYGAEUS] By the way, should I give her anything to eat?

TRYGAEUS: No, nothing. Do you expect her to accept bread or barley cakes, when she's been used to licking ambrosia with the gods above?

SLAVE: She'd better be prepared for a bit of licking here too! [*He takes* HARVEST *into the house.*]

CHORUS:
> How happy you are, how fortune smiles!
> Your course is righter than right.

TRYGAEUS:
> What will you say when I soon become
> A bridegroom shining and bright?

CHORUS:
> We'll envy you your youth regained
> And the way you're anointed all o'er.

TRYGAEUS:
> What will you say when I feel her tits
> And my cock's all ready for more?

CHORUS:
> You'll be the happiest of men, unlike
> The rotating Carcinus clan.[57]

TRYGAEUS:
> And happiness has never blessed
> A more meritorious man.

    I mounted my sturdy beetle-steed,
       I saved all Greece from war,
    So that now you can all go back to your fields
       And work, or screw, or snore.

[*Re-enter* SLAVE.]

SLAVE: She's had her bath, and her rump's shining. All the wedding cakes are ready and baked. Everything's shipshape and done to a T. We're just waiting to pipe your cock aboard, sir!

TRYGAEUS: Fine. Now let's hand over Festival here to the Council.

SLAVE: What? You mean *she's* Festival? The same Festival that we had down at Brauron[58] after that booze-up?

TRYGAEUS: That's right. And I can tell you, it was no easy task getting hold of her.

SLAVE [*who has been examining* FESTIVAL]: Master, you're right! Just look at that ten-gallon arse!

TRYGAEUS: Now then – [*to the audience*] is there an upright man down there? Hmm, there is. I mean, is there anybody who will take charge of this lady for the Council? [*To* SLAVE] Here, you, what do you think you're doing to her with that tool of yours? Drawing maps or something?

SLAVE: Um . . . ah . . . I'm staking a claim to space for a tent for the duration of the Isthmian Games.[59]

TRYGAEUS [*to the audience*]: Decided yet who's going to take charge of her? Come on, Festival, I'll hand you over to them myself. [*He is about to take her down to the auditorium.*]

SLAVE: Wait a minute, there's someone says he will.

TRYGAEUS: Who is it?

SLAVE: Ariphrades. He's dying for you to give her to him.

TRYGAEUS: So he can lap up all her oxtail soup,[60] I suppose. No thanks. Come on now, get rid of this gear.

    [FESTIVAL *removes her clothes.* TRYGAEUS *leads her forward and displays her to the audience.*]

Gentlemen of the Council, Members of the Executive Committee, may I present to you Festival. Have a good look at all the delights I'm providing you with. You will be able without delay to lift her legs high in the air and then have yourself a feast of a time![61] You will observe her capacious oven.

SLAVE [*who is observing very closely*]: Whee-whew! It's gorgeous!

Lovely and sooty too! I bet the Council stirred things up a bit in there before the war!

TRYGAEUS: As soon as you are in possession of this lady, you will immediately be able to announce for tomorrow a grand sports gala, consisting of wrestling on the mat, exercising on all fours, sideways throws, gripping in a kneeling position, and no-holds-barred. The latter will comprise – after the application of suitable ointments, of course – shoving and prodding with two fists and one prick simultaneously! On the following day will be held the horse-racing, with all the jockeys striving to outdo one another, and all the competitors piling one on top of the other, gasping and panting, trying to be first into the finishing stretch! And some will fall by the wayside and lie still and rigid. So, members of the Executive Committee, I hereby give you Festival. [He presents FESTIVAL to the CHAIRMAN of the Executive Committee who is sitting in the front row.] Grabbed her sharp enough, didn't he? Wouldn't have been like that if you'd had to do the job for nothing! You'd have insisted on your pound of flesh all right!

[For the rest of the play FESTIVAL goes about comforting various members of the audience.]

CHORUS:
What rapture through you will each citizen win!

TRYGAEUS:
You'll see just how much when the vintage comes in!

CHORUS:
We see it already: our saviour are you.

TRYGAEUS:
Think of drinking a goblet of wine that is new!

CHORUS:
We'll ever admire you, your virtue relate,
And next to the gods 'tis your name will be great.

TRYGAEUS:
Trygaeus my name, an Athmonian by deme,
And well, my good friends, I deserve your esteem;
I've released all the People from toil and alarm,
And sent them back home to the peace of the farm;
And I've saved all of Hellas, east, west, north and south,
By finally stopping Hyperbolus' mouth.

SLAVE: Well, where do we go from here?

TRYGAEUS: Why, we must dedicate the statue of Peace, with offerings of cooked vegetables.

SLAVE: Vegetables? This isn't a piffling little Hermes, you know.

TRYGAEUS: Well, what would you suggest? A fatted bull?

SLAVE: No thanks. No more *bull* for us now – the war's over.[62]

TRYGAEUS: Then a well-proportioned pig?

SLAVE: No, no!

TRYGAEUS: Why not?

SLAVE: Reminds me too much of Theagenes.[63]

TRYGAEUS: Then what?

SLAVE: A la-a-amb.[64]

TRYGAEUS: A la-a-amb?

SLAVE: That's right.

TRYGAEUS: Why pronounced like that?

SLAVE: Well, the idea is that in future, in the Assembly, if someone says we ought to go to war, everybody will be terrified and go a-a-ah –

TRYGAEUS: Good idea!

SLAVE: – and be as gentle as lambs in every other way too. Then we'll all be kind to each other, and not so severe on our allies either.

TRYGAEUS: All right then, bring out a lamb, and I'll fetch an altar so we can sacrifice.

[*They go separately into the house, the* SLAVE *first.*]

CHORUS:

> God wills and Fortune guides,
>   And all proceeds correctly,
> Good things upon good things,
>   Each blessing timed per*fectly*!

TRYGAEUS [*reappearing with a portable altar*]:
> You've got the right idea;
> Just look, the altar's here.

CHORUS:

> Now hurry, hurry, quick!
> The omens now are cheering.
> The breeze of heaven's will
>   Away from war is veering.

So while the skies are fair,
Let's use that altar there!

[*Re-enter* SLAVE *with a basket containing various items mentioned in the following lines, and a brazier.*]

TRYGAEUS [*recitative*]:

Here is the garland and the barley grain;
Here is the knife to slaughter; here again
Is fire to roast the victim; here I am;
We're ready – hey! *We haven't got a lamb!*

[*Exit* SLAVE.]

CHORUS [*ignoring this problem*]:

Hurry up, hurry up!
If that Chaeris[65] sees,
He'll come here, play his flute,
And demand his fees!
See him blow, pant and toil,
And pretend to play;
At the end, sure as sure,
You will have to pay!

[*Re-enter* SLAVE *with lamb.*]

TRYGAEUS [*to* SLAVE]: Now take the basket and the bowl of lustral water, and walk round the altar once clockwise.

SLAVE [*doing so*]: There. What next? I've gone right round.

TRYGAEUS: Now let me see. I'll dip this torch in the water, so [*he does so*]. Now then, lambkin [*letting the torch drip over the lamb*], shake your head quickly, that's a good little beast.[66] [*To* SLAVE] Give me some of the barley-grains.

[*The* SLAVE *does so, and* TRYGAEUS *sprinkles them over the lamb.*] Now let me have the bowl, so you can wash your hands. And now you can throw the rest of the barley to the audience.

SLAVE [*scattering the barley among the audience*]: There.

TRYGAEUS: Have you given it them?

SLAVE: Yes, I swear. Every one of the spectators now has some barley – or at least some wild oats to sow.[67]

TRYGAEUS: Not the women, though, they haven't got any.

SLAVE: You just wait till tonight!

TRYGAEUS: Now let's pray. Who is here? [*Silence.*] Here, we haven't got a quorum of virtuous men![68]

SLAVE: How about the Chorus? There's enough of them, and they're very virtuous. I'll give them the ritual sprinkling. [*He empties a bucket of water over the* CHORUS.]

TRYGAEUS: You think *they're* virtuous?

SLAVE: Well, they've got a stiff upper lip, anyway. All that cold water, and they haven't stirred a muscle!

TRYGAEUS: Now may we pray?

LEADER: Let – us – pray.

TRYGAEUS: O most holy and sovereign goddess, our Lady of Peace, protectress of all sacred choruses and all marriages, accept, we pray thee, our sacrifice.

SLAVE: Yes, indeed, most holy Peace. And don't do what the women do when they're looking for their lovers. They just open the door a fraction and peep out, and if anyone notices them they pop back in again, and then when he goes away they peep out again. Don't do that kind of thing to us.

TRYGAEUS: No; rather show thyself in the entirety of thy noble beauty to us thy lovers, who for thirteen years[69] have been worn out with longing for thee. Make an end of battle and tumult, and may thy works be peace, even as thy name is Peace. Blot out from our minds the too clever hidden meanings which we put into every-thing we say to one another. Re-mix our elements and the elements of all the Greeks, with a more generous portion of friendship and compassion. And fill, we pray thee, our market with all good things, even Megarian garlic, early figs, apples, pomegranates, and little woolly cloaks for our slaves; and may we again see the Boeotians bringing their wares, geese, ducks, pigeons, sandpipers, and baskets full of eels fresh from Lake Copais; and may we all jostle one another to buy them, and may Morychus, Teleas, Glaucetes, and many another gourmet be in that happy throng; and may Melanthius[70] come late to the market, and may all the eels have been sold, and may he utter cries of distress and sing a song out of his brother's *Medea*, even this song,

'Alas, alack! I mourn, I pine, I reel,
Bereavèd of my beetroot-loving eel!'

And at his discomfiture may all men rejoice. Grant, we beseech thee, O most glorious Peace, this our humble prayer. Amen. [*To*

SLAVE] Now take the knife and slaughter the victim. Make a professional job of it.

SLAVE: We can't do that.

TRYGAEUS: Why not?

SLAVE: I'm sure Peace wouldn't approve of a slaughter with blood running all over her altar and everything.

TRYGAEUS: All right, take it inside and sacrifice it there, and bring us back the thigh-bones, will you? [*Confidentially to the audience*] That way our sponsor won't lose his lamb.

[*Exit* SLAVE *with lamb.*]

CHORUS:
>Now lay the faggots out
>And do the necessary.

TRYGAEUS [*arranging faggots on the altar*]:
>Now don't you think my skill
>   Is extraordinary?
>Would any learned seer
>   Disturb one item here?

CHORUS:
>Not one, I do declare!
>   There's nothing you've omitted!
>You've shown that you're aware
>   Of everything, and fitted
>To be accounted clever,
>Because you're baffled never.

TRYGAEUS:
>That's lit it! See, the prophets71 are annoyed,
>Afraid that they will soon be unemployed!
>The table, boy! No answer to my shout?
>Then I myself will bring the table out!

[*He goes into the house.*]

CHORUS:
>Praise the man of courage who
>Saved the City, us and you!
>He has won eternal fame,
>Envied now his glorious name!

[TRYGAEUS *returns with a table and the* SLAVE *with thighs ready for cooking.*]

TRYGAEUS: There we are. Put the thighs on the fire, will you? I'll go and get the offal and the sacrificial cakes.

SLAVE: No, I'll go. [*Dashes into the house.*]

TRYGAEUS [*after a moment*]: You ought to have brought them by now!

SLAVE [*returning*]: Here I am, sir. Tell me, sir, did I dawdle?

TRYGAEUS: Now make sure you roast them well. I see someone coming. He's got a laurel wreath on his head.

SLAVE [*looking off*]: Who is he? *Some* kind of puffed-up quack, I can see that, but –. Is he an omen expert?

TRYGAEUS: Not quite. It's Hierocles the oracle-monger, from Oreus.

SLAVE: What do you think he's going to say?

TRYGAEUS: Obviously he'll object to our ending the war.[72]

SLAVE: Are you sure he hasn't just run to the smell of cooking?

TRYGAEUS: Let's pretend not to see him.

SLAVE: Right you are.

> [*Enter* HIEROCLES, *clothed in a thick fleece, and carrying a roll of oracles.*]

HIEROCLES: What is this sacrifice and to whom is it being made?

TRYGAEUS [*to* SLAVE]: Be careful how you cook it. Don't touch the loin part.[73]

HIEROCLES: Please tell me to whom you are sacrificing.

TRYGAEUS [*to* SLAVE]: The tail's doing nicely.

SLAVE: Very nicely, thank you, holy Peace!

HIEROCLES: Begin carving, please, and let me have the priest's dues.

TRYGAEUS: We need to cook it first.

HIEROCLES: This is already cooked.

TRYGAEUS: Please don't interfere. [*To* SLAVE] Cut it up now. – What's happened to the table? – Bring the wine for the libation.

HIEROCLES: Don't forget to cut the tongue out.

TRYGAEUS: We're not forgetting. And do you know what you can do?

HIEROCLES: If you'll be so kind as to tell me.

TRYGAEUS: Keep your mouth shut. We are in the middle of a sacrifice to Peace.

HIEROCLES [*opening his roll*]:
> O how wretched and foolish are men –

TRYGAEUS: You can speak for yourself, sir.

HIEROCLES [*ignoring him*]:
  Who in their folly, not knowing th'inscrutable purpose of heaven,
  Rashly, though human, made peace with the golden-eyed monkeys
                                            of Sparta –
TRYGAEUS: Ha! ha! ha!
HIEROCLES: What, may I ask, is amusing you?
TRYGAEUS: Golden-eyed monkeys! Ha! ha! ha!
HIEROCLES:
  You like storm-fearing petrels are trusting the word of the foxes,
  Treacherous of heart and treacherous of mind –
TRYGAEUS: This meat is roasting beautifully. I hope the same happens
  to your windbag lungs!
HIEROCLES:
  For if the Nymphs tell the truth unto Bakis and Bakis to mortals,
  And if the Nymphs tell the truth unto Bakis[74] –
TRYGAEUS: One more Bakis and I'll murder you!
HIEROCLES:
  Not, not yet is it fated that Peace should be loosed from her fetters,
  Not till –
  [*The* SLAVE *has now returned with the libation cup and wine.*]
TRYGAEUS [*to* SLAVE]: Sprinkle some salt on the meat, will you?
HIEROCLES:
  Not, not yet do the gods consent that the war should be ended,
  Till that a wolf shall mate with a sheep.
TRYGAEUS: And how the hell do you expect a wolf to mate with a
  sheep?
HIEROCLES:
  While that the beetle in flight farts foully, and while that the
                                            goldfinch
  Crossed with a bell[75] brings forth prematurely, and blind are her
                                            offspring,
  Still is the time not ripe that peace should be made by the Hellenes.
TRYGAEUS: You mean we should just go on fighting? Have a lottery
  which of us is going to be more severely crippled, when we've the
  opportunity to make peace and rule all Greece together?[76]
HIEROCLES:
  Never can anyone make the crab to walk straight and go forwards.
TRYGAEUS: You mean, never will you be invited to dine in the City

Hall again, in fact now the war's over never will you be able to
make a living at all!

HIEROCLES:

None can bring it about that the hedgehog should cease to be
prickly.

TRYGAEUS: Are you ever going to stop trying to pull the wool over
the City's eyes?

HIEROCLES: What oracle can you cite to justify your sacrifice?

TRYGAEUS: An excellent one, straight out of Homer.[77]

'Thus they thrust clean away the hateful darkness of warfare,

Then took Peace for themselves, and enshrined her and gave her
an altar.

Then when the thighs had been burnt and the entrails been dressed
for the roasting,

From their cups they poured their libations, and I was their
leader' –

And to the oracle-monger a cup was given by *no-one*!

HIEROCLES: That's a fake! That's not in the Sibylline collection.[78]

TRYGAEUS: But *this* is a very shrewd and relevant remark of Homer's:

'Clanless and homeless is he, an outcast by law unprotected,

Whoso has War for his love, even War the destructive and gory.'[79]

HIEROCLES:

Mortals beware, lest the kite with guile should deceive you and
swooping –

TRYGAEUS [*to* SLAVE]: You've been warned – make sure he doesn't
swoop on our roast meat. Now pour the wine into the cup and
bring the offals here.

[*The* SLAVE *does so.*]

HIEROCLES: Oh, well, in that case, I'll help myself. [*He attempts to
reach the plate which the* SLAVE *has just placed before the altar but is
beaten off.*]

TRYGAEUS: A drink-offering to the gods! [*He takes up the cup.*]

HIEROCLES: Aren't you going to give me any? And what about those
offals?

TRYGAEUS:

Not, not yet do the gods consent, for they strictly enjoin us

First to pour our libation, and *you* to get out of it pronto!

[*Pours a little wine out of the cup.*] Our Lady of Peace, be with us and remain with us all our life long. Amen. [*He and the* SLAVE *drink from the cup.*]

HIEROCLES: Could I have the tongue, please?

TRYGAEUS: You've got one already – so kindly take it away from here.

HIEROCLES [*grabbing the wine-skin*]: A drink-offering!

TRYGAEUS: Here, have something to go with it! [*Throws some rubbish in his face, enabling the* SLAVE *to snatch the skin back.*]

HIEROCLES: Is nobody going to give me any of the meat?

TRYGAEUS: Not yet is it lawful to do so,
Till that a wolf shall mate with a sheep.

HIEROCLES [*on his bended knees*]: I beg you, I beseech you!

TRYGAEUS: No good beseeching. 'None can bring it about that the hedgehog should cease to be prickly.' [*To the audience*] Come here, everyone, let's have a feast!

HIEROCLES: What about me?

TRYGAEUS: Oh, go and eat Sibyllines!

HIEROCLES: I swear I'm not going to let you eat the whole lot yourselves! I'll get 'em, see if I don't! [*He again makes for the plate but is intercepted.*]

TRYGAEUS: Let's get this Bakis! Hit him good and hard!

[TRYGAEUS *and the* SLAVE *belabour* HIEROCLES *with blows, the* SLAVE *having produced a large cudgel.*]

HIEROCLES: Help! Assault! Is there a witness? Help!

TRYGAEUS: Yes, I'm a witness! I witness that you're a greedy swine who talks a lot of rot! [*To the* SLAVE] Give the bastard some more!

SLAVE: No, you [*giving the cudgel to* TRYGAEUS, *who carries on the good work*]. I'll peel off this sheepskin. It's not his – he picked it up on the sly. [*To* HIEROCLES] Put it down, priest, do you hear? [*He strips* HIEROCLES *of his coat.*] We'll send this thieving raven back to Oreus without his feathers. Off you go to Elymnium! Shoo!

[HIEROCLES *is driven off.* TRYGAEUS *and the* SLAVE *assisted by other slaves take the roast meat and other paraphernalia into the house.*]

CHORUS:
> What joy to cast one's helmet off
>   And live a life of ease,
> No more to taste the army food,
>   The onions and the cheese!

I never was a warrior man,
　　And now I'll make amends
By drinking deep beside the fire
　　With my devoted friends.

Uproot an olive-tree or two
　　When parched in summer's heat,
Roast peas and acorns while it burns –
　　That's what I like to eat!

For that's the way to raise a thirst,
　　And when I'm slightly tips-
-y and the wife is in the bath,
　　I'll taste young Thratta's lips!

LEADER:
There's nothing sweeter when the sowing's done
Than having rain instead of blazing sun;
On such occasions neighbours tend to say
'Comarchides, what shall we do today?'
To which I answer, 'Well, my friend, I think,
As Zeus has been so kind, we ought to *drink*!
Here, missus, parch the beans, three quarts or more,
Mix in some wheat and take some figs from store,
And send our Syra to the fields to call
Our Manes back, 'cos there's no point at all
In breaking clods or pruning trees just yet
Nor any time today – the ground's too wet.'
'And I've a thrush at home,' my friend declares,
'Beestings, two finches, yes, and four fine hares.
(Or were they pinched last evening by the cat?
I heard a noise – I wonder, was it that?)
Three hares for us now, boy, and one for dad!
And ask Aeschinades – I heard he had
Some myrtle boughs – with berries on, I think –
And tell Charinades to come and drink,
Now that the god has given with open hand
His largess to us, and has blessed our land!'

138

CHORUS:

What joy to hear the cricket chirp
   A merry tune and sweet,
And then inspect my Lemnian vines
   Arranged in order neat –

(I wonder, have they ripened yet?
   The type, so experts tell,
Is often early) – and to see
   The figs begin to swell!

And when they're ripe I'll eat with zest
   And sing 'O Seasons dear',
And grind some thyme and mix myself
   A posset of good cheer!

Yes, that's the kind of summer-time
   That I to spend would seek,
That's just the way to make myself
   Look rich and fat and sleek –

LEADER:

Not marching with some blasted brigadier
Who wears three crests (one *here*, one *here*, one *here*)
And dons a cloak of brightest scarlet, made
In Sardis, which he calls 'a Lydian shade'.
If ever in that cloak he has to fight,
He's dyed a Shittian shade from utter fright!
And while I firmly stand the battle's shock,
He scarpers like a tawny hippocock[80]
Shaking his crests (one *here*, one *here*) like so:
I'll give him this – he's always first to go!
Back home he rigs the call-up, past all doubt,
Writes in some names and crosses others out,
Twice, thrice, till all is chaos. On the board
It says 'We leave tomorrow', but a horde
Of privates haven't bought their ration-fare
Because they didn't know their names were there.
Then at Pandion's plinth[81] they see by chance

They're in – and, looking acidly askance,
Run to and fro demented. Country folk
Suffer this way; the townsmen dodge the yoke.
All officers, so gods and mortals say,
Are cowards, and they'll pay for it one day.
They cheat us, and what's more they drop their shield,
Lions at home, but foxes in the field!

[*Re-enter* TRYGAEUS. *He is wearing a bright new tunic.*]

TRYGAEUS: Whew! You never saw such a crowd as has come to our wedding feast!

[*A* SLAVE *comes out and whispers to him.*]

You want something to clean the tables with? Here, use this [*handing him his ragged old cloak*]; I've no more need of it now. Then if you can bring out the cake, the thrushes and plenty of hare, and some rolls as well. [*These, a pot and fire are brought, and* TRYGAEUS *begins cooking again.*]

[*Enter a* SICKLE-MAKER *and a* JAR-MAKER, *loaded down with their wares.*]

SICKLE-MAKER: Where's Trygaeus?

TRYGAEUS: Here, boiling thrush.

SICKLE-MAKER: Oh, my dearest Trygaeus! You can't imagine what you've done for me by making peace. Before nobody would pay an obol for one of my sickles, or even for five dozen of them. Now I sell them at five drachmas apiece, and my friend here gets three drachmas for his jars. Trygaeus, any of these you want are yours, free. The sickles *and* the jars. These too [*giving* TRYGAEUS *a large hamper*]: out of our profit on sales we've been able to buy you all these as wedding presents.

TRYGAEUS: Come in to dinner. You can leave the presents in the hall. Better hurry. I can see an arms salesman coming – and he's annoyed, by the look of him.

[*He shows the* SICKLE-MAKER *and* JAR-MAKER *into the house. Enter an* ARMS SALESMAN *accompanied by a* SPEAR-POLISHER *and* HELMET-MAKER.]

ARMS SALESMAN: Trygaeus, you've ruined me. Absolutely ruined me.

TRYGAEUS: What's wrong with you? Poor chap. You look so very crestfallen.

ARMS SALESMAN: You have deprived me of my trade and my living, and the same goes for my two friends here.

TRYGAEUS [*noticing two crests protruding from the* ARMS SALESMAN's *bag*]: What would you like me to pay for those two crests?

ARMS SALESMAN: What would you like to pay?

TRYGAEUS: What would I give for them? Oh, I really don't think I should name the price ... But I must say, the fastening shows exquisite workmanship. What do you say to – three quarts of figs?

ARMS SALESMAN: All right, then, fetch the figs. [*To* HELMET-MAKER] After all, it's better than nothing.

TRYGAEUS [*who has been examining the crests further*]: Here, you can bloody well take these blasted things away! Look at them! They're going bald – they've disintegrated in my hands! I won't give a fig for them, do you hear? I won't give one fig!

ARMS SALESMAN:
         And what of this my thousand-drachma corslet,
         Most curiously jointed, truly noble?[82]

TRYGAEUS: Well, I wouldn't like you to make a loss on it. I'll take it at cost price. I do need a new commode, actually.

ARMS SALESMAN: Do you mind not insulting my stock-in-trade?

TRYGAEUS [*who has been setting the cuirass on the ground*]: Like this. Three stones to wipe my arse, and there we are. [*Squats over it.*] Isn't it perfect?

ARMS SALESMAN: You won't be able to wipe your arse like that, you idiot.

TRYGAEUS: No? Look. Hand through the oar-hole – so. [*He means, as he demonstrates, the armhole.*] And I can use the other hand too.

ARMS SALESMAN: Both hands at once?

TRYGAEUS: Well, yes. An oar to every hole, surely. Otherwise I might be charged with undermanning the ship.[83]

ARMS SALESMAN: So you mean to use a thousand-drachma cuirass for shitting on?

TRYGAEUS: Why not, you fool? D'you think my arse isn't worth more than that to me?

ARMS SALESMAN: All right, then, a thousand drachmas, please.

TRYGAEUS: It's no good. It hurts my backside. Take it away. I'm not buying it.

ARMS SALESMAN: And what about this trumpet? I bought it for sixty drachmas.

TRYGAEUS: Why, weight the bell with lead, put a rod a few inches long in the mouthpiece here, and it'll make a capital adjustable target for a wine-flicking game.[84]

ARMS SALESMAN: You're making fun of me.

TRYGAEUS: Or another suggestion. Weight the bell with lead as before, hang a scale-pan on a string from here, and you can use it to weigh out figs in the orchard for your slaves!

ARMS SALESMAN:
>   O god implacable, how am I ruined!
>   What of these helmets, for the which I paid
>   An hundred drachmas? Who will buy them now?

TRYGAEUS: Try marketing them in Egypt. They'll do fine for measuring out emetics.[85]

ARMS SALESMAN [to HELMET-MAKER]: We're in a bad way, old man!

TRYGAEUS: *He's* not.

ARMS SALESMAN: Why, what will anyone want with helmets now?

TRYGAEUS: Why, all he needs to do is add handles like this [*pointing to the* HELMET-MAKER'*s ears*], and he'll get more for them than he ever did before![86]

ARMS SALESMAN [to SPEAR-POLISHER]: Come on, let's go.

TRYGAEUS: Don't go yet. I want to buy his spears off him.

ARMS SALESMAN: How much will you give?

TRYGAEUS: Well, if you sawed them in half, I'd buy them to use as vine props. Would you say one drachma a hundred?

ARMS SALESMAN: We're being made fun of. Come on, let's be off. [*He and his companions leave.*]

TRYGAEUS: And good riddance!

[*Two* BOYS *come out of the house.*]

Two of my guests' children! I bet they said they wanted to wee − and I bet they really want to practise their songs for the party. [*To* FIRST BOY] Here, my lad, what have you got in mind to sing? Come here next to me, and let's have a run through.

FIRST BOY [*sings*]:
>   The deeds of younger arms I sing −[87]

TRYGAEUS: Not here you don't! No arms now – we've made peace, blast you, you stupid good-for-nothing!

FIRST BOY:

> And when the armies came to grips
> Upon the stricken field,
> The oxhide then with oxhide clashed
> And shield encountered shield.

TRYGAEUS: Shield, shield, shield – will you stop reminding us?

FIRST BOY:

> Then some did shout and some did moan –

TRYGAEUS: Oh, they did, did they? If you sing one note more about moans, oxhide or otherwise, you'll do some moaning yourself, I swear!

FIRST BOY: What *am* I suppose to sing about? What kind of thing do you like?

TRYGAEUS: Well, for instance, 'So then on beef they banqueted' – how does it go on? – 'and took a hearty lunch, and dum–de–dum–de–dum–de–dum, and all that's nice to munch'.

FIRST BOY:

> So then on beef they banqueted,
> The while their steeds perspired
> Unbridled, since they'd had of war
> As much as they desired.

TRYGAEUS: Good, good. They'd had enough of war, so they ate. Now go on, sing more about them eating after they'd had enough!

FIRST BOY:

> They fortified themselves –

TRYGAEUS: With good wine, and I'll bet they enjoyed it!

FIRST BOY:

> – with arms,
> And from the gates poured out,
> And once again upon the field
> Was heard their battle-shout.

TRYGAEUS: Hell take you and your battles! You sing nothing but war, war, war! Whose boy are you?

FIRST BOY: Me, sir?

TRYGAEUS: You, sir.

FIRST BOY: My daddy's Lamachus.[88]

TRYGAEUS: Lamachus! Ugh! I *thought* it must have been one of the *lam*basting type – in future to be the *lam*enting type! You buzz off and sing to your spearmen!

[FIRST BOY *runs off.*]

What's happened to Cleonymus' son?[89] [*To* SECOND BOY, *whose back has been to the audience all this time*] Here, boy, let us have a song before you go back inside. I know *you* won't sing about toil and trouble – *you've* got a *sensible* father.

SECOND BOY [*sings*]:

Now is a Thracian decked with the shield which once by a thicket,
Though it had done me no ill, I most unwillingly left –[90]

TRYGAEUS: Tell me, my little cockerel, are you thinking of your father?

SECOND BOY:

'Thus I preserved my life' –

TRYGAEUS: And ruined your family's honour. Let's go inside. With a father like yours you'll never forget any song about dropping a shield, I know that. [*They go into the house. A moment later the front of the house swings open revealing a magnificent feast and* TRYGAEUS *comes out.*]

TRYGAEUS [*recitative*]:

I now declare the banquet open wide
To every one of you good folk outside.
Tuck in, and let no stomach empty stay;
Lay to like men, and give both jaws full play!
A set of teeth that all are gleaming white
Are very little use unless they bite!

[*He goes back into the house.*]

CHORUS:

Thanks for the tip! We will see that its done!
  You that so long have starved,
On with the feast! Attack the jugged hare,
  Perfectly cooked and carved!
Not every day do you meet lovely cakes
  Unguarded, an easy prey;
Come quickly and get it, or else you'll regret it,
  Grab it and munch away!

[TRYGAEUS *reappears, arrayed as a bridegroom.*]

TRYGAEUS [*recitative*]:
> Let silence be observed on every side,
> And from the house escort my lovely bride!
> Let all rejoice and cheer and torches burn,
> As homeward to the country we return!
> Let us all dance and all libation pour,
> And pray to see Hyperbolus no more!

[*Slaves appear, lining the way out of the house with flaming torches.*
TRYGAEUS *advances to the altar and raises his hands.*]

FINALE

TRYGAEUS:
> Let us now to heaven pray
> To bless us this and every day,
> To give us lots of bread to eat
> And wine to drink, and figs so sweet,
> To give all Greece abundant wealth,
> Our wives fertility and health,
> Restore us all the joys of yore,
> And make at last an end of war
>> For ever and ever, Amen!

ALL: Amen!

[*Enter* HARVEST, *attended, as bride.*]

TRYGAEUS: Come hither, my pretty, and under the sky –
CHORUS: Sing hey for Hymen, Hymen i-o!
TRYGAEUS: Away from the city together we'll lie –
CHORUS: Sing hey for Hymen, Hymen i-o!
LEADER: Hymen, Hymen, sing unto Hymen,
> Happy the man to whose wedding we go,
> He merits the right to such heavenly delight –

CHORUS: Sing hey for Hymen, Hymen i-o!

LEADER: What shall we do with Harvest so fair?
CHORUS: Sing hey for Hymen, Hymen i-o!
LEADER: We'll gather her in and lay her all bare!
CHORUS: Sing hey for Hymen, Hymen i-o!
LEADER: Hymen, Hymen, sing unto Hymen,

          Lift him on high and away we will go,
          Rejoicing they're wedded and soon will be bedded –

CHORUS: Sing hey for Hymen, Hymen i–o!

[*The couple are lifted on to the shoulders of groups of the* CHORUS.]

TRYGAEUS: How free you will live from all trouble and shock!

CHORUS: Sing hey for Hymen, Hymen i–o!

LEADER: How sweet is her fig, how ripe is your cock!

CHORUS: Sing hey for Hymen, Hymen i–o!

TRYGAEUS: Hymen, Hymen, sing unto Hymen,
          Now to the banquet I bid you all go,
          Be eating and drinking, of happiness thinking –

CHORUS: Sing hey for Hymen, Hymen i–o!

LEADER: Goodbye, dear spectators, we wish you all joy –

CHORUS: Sing hey for Hymen, Hymen i–o!

LEADER: For now other business our minds must employ –

CHORUS: Sing hey for Hymen, Hymen i–o!

LEADER: Hymen, Hymen, sing unto Hymen,
          Follow me now, it's the end of the show,
          Let's go and partake of the wine and the cake –

CHORUS: Sing hey for Hymen, Hymen i–o!

[*Still repeating the refrain, they chair* TRYGAEUS *and* HARVEST *into the house, which closes behind them.*]

The Birds

Translated by David Barrett

Introductory Note to *The Birds*

The Birds was produced at the City Dionysia festival at Athens in the year 414 B.C. The city was still at war with Sparta and her allies, but things had not been going too badly for the Athenians, and hopes were still running high for the success of the great expedition which had been sent off to Sicily in the preceding year, with the aim of gaining control over the Greek cities of the island and establishing a kind of Western Empire which would assure the supremacy of Athens over all her rivals.

In this comparatively prosperous year the festival of Dionysus was celebrated with the usual splendour, and Aristophanes was able to mount his comedy with a full chorus of twenty-four, all costumed as different birds, not to mention an unusual number of extras – the special flute player who took the part of the Nightingale, the four 'birds' who walked on (and perhaps danced) in especially elaborate costumes before the entry of the Chorus proper, and a professional singer for the Hoopoe's two songs, which in the original production would have been sung off-stage. His Chorus, too, must have included trained singers, for some of the lyrics in *The Birds* (like the song to the Woodland Muse) are graceful poems quite free of the usual comic material, and demand a musical setting equally elegant in style.

The Birds is the longest of Aristophanes' surviving plays; it is also the richest in incident and variety, and the most consistent in tone. Current events are hardly referred to at all; the war is not mentioned, and apart from the obligatory lampoons and a fair number of passing references to individual citizens (notably in the list of bird-nicknames in the Third Messenger's speech) there are few allusions to politics. Peisthetaerus and Euelpides have no special reason for wanting to quit Athens apart from the time-honoured one: they are tired of paying fees and fines, of the city's obsession with laws and litigation. The play is justly admired as a fine example of a perfectly worked-out fantasy. This dream of a new republic 'where Wisdom, Grace and

Love pervade the scene' is presented throughout in a simple and charming style, almost like a tale for children. One is unusually conscious of the author's affection for his audience.

Would it be rash, or sentimental, to credit him also with an affection for the birds themselves? Neither he nor his audience possessed the ornithological textbooks which are available to every amateur bird-watcher today. Yet he makes Peisthetaerus identify every single bird in the Chorus as it enters – no fewer than twenty-four species, only one of which (the Barber-bird, introduced for the sake of an elaborate and untranslatable joke) is a product of the imagination. The Hoopoe, summoning the birds to conference, classifies them by habitat. (We note that woodland birds are not included: they may well have been less familiar to an Athenian audience.) Many other species are mentioned in the course of the play, nearly always with some appropriate reference to their habits or appearance. Most striking of all is the characterization of the bird community as a whole. From fluttering excitement through wary mistrust to cocky impudence, the Chorus is convincingly bird-like throughout (even in their direct addresses to the audience they never abandon the role and become human beings); by a hundred subtle and imaginative touches we are persuaded that if birds could think and speak, this is exactly what they would be like. Paradoxically, by their very truth to nature, they sustain the fantasy of the play.

In *The Birds*, the traditional pattern (prologue, entry of Chorus, contest, *parabasis*, short episodes, finale) is followed, but with many modifications, the section following the *parabasis* being greatly expanded. There is the usual procession of unwanted visitors, who are duly discomfited and sent packing. But there is now a second (though shorter) *parabasis*, after which the main action of the play is seen to be continuing. The wall is completed; and then, in skilfully alternating scenes, interspersed with lampoons from the Chorus, the effects on the gods and on men are illustrated. By this means a steady crescendo of fantasy is achieved: the scenes with Iris and Prometheus prepare the way for the deputation from Olympus; and the arrival of a second series of human visitors (not mere busybodies like the first group, but misguided enthusiasts in need of advice and correction) enables Peisthetaerus to develop in stature, becoming a kind of Prosperofigure – a necessary preliminary to the culminating (and outrageous) fantasy of his elevation to the throne of Zeus.

So far as one can judge from internal evidence, the play appears to have been staged on at least two levels, the Hoopoe's kitchen (outside which the battle with the birds takes place) being at ground level, while his living quarters are clearly higher up. Extensive use was probably made of the stage crane, for flights of birds and the exit of Euelpides as well as for the arrival and departure of Iris. The 'pot' used by the two Athenians in their defence against the birds may be the brazier they have brought with them (see p. 156) or a larger vessel belonging to the Hoopoe.

In comparatively recent years, the phrase 'Cloud Cuckoo Land' has crept into everyday English: it is, of course, derived from the *Nephelococcygia* of this play, and some readers may regret that it is not used in this translation. But a 'land' (even in the sky) is not something that can be set up, and have a wall built round it; and anyway, Greek states were cities, not countries. This translator has chosen 'in the clouds' as the obvious English place-name tag to correspond with *Nephelo-*; if this is used, then *-coccygia* must inevitably become 'Much Cuckoo'. If, at the same time, one is reminded of a much-loved radio entertainment of the 1950s, the tribute is not inappropriate. 'Much Binding', too, was a fantasy republic of the air, and in it the spirit of Aristophanes lived on.

It should be added that the original production of *The Birds* won the second prize in the comedy competition, the first being awarded to Ameipsias for a play called *The Revellers*, of which not a single line has survived.

CHARACTERS

PEISTHETAERUS ⎱ *citizens of Athens*
EUELPIDES ⎰

THE FOOTBIRD *servant to the Hoopoe*

THE HOOPOE *formerly Tereus, an Athenian prince*

CHORUS LEADER *the Partridge (see opposite)*

A PRIEST *(masked as a bird)*

A RAGGED POET

AN ORACLE MAN

METON *the famous mathematician*

A STATUTE SELLER

AN INSPECTOR

FIRST MESSENGER *(a bird)*

SECOND MESSENGER *(a bird)*

IRIS *goddess of the Rainbow, daughter of Zeus*

THIRD MESSENGER *(a bird)*

A REBELLIOUS YOUTH

CINESIAS *the famous dithyrambic poet*

AN INFORMER

PROMETHEUS *the demigod ('the Friend of Man')*

POSEIDON *god of the Sea*

HERACLES *the demigod*

GOD OF THE TRIBALLIANS

HEAVENLY HERALD

CHORUS OF BIRDS

Partridge	*Crested Lark*	*Stockdove*
Francolin	*Reed Warbler*	*Firecrest*
Mallard	*Wheatear*	*Rail*
Halcyon (kingfisher)	*Pigeon*	*Kestrel*
Barber-bird (sparrow)	*Merlin*	*Dabchick*
Owl	*Sparrowhawk*	*Waxwing*
Jay	*Ringdove*	*Vulture*
Turtledove	*Cuckoo*	*Woodpecker*

Other characters (silent, except for Xanthias, who speaks one line)

XANTHIAS⎫
MANES ⎭ *slaves to Peisthetaerus*

BIRD DANCERS (*Flamingo, Cock, Second Hoopoe and Gobbler*)
NIGHTINGALE *formerly Procne, wife of Tereus: flute-player*
RAVEN *piper*
SOVEREIGNTY *a beauteous maiden*
ATTENDANTS, etc. *as required*

SCENE: *The play opens in a desolate stretch of country at some distance from Athens. At the rear of the stage rises a steep, rocky cliff.*

[PEISTHETAERUS *and* EUELPIDES *enter, followed by* XANTHIAS *and* MANES *carrying their baggage.* PEISTHETAERUS *carries on his wrist a crow,* EUELPIDES *a jackdaw.*]

EUELPIDES [*to his jackdaw*]: What's that? Straight on? Where the tree is?

PEISTHETAERUS [*to his crow*]: Make up your mind, damn you. [*To* EUELPIDES] She's cawing back the way we came, now.

EUELPIDES [*to his jackdaw*]: Up and down, this way, that way, what the dickens are you playing at? We're not getting anywhere.

PEISTHETAERUS: A hundred miles I must have walked by now. This crow of mine's been leading me round in circles.

EUELPIDES: What about me, with this ruddy jackdaw? I've just about worn the nails off my toes, trying to go where she says.

PEISTHETAERUS: And where are we now, I should like to know?

EUELPIDES: Could you find your way back to Athens, do you think?

PEISTHETAERUS: I don't think even Execestides could, from here.[1]

[EUELPIDES *groans as he tries to keep his footing on the steep, rocky slope.*]

All very well for *you* to groan, try coming up this way!

EUELPIDES: The fact is, we've been swindled. That fellow in the bird market must have seen us coming. Told us these birds would take us straight to Tereus, the king who turned into a hoopoe. One obol for this jackass of a jackdaw, and three for your confounded crow. Talk about rooking! And all they can do is bite. [*To his jackdaw*] Well, what are you gaping at now? Trying to lead me straight into the cliff? There's no way up here.

PEISTHETAERUS: No sign of a path here either.

[PEISTHETAERUS' *crow begins to caw excitedly.*]

EUELPIDES: Here, what's she saying: Which way now?

PEISTHETAERUS: She's changed her mind. There's a new note in her caw.

EUELPIDES: Yes, but which way do we go? What does she say? [*The crow goes on cawing.*]

PEISTHETAERUS: She says – Ow! She says she's going to peck my fingers to bits.

EUELPIDES [*to the audience*]: It's a bit hard, isn't it, that when you've got two people who actually *want* to 'go to the crows', they can't find the way!² You see, gentlemen (you do realize, by the way, that strictly speaking you aren't here at all), we've got Acestor's disease³ – only in our case it's the other way round. He spends all his time, as an outsider, trying to find a way *in*; whereas we – respectable citizens, born of the purest Athenian stock, and acting under no compulsion whatever – are clearing out. And why, you may ask, have we taken wing (on foot) from our native city? Well, it isn't that we've anything against the city as such: it's as grand and happy a place as ever a man paid a fine in. But there it is: the cicadas chirp away in the trees for a month on end, perhaps even two; but the Athenians yammer away in the lawcourts for the whole of their lives. Which is why you see us on the march, with our basket and our brazier and our myrtle, looking for a land without lawsuits, where we can settle down and live in peace. We're trying to find Tereus the Hoopoe: he must do quite a lot of flying around, he may have come across the kind of place we're looking for.

PEISTHETAERUS: Hey!

EUELPIDES: What's up?

PEISTHETAERUS: My crow keeps cawing sort of upwards.

EUELPIDES: Oh, yes – and look, my jackdaw's gawping upwards too: I think she's trying to show me something. Must be some birds around here somewhere. We can soon find out if we make a noise.

[*They climb a little way up the cliff, shouting and making as much noise as they can.*]

PEISTHETAERUS: Remember the old nursery rhyme? 'Kick the rock with both your feet, Down come the dicky-birds, tweet tweet tweet.' [*He kicks the rock.*]

EUELPIDES: Why don't you use your head, it'll make more noise.

PEISTHETAERUS: Get a stone and bang the rock with that.

EUELPIDES: All right. [*He picks up a stone and starts banging it on a smooth piece of rock. Without knowing it, he is banging on the door of the Hoopoe's kitchen.*] Boy!

PEISTHETAERUS: Here, what are you thinking of? You can't say 'boy' to a hoopoe!

EUELPIDES: Well, hoopoe then. Hoop ho! Hoop ho! I'll have to knock again. [*He does so.*] Hoop ho!

[*A door in the rock suddenly opens and they are confronted by the* HOOPOE's *servant the* FOOTBIRD. *He wears a bird-mask with an enormous beak.* PEISTHETAERUS *falls to the ground in terror. The crow and the jackdaw fly away.*]

FOOTBIRD: Who's this? Who's shouting for my master?

EUELPIDES: Heaven preserve us, what an orifice!

FOOTBIRD [*equally terrified*]: Horrors, two bird-catchers!

EUELPIDES: I don't like his looks, and I don't like his tone.

FOOTBIRD [*recovering quickly*]: Clear off!

EUELPIDES: It's all right, w-we're not human b-beings.

FOOTBIRD: What are you, then?

EUELPIDES: To t-tell you the truth, I'm a wee bit –

FOOTBIRD: A weebit? No such bird. You mean a peewit.

EUELPIDES: No, a weebit. A Libyan bird.

FOOTBIRD: Nonsense! [*To* PEISTHETAERUS] And what kind of bird are you? Come on, answer.

PEISTHETAERUS: I'm – a puddle duck. If you don't believe me, look down there.

EUELPIDES: And what kind of creature are you, for goodness' sake?

FOOTBIRD: Oh, I'm a footbird, a gentlebird's gentlebird.

EUELPIDES: I suppose he beat you in a cockfight and took you prisoner.

FOOTBIRD: Well, no, not exactly. When my master was turned into a hoopoe he realized that he'd still need a reliable servant, so he asked for me to be turned into a bird too.

EUELPIDES: I didn't know birds needed servants.

FOOTBIRD: Well, he did: having been a man, he'd got used to the idea, I suppose. So now, if ever he feels like having a couple of sardines for breakfast, off I run with my little jar and fetch some

from Phalēron. Or say he wants some soup: we need a cooking-
pot, and a spoon for stirring. I fetch the spoon.

EUELPIDES: I see, a sort of errand-bird. Well, listen, Mr Errand-bird,
I'll tell you what you can do: you can go and call your master.

FOOTBIRD: Quite impossible. He's just sleeping off the effects of his
lunch.

EUELPIDES: Why, what did he have?

FOOTBIRD: Oh, the usual: myrtleberries, and a few gnats.

EUELPIDES: Well, go and wake him all the same.

FOOTBIRD [*holding out a claw into which* EUELPIDES *puts a grape*]: He
won't like it, but – oh, very well, just to oblige you. [*He retires into
the cliffside.*]

PEISTHETAERUS: Blast the bird, I nearly died of fright when he
came out.

EUELPIDES: My jackdaw was so scared he flew away.

PEISTHETAERUS: You mean *you* were so scared you let go of him:
coward!

EUELPIDES: And *you* were so scared you fell down in a heap, *and* let
go of your crow.

PEISTHETAERUS: I never let go of her, what are you talking
about?

EUELPIDES: Where is she now, then?

PEISTHETAERUS [*pompously*]: She flew away of her own volition.

EUELPIDES: In other words, you didn't let go, she just flew away.
How brave of you.

[*The* HOOPOE's *voice is heard.*]

HOOPOE: Open the wood, I'm going out.

[*The bushes high up on the cliffside roll apart revealing the* HOOPOE's
luxurious 'nest'. The HOOPOE *himself steps out.*]

EUELPIDES: Great heavens, what kind of a creature is this? Look at
those feathers! And that triple crest!

HOOPOE: Who is it wants to see me?

EUELPIDES: Looks as though the gods have had a good go at *him*, I
must say.

HOOPOE: Ah, my plumage amuses you, does it? I used to be a man
once, you know, that's why it looks a little odd.

EUELPIDES: Oh no, we weren't laughing at *you*.

HOOPOE: What's so funny, then?

EUELPIDES: It's that beak of yours.

HOOPOE: I'd have you know it's copied exactly from the description of me in the Tragedy of Tereus, by Sophocles.[4]

EUELPIDES: Oh, so you're Tereus. What are you, a bird or a peacock?

HOOPOE: A bird.

EUELPIDES: Then what's happened to your feathers?[5]

HOOPOE: They've moulted.

EUELPIDES: Have you been ill, or what?

HOOPOE: No, we birds always lose our feathers in the winter, and then we grow new ones. And now would you mind telling me who you are?

EUELPIDES: Who are we? Oh, we're human beings.

HOOPOE: What kind? Where are you from?

EUELPIDES: Where the best warships come from.

HOOPOE: Not lawcourt men?

EUELPIDES: No, quite the opposite: we're *anti*-lawcourt men.

HOOPOE: I didn't know such a species existed, where you come from.

EUELPIDES: Oh, in the rural areas you can still find a few specimens, if you look hard enough.

HOOPOE: And what business brings you here?

EUELPIDES: We wanted to consult you.

HOOPOE: What about?

EUELPIDES: Well, you were once a man, just like us. And you used to get into debt, just like us. And you liked to get out of paying, just like us. And then suddenly you got turned into a bird. And you flew over the land, and you circled over the sea, and you got a bird's eye view of everything. But a man's eye view at the same time. And that's why we've come here to see you. Perhaps *you* can tell us where to find a really comfortable city: warm and welcoming, like a soft, warm, fleecy blanket.

HOOPOE: So you're looking for a city that's greater than Athens?

EUELPIDES: Not greater. Just easier to live in.

HOOPOE: You favour an aristocratic form of government, I take it.

EUELPIDES: Heaven forbid: the very idea gives me the shivers.

HOOPOE: Then I don't understand. What kind of city *do* you want to live in?

EUELPIDES: A place where the very worst thing that could happen

to you would be something like this: early in the morning a
neighbour knocks at your door and says [*he puts on a tone of
hysterical entreaty*] 'For God's sake, I implore you, have your bath
early today – we're having a wedding feast and you simply must
come, and bring the children too, if you don't come I'll never for-
give you, I'd do the same for you if you were celebrating, really I
would, oh do come, do come.'

HOOPOE: A tragic situation indeed. [*To* PEISTHETAERUS] And
what about you?

PEISTHETAERUS: That's exactly the kind of thing I dream of too.

HOOPOE: What kind of thing? Give me an example.

PEISTHETAERUS: Well, a chap comes up to you and he's quite
purple in the face with fury, and he's got this very good-looking
young son, you see, and he says: 'What's all this I hear about you
and my boy? This is a fine way to go on, I must say. You meet him
coming away from the gymnasium, clean and gleaming after his
bath – and you don't make love to him, you don't speak to him,
you don't go near him, you don't even tickle his balls. And you call
yourself a friend of mine.'

HOOPOE: My poor fellow, what a taste for calamity you seem to
have. But actually I think I do know of a happy place of the kind
you describe. It's on the Red Sea.

EUELPIDES: Oh, not by the sea – that wouldn't do at all. The very
first morning we'd wake up to find they'd sent the *Salaminia* after
us, with a summons-server on board.[6] Don't you know of anywhere in Greece?

HOOPOE: Why not go and live with the Lepreans, in Elis?

EUELPIDES: No thank you: I've never been there, but I've met
Melanthios. One leprous poet's quite enough for me.

HOOPOE: Then there are those other fellows, the Opuntians, in
Locris, that's where you should settle.

EUELPIDES: And be labelled 'Opuntios'?[7] Not for a bag of gold!
But – I say! What about the life you birds lead here? How do you
find it, personally?

HOOPOE: Oh, the time passes pleasantly enough. For one thing, you
have to live without a purse.

EUELPIDES: Well, that cuts out a good deal of the seamy side of life,
for a start.

HOOPOE: We feed pretty well too, in the gardens: sesame, myrtle-berries, poppyseed, mint. . . .

EUELPIDES: Spiced wedding cake every day, what?

PEISTHETAERUS [*suddenly*]: My goodness, the possibilities I can see for you birds – and power too, if you'll let yourselves be guided by me.

HOOPOE: Guided by you? In what way?

PEISTHETAERUS: You want my advice? Very well. In the first place, give up this habit of flying stupidly around all day; it's getting you a bad name. I mean, where we come from, ask someone like Teleas about one of these flighty types we have, and he'll say 'Oh, the man's an absolute *bird* – restless, shifty, flighty, unreliable, can't stay in one place for two minutes on end.'

HOOPOE: I see what you mean: a fair criticism. But what *should* we do?

PEISTHETAERUS: Stay in one place and found a city.

HOOPOE: What kind of a city could birds found, I ask you.

PEISTHETAERUS: That's a stupid question if ever there was one: look down there!

HOOPOE [*looking down*]: Well?

PEISTHETAERUS: Now look up there.

HOOPOE [*looking up*]: Well?

PEISTHETAERUS: Turn your head, look around you, that way, this way, behind you . . .

HOOPOE [*doing his best*]: All I'm getting out of this is a crick in the neck.

PEISTHETAERUS: And what do you see?

HOOPOE: Only the clouds and the sky.

PEISTHETAERUS: The sky, exactly: the great vault of heaven. Revolving on its axis – to which only the birds have access. Build a wall around it, turn this vast immensity into a vast, immense city, and then – you'll rule over man as you now rule over the insects; and as for the gods, they'll starve to death, like the Melians.

HOOPOE: How?

PEISTHETAERUS: The air lies between the earth and the sky, doesn't it? If we Athenians want to consult the oracle at Delphi, we have to ask the Boeotians to allow us through. Well, in future, when men offer sacrifices to the gods, the gods will have to pay duty on them, otherwise you won't grant transit rights for those fragrant meaty odours to pass through space, across foreign territory.

HOOPOE: Well, I'll be snared! Ods nets, traps and scarecrows, it's the most brilliant idea I ever heard. I'll be delighted to help you found this city – provided the other birds agree, of course.

PEISTHETAERUS: Who's going to put it to them?

HOOPOE: Oh, you can do that yourself. They're not barbarians any more, you know; I've been with them a long time and I've taught them to speak.

PEISTHETAERUS: How will you call them together, though?

HOOPOE: That's easy. I can just step back into the wood here and wake up my nightingale, and we'll send out a call. As soon as they hear our voices they'll come here at the double.

PEISTHETAERUS: All right then, you splendid bird, please don't let's waste a minute. Off with you into the wood, there's a good fellow, and wake that nightingale.

[*The* HOOPOE *retires into the wood, and is soon heard singing his Song to the Nightingale.*]

HOOPOE [*sings*]:
Come, dearest mate, shake off your sleep,
Set free the notes of the hallowed songs
That pour divinely from you, lamenting
Itys our dear dead son,
Your tawny throat throbbing with liquid music –
Through the tracery of leaves the pure sound is heard
And echoes up to the very throne of Zeus,
Where golden Phoebus, hearing,
Takes up his lyre inlaid with ivory,
Catches the notes as they fly, and soon
To his sad music the gods are dancing, and your cry of grief
Is echoed by the voices of the Blest.

[*The sound of a flute, representing the song of the Nightingale, is heard offstage.*]

EUELPIDES: What a voice that little bird has! Makes you feel as if – [*he searches for a poetical phrase*] the woods were being drenched with honey.

PEISTHETAERUS: Shut up!

EUELPIDES: Eh? What's the matter?

PEISTHETAERUS: The Hoopoe's getting ready to sing again.

HOOPOE [*sings*]:
        Epo popo popo popo, popo popo poi!
        Ió, ió, itó, itó, itó, itó!
        Come along, come along, birds of my own feather,
        Birds who live in the farmers' well-sown fields,
        Eaters of seed and of barley, myriad flocks
        Of a hundred species, fluttering quickly,
        Uttering gentle calls,
        Twittering together on the furrowed soil
        In a pleased voice, tió, tió, tió!

        Birds who live in gardens, or in the mountains,
        Birds who feed on the wild olive
        And the fruit of the arbutus,
        Quickly fly to my call. triotó, triotó totobrix.

        Birds of the watery places,
        Snapping up the sharp-mouthed midges
        Along the ditches in the marshland,
        Birds of the swamp and the fenland
        And the pleasant meadow of Marathon;
        Bird of the stripy wing, godwit, godwit, godwit!

        And all the tribes that fly with the halcyon
        Over the waves of the sea, come along, come along!
        Come here to be informed
        Of a revolution, hi! all long-necked birds, you too
        Come along!

        Come and meet a shrewd old fellow,
        Full of wisdom, new in outlook,
        Enterprising. Come along now,
        Come along now, join the meeting!

        Toro toro toro torotix!
        Kikkabau! Kikkabau!
        Toro toro toro toro lililix!
PEISTHETAERUS [*scanning the sky*]: Can't see any birds: can you?
EUELPIDES: Not a bird to be seen in the whole sky.

PEISTHETAERUS: Looks as though the old Hoopoe's been wasting his time in the wood there, whistling away like a whimbrel.

HOOPOE [*off*]: Torotix, torotix! [*He returns to the stage.*]

PEISTHETAERUS [*lowering his eyes to ground level*]: Oh, but look, this must be a bird of some kind, coming in now.
    [*The* FLAMINGO *enters.*]

EUELPIDES: Yes, it's a bird all right, but what can it be? A peacock, d'you think?

PEISTHETAERUS: Let's ask the Hoopoe. [*To the* HOOPOE] What is it?

HOOPOE: Ah, he's not one of the birds you'd be familiar with. He lives in the marshes.

EUELPIDES: My, what a beauty: flaming pink!

HOOPOE: That's why we call him flaming-go.

EUELPIDES: Hey!

PEISTHETAERUS: What are you yelling about?

EUELPIDES: There's another bird coming. Not a bit like the other one.
    [*The* COCK *enters.*]

PEISTHETAERUS: You're right: a bird of ill omen, if you ask me. [*To the* HOOPOE] What is this sinister, soft-stepping, prophetic-looking creature?

HOOPOE: Oh, that's a Persian bird.

PEISTHETAERUS: A Persian, eh? How did he get here, without a camel?

EUELPIDES: Here comes another. This one's got a crest.
    [*The* SECOND HOOPOE *enters.*]

PEISTHETAERUS: Extraordinary! Do you mean to say you're not the only Hoopoe?

HOOPOE: This is the son of the one in the play by Philocles: my grandson,[8] you might say. Just as you have Hipponicus son of Callias, and then – next generation – Callias son of Hipponicus.

PEISTHETAERUS: So this one's Callias. Moulting badly, isn't he?

HOOPOE: Well, being an honest fellow, he's always getting plucked by the informers; and any feathers he's got left are pulled out by the females.

PEISTHETAERUS: Oh Poseidon, look at this one: what colours!
    [*The* GOBBLER *enters.*]
What's this one called, Hoopoe?

HOOPOE: That's a gobbler.

PEISTHETAERUS: The only gobbler I know is Cleonymus.⁹

EUELPIDES: Ah, but this one's still got its crest.

PEISTHETAERUS: Why are all these birds wearing crests anyway? Are they going to race in full armour?

HOOPOE: No, they live on the hill crests, like the Carians: it's safer.

[FLAMINGO, SECOND HOOPOE, COCK and GOBBLER *dance a ballet together and depart.*]

PEISTHETAERUS: Help, look at this mob of birds coming in now!

[*The 24 members of the* CHORUS *swarm in.*]

EUELPIDES: Lord Apollo, what a swarm. You can't see the gangways for them.

PEISTHETAERUS: A partridge and a francolin; a mallard; and that's a a halcyon¹⁰ –

EUELPIDES: What's that behind the halcyon?

PEISTHETAERUS: The halcyon's barber, of course.

EUELPIDES: A barber's not a bird.

PEISTHETAERUS: Isn't he? My barber's called Sparrow and he's a very queer bird indeed. And here's an owl.

EUELPIDES [*to audience*]: Bringing owls to Athens, as the saying is.¹¹

PEISTHETAERUS: Look at them all! Jay, turtledove, crested lark, reed warbler, wheatear, pigeon, merlin, sparrowhawk, ringdove, cuckoo, stockdove, firecrest, rail, kestrel and – oh look, a dabchick! Waxwing – vulture – woodpecker – and that seems to be the lot.

EUELPIDES: What a commotion they're making! All twittering and screeching and – hey! is this all directed against us, by any chance? Look, they've all got their beaks open. And what's more, they're all looking this way!

PEISTHETAERUS: I have that impression too.

CHORUS:

> Ca–ca–ca–ca– can you lead me
> To the bird that caw– caw– called us?
> Is he here or has he hopped it?

HOOPOE: Here I am, my friends, waiting for you.

CHORUS:

> What, a friendly message for us?
> Cwic–cwic–cwic–cwic–quickly tell us
> What–twhat–twhat–twhat–twhat's the matter?

HOOPOE: I have an announcement to make that affects you all. No, calm down, no need to be alarmed. It's good news. Two men of great sagacity have come here to see me.

CHORUS LEADER: Who? Where? What are you saying?

HOOPOE: I'm telling you, two human gentlemen have arrived among us, with an idea for the most stupendous scheme.

CHORUS LEADER: Two *men* here? Never since I left the nest have I heard of such lunacy. Do you mean to say –

HOOPOE: There's nothing to be frightened of.

CHORUS LEADER: What have you done, you fool?

HOOPOE: I've admitted two men. Who are *friendly* to our community.

CHORUS LEADER: How could you?

HOOPOE: And I stand by what I've done.

CHORUS LEADER: Are they here among us now?

HOOPOE: Just as surely as I am.

CHORUS LEADER: Birds, we have been betrayed and wickedly deceived. One who was our friend and fed beside us in the fields has been false to the ancient oath and broken the sacred law of the birds: he has lured us into a trap, he has betrayed us to an accursed race, brought up from birth to be our enemies. – But we'll deal with him later: first the two men must pay for their crimes. I propose that they be put to death forthwith. And we'll carry out the sentence ourselves.

[*The* CHORUS *shout assent, and the* LEADER *sets about marshalling them for battle.*]

PEISTHETAERUS: We're for it now.

EUELPIDES: It's all your fault, if it hadn't been for you, none of this would have happened. Why did you have to bring me with you?

PEISTHETAERUS: To be my trusty comrade in arms.

EUELPIDES: To weep my tragic fate, more like it.

PEISTHETAERUS: That's a silly thing to say: you won't be able to weep when they've pecked your eyes out.

CHORUS:

Iaa-uuu!
Let the war-cry rasp and rattle
As the birds prepare for battle.
Form your ranks! Advance, and rend them!
Soon to Hades we will send them.

Closely with your wings surround them,
Bash them, stun them and confound them.
If they fly you, helter skelter,
Vainly shall they seek for shelter;
No remote and wooded highland,
Ocean, cloud or rocky island
Shall protect them from our talons:
Let the blood run down in gallons!
　　Strike, and strike again!
　　Soon shall both be slain!

CHORUS LEADER: Come on, then, no time to waste! Captain, bring up the right wing!

EUELPIDES: Here they come! Help! I'm off!

PEISTHETAERUS: Stay where you are!

EUELPIDES: What, and get pecked to pieces?

PEISTHETAERUS: How do you expect to get away from this lot?

EUELPIDES: Don't ask me!

PEISTHETAERUS: We'll have to stay and fight it out, I tell you. Come on, let's grab hold of these pots. [*They have edged back to the entrance to the kitchen.*]

EUELPIDES: What use is a pot going to be?

PEISTHETAERUS: It'll keep the owls off, anyway.

EUELPIDES: Yes, but what about these vicious-looking eagles and things?

PEISTHETAERUS [*rummaging in the kitchen*]: Here, take this spit and hold it out in front of you.

　　[PEISTHETAERUS *himself does the same and they barricade themselves behind a random selection of the* HOOPOE's *cooking utensils.*]

EUELPIDES: What about our eyes?

PEISTHETAERUS: Here you are, take one of these sauce-bowls. Or a basin.

EUELPIDES [*as they don their 'helmets'*]: Quite a military genius, aren't you? Talk about resourceful, Nicias isn't in it.

CHORUS LEADER: Beaks at the ready! By the right – charge!

　　[*The* CHORUS *surges forward.*]

Come along, keep up the pace there! Peck them, pluck them, strip them, skin them – smash the pot first!

HOOPOE: What are you doing, you brutes, attacking two men who haven't done you any harm? You can't do this, they're Athenians; dammit, they're related to my wife![12]

CHORUS LEADER: Why should we spare them, any more than we'd spare a couple of wolves? Where could we find worse enemies?

HOOPOE: They may be enemies by birth, but they've come here with friendly intentions. They've come to teach us something useful.

CHORUS LEADER: How could they have anything useful to teach us – enemies of our race from time immemorial?

HOOPOE: The wise can learn a great deal even from enemies. Take a proverb like 'Safety lies in circumspection'. You don't learn the truth of that from your friends, you learn it from your enemies, and pretty quickly too. It wasn't from their friends that cities learned to perfect their fortifications and build up their navies: it was from their enemies. Yet it's only through having learnt this lesson that they can protect their children, their homes and their property.

CHORUS LEADER: Well, perhaps it might be a good thing to listen to them first. As you say, one can learn something even from enemies.

PEISTHETAERUS: They seem to be calming down a bit. Draw back gently, one step at a time.

HOOPOE [to CHORUS]: Besides, it's only right that you should do me a favour when I specially ask it.

CHORUS LEADER: Well, we've never gone against you before, have we?

PEISTHETAERUS: Now they're behaving much more peaceably: I think we can take our helmets off now. We'd better hang on to the spits, though, and patrol the battlements. Keep a sharp look-out over the top of your pot. Whatever happens, we mustn't run for it.

EUELPIDES: Suppose we get killed, I wonder where our graves will be.

PEISTHETAERUS: In the Potters' Quarter, obviously. If we want a state funeral we'll have to tell the generals we died fighting the enemy at Orneai.

CHORUS LEADER [to his troops]: Fall back into line! On the command one, calm yourselves down. On the command two, assume a friendly expression. One . . . two! And now we can ask who these men are, where they come from and what they want. Hey! Hoopoe! I'm talking to you!

HOOPOE: What is it you want to know?

CHORUS LEADER: Who are these people and where do they come from?

HOOPOE: Two visitors from Hellas, the land of wisdom.

CHORUS LEADER: And what strange chance brings them to Birdland?

HOOPOE: Their love for you has brought them here: love for you and your way of life. They want to live with you and be with you always.

CHORUS LEADER: What do you say? What has that fellow been telling you?

HOOPOE: Marvels beyond belief.

CHORUS LEADER: What can he possibly have to gain by staying with us? Will it help his friends or harm his enemies?

HOOPOE: He brings you word of a bliss beyond all your imaginings: everything, he says, is yours – he can prove it to you. Everything, everywhere, yours!

CHORUS LEADER: Is he off his head or something?

HOOPOE: Far from it: he couldn't be saner.

CHORUS LEADER: Crazy, absolutely crazy.

HOOPOE: No, no, he's very crafty: a master of schemes and devices, ruses and inventions.

CHORUS LEADER: Tell him to speak to us: I can hardly wait.

HOOPOE [calling to two slave-birds]: Come and pick up all these armaments, please; take them back into the kitchen and hang them up beside the what's-it. [To PEISTHETAERUS] And now tell them the news I've summoned them to hear.

PEISTHETAERUS: Not unless they swear a solemn oath, like the one that ass of a cutler dictated to his wife: not to bite me or scrag me or poke me in the –

CHORUS LEADER: Heaven forbid!

PEISTHETAERUS: Eyes, I was going to say.

CHORUS LEADER: We promise.

PEISTHETAERUS: Swear it.

CHORUS LEADER: We swear: on condition that we win the first prize, by the unanimous vote of the judges and the audience.

PEISTHETAERUS: You will, don't worry.

CHORUS LEADER: And if we break our word, may we – win by only one vote.

PEISTHETAERUS [to his imaginary army]: Attention all heavy-armed

troops! All ranks will return home with their equipment and await
further orders, which will be posted on the notice-boards in the
usual manner.

CHORUS:

> Though man is a master
> Of fraud and deception,
> We're ready to grant
> That we probably aren't
> His equals in wit
> Or in powers of perception.
> So if you have hit
> On a way for the birds
> To win glory and power,
> We'll hang on your words
> Though they last half an hour.

CHORUS LEADER: So speak out confidently and tell us what you had
in mind in coming here: we won't be the first to break the truce.

PEISTHETAERUS: I'm more than ready: I've worked up my speech
like a baker working up a lump of dough, and all it needs is kneading.
Bring me a wreath, boy, and water for my hands, quickly, somebody.

EUELPIDES: Are we going to have dinner, or what?

PEISTHETAERUS: No, I've been waiting for ages to make my speech,
and it's a real meaty one: it'll shatter their morale. [*The wreath and
water are brought: he puts on the wreath and water is poured over his
hands. He clears his throat and begins his speech.*] Oh, how I grieve for
you birds: once you were kings!

CHORUS LEADER: Kings? Of what?

PEISTHETAERUS: Of all creation. Of me, of him, of Zeus himself.
Before Kronos and the Titans, before Earth itself, You existed.

CHORUS LEADER: Before Earth itself?

PEISTHETAERUS: Yes, indeed.

CHORUS LEADER: That's news to me.

PEISTHETAERUS: Then you must be very unobservant, or very
uneducated: you don't know your Aesop. According to him,
surely, the Lark was the first of all the birds to be born, and this was
before the Earth existed: so when her father took sick and died,
what was the poor creature to do, with no Earth to bury him in? He

lay in state for four days and then she buried him in her own head.

EUELPIDES: What a lark!

PEISTHETAERUS: And obviously, if you birds existed before the Earth and before the gods, the sovereignty belongs rightly to you.

EUELPIDES: You'd better keep your beaks well sharpened: I can't see Zeus handing over his sceptre to a woodpecker – especially if it's been making holes in his sacred oaks.

PEISTHETAERUS: There's any amount of evidence to prove that it wasn't the gods who ruled over men in ancient times, but the birds. I need only remind you of the Cock, who ruled over the Persians long before Darius or Megabazus were ever heard of. That's why we still call him the Persian Fowl.

EUELPIDES: And he's the only bird to wear an upright tiara – like the king of the Persians.

PEISTHETAERUS: Great and powerful he was in those days, and even now, when he sings his song in the morning, men feel his ancient power: they leap from their beds and start working – smiths, potters, tanners, cobblers, bath attendants, millers, and even those fellows who can turn anything on a lathe from a lyre to a shield. Some people put on their shoes and go out, even if it's still the middle of the night.

EUELPIDES: You don't have to tell me: that's how I lost a perfectly good Phrygian cloak, a beautiful soft woolly one. I'd been invited to a naming-day party for some child, and I had a few drinks down town beforehand. When I got there I fell asleep. Suddenly the cock crew – the party hadn't even begun, but I thought it was morning and set off in a great hurry to walk back to Alimous. I'd hardly got one foot outside the Wall when I was attacked from behind by a bandit with a cosh. Down I went, naturally; and before I had time to shout he'd made off with my cloak.

PEISTHETAERUS: It was the kite who ruled over the Greeks in those early days.

CHORUS LEADER: Oh, really?

PEISTHETAERUS: Yes, it's because he was our first king that we always fling ourselves flat on the ground when a kite appears.

EUELPIDES: Yes, I did that once when I saw a kite, and when I rolled over on my back to see if he'd gone I swallowed the coin I had in my mouth. Nothing left to buy the dinner with.

PEISTHETAERUS: And in Egypt and the whole of Phoenicia it was the cuckoo who reigned supreme. And whenever he called 'Cuckoo!' all the Phoenicians used to grab their tools and get down to cutting the –

EUELPIDES: Foreskins off. Yes, I've heard about that.

PEISTHETAERUS: – hay in the fields. So firmly established was the rule of the birds that even when the Greek cities began to have kings of their own, like Agamemnon and Menelaus, there was always a bird perched on the royal sceptre, making sure it got a fair share of any gifts that were offered.

EUELPIDES: Well, I never knew that before. I often used to wonder about that bird, when King Priam came on in some tragedy: it was watching Lysicrates,[13] of course, hoping for a share in – how did you put it, now? – 'any gifts that were offered'.

PEISTHETAERUS: But the most impressive proof of all is that Zeus, who now has the sovereignty, always stands with an eagle on his head as the sign of kingship; and his daughter Athene has an owl, and Apollo, as his henchman, has a falcon.

EUELPIDES: How right you are. Why do they have them, though?

PEISTHETAERUS: It's so that when anyone sacrifices and places the offerings in the god's hand as the custom is, the bird can get at the meat before even Zeus does. In the old days people never used to swear by a god but always by a bird: even in our own time the fortune-tellers say 'By Goose' instead of 'By Zeus' when they're not telling the truth. So there you are: in the olden days everyone considered you great and holy, but now they treat you like slaves or fools and throw things at you as they do at madmen; even inside the sanctuaries they hunt you down with nooses and traps, sticks, nets, webs, snares and cages; and when they've caught you they sell you at so much a dozen. And the customers prod your flesh, and if they decide you're good enough to roast they don't just roast you and have done with it. Oh no, you have to have cheese grated over you and oil and silphium and vinegar thrown on, and after that they make another sauce, all sweet and greasy, and pour it over you – hot! – as though you were some kind of noisome carrion.

CHORUS:
| Hard, friends, hard | is the tale that he has told us: |
| How I weep | for the folly of our fathers! |

Oh, what a crime	to cast away a kingdom!
Thank you, sir,	for coming here to save us.
Life henceforth	will hardly be worth living
If we can't	regain our former glory.
We'll place all	our confidence in you, sir,
Trusting you	with all our little nestlings;
You shall help	us build another kingdom:
Please instruct	us how to set about it.

PEISTHETAERUS: Well, the first essential is that there should be a single bird city. And the whole sky between Earth and Heaven should have a wall of huge baked bricks around it, like Babylon.

HOOPOE: Bitterns and bustards! A fearsome city indeed!

PEISTHETAERUS: And when it has been set up, Zeus should be told to hand over his powers. And if he refuses or is reluctant, and won't climb down at once, war must be declared on him. A holy war. And you can tell the gods they'll no longer be allowed to go rampaging across your territory whenever they want to go down and rape some mortal maiden: otherwise they'll have seals put on their foreskins so that they can't rape anyone at all. And to men you must send another bird envoy to explain that in future they must sacrifice to the birds, who have the sovereign power. If they want to sacrifice to the gods as well, they can do that afterwards. For every god there must be a corresponding bird, appropriately chosen of course: for example if a man wants to sacrifice to Aphrodite he must put out some grain for the coot; if he is offering a sheep to Poseidon he must burn wheat for the duck; if his offering is to Heracles, there must be, not a honey-cake, but a great quartern loaf for the hungry gull. And before he can sacrifice a ram to Zeus, the wren must be appeased with a sturdy uncastrated gnat.

EUELPIDES: I like the idea of sacrificing a gnat. What price Zeus's thunder now?

CHORUS LEADER: And how are men to know that we are gods, and not just jackdaws and so on, when they see us flying around with wings on?

PEISTHETAERUS: Why, Hermes is a god, and he flies, doesn't he, and wears wings? And so do lots of the other gods. Victory flies – and on golden wings at that. And what about Eros? And then there's Iris: doesn't Homer compare her to a timorous dove?

EUELPIDES: Zeus's thunderbolts are winged too: we'll be lucky if he doesn't launch one at us.

PEISTHETAERUS: If, in their ignorance, men think you count for nothing, and that the real gods are the ones on Olympus, just let a cloud of sparrows descend on their fields and gobble up every single grain: and then, when they're starving, let them look to Demeter for their dole of corn.

EUELPIDES: The only thing she'll dole out will be excuses.

PEISTHETAERUS: Just as a demonstration, let the crows pluck out the eyes of their sheep and their cattle and the oxen that draw their ploughs: they can ask Apollo the Healer to cure them. He'd want a pretty big fee, I reckon.

EUELPIDES: Tell them to wait till I've sold my pair of bullocks.

PEISTHETAERUS: But if they acknowledge that *you* are God, *you* are Life, *you* are Earth, *you* are Kronos, *you* are Poseidon – ah, then what blessings will be showered upon them.

CHORUS LEADER: What kind of blessings? Could you name some of them?

PEISTHETAERUS: To begin with, the locusts will no longer devour the vine blossoms: a squadron of owls and kestrels will wipe out the whole swarm. No longer will the figs be eaten by ants and grubs: one flock of thrushes will make a clean sweep of the pests.

CHORUS LEADER: But how can we make men rich? – because that's what they want most.

PEISTHETAERUS: When they watch you for omens you can guide them to the richest silver mines, you can forecast the luck of a trading venture: never again will any seafarer be drowned.

CHORUS LEADER: How can we stop that happening?

PEISTHETAERUS: Before a voyage they will always take the omens from your flight: 'Don't sail today, there'll be a storm'; 'Sail now, the voyage will bring you profit'.

EUELPIDES: I think I'll change my mind about staying with you, and buy a ship instead.

PEISTHETAERUS: And you can show them hoards of silver, hidden away by people of long ago: because you are the ones who know where it is. Don't they always say 'Nobody knows where my treasure is hidden, except the birds and me'?

EUELPIDES: Perhaps I'll sell the ship, buy a spade, and dig up a crock of gold.

CHORUS LEADER: And how can the birds give men health? Surely that comes from the gods?

PEISTHETAERUS: If they prosper, isn't that health?

EUELPIDES: Obviously, if a man's doing badly you can't call him healthy.

CHORUS LEADER: And what about long life? That's a gift of the gods too. Must they all die in infancy?

PEISTHETAERUS: Far from it: the birds can give them three hundred years or more of extra life.

CHORUS LEADER: Where are we going to get those from?

PEISTHETAERUS: You've got lots of your own to spare. Have you forgotten your Hesiod? 'And in the lifetime of one squawking crow, Five human generations come and go.'

EUELPIDES: They'll make jolly good kings, won't they! Much better than Zeus.

PEISTHETAERUS: Much better. For one thing, we won't have to build stone temples for them, with magnificent golden doors: they'll live among the oaks and under the bushes; an olive tree will do as a temple for the proudest of them. And we won't have to go to Delphi or the shrine of Ammon to sacrifice; we shall just stand among the strawberry trees and the wild olives with our offerings of barley and wheat, hold out our hands and pray to the birds for a share of the good things they can give; and we shall get them at once – very good value for a handful of wheat grains.

CHORUS LEADER: And to think that we took you at first for our worst enemy! From now on we'll take your advice in everything, if we possibly can.

[CHORUS *cheer and applaud.*]

After listening to your inspiring words, we solemnly swear that if you will march with us against the gods, and remain a true ally to us, the gods shall not long continue to handle the sceptre that is ours by right!

[CHORUS *cheer and applaud.*]

We have the strength, and whatever needs doing, we can do: the planning we leave to you.

HOOPOE: And now, by Zeus, it's time to stop dreaming and drowsing, and dithering about like old Nicias: we must get down to work right away. But first I hope you'll come up and see my nest – just a little shack I knocked together myself from a few twigs and sticks I found lying around. By the way, I don't know your names.

PEISTHETAERUS: Well, that's easily remedied. My name is Peisthetaerus.

EUELPIDES: And mine's Euelpides. From Crio.

HOOPOE: Well, come along up, you're both very welcome.

PEISTHETAERUS: Thanks very much. [*He looks a bit doubtfully at the precipitous path leading up to the nest.*]

HOOPOE: This way, gentlemen.

PEISTHETAERUS: Er – thank you. [*He steps on to the path trips and falls.*] You lead the way, then you can give us a hand.

HOOPOE: Come along, then.

PEISTHETAERUS [*wondering how they will ever get down again*]: Hold on a minute: how do we sort of . . . I mean how are we two going to manage to live your kind of life, when you've got wings and we haven't?

HOOPOE: You'll manage all right.

PEISTHETAERUS: Isn't there a fable by Aesop about a fox who tried to set up house with an eagle, and fared rather badly?

HOOPOE: Don't worry. I know of a root you can chew: it'll make you grow wings.

PEISTHETAERUS: Oh, good. Let's go in, then. Xanthias! Manodorus! Bring up the luggage!

CHORUS LEADER: Hi! Hoopoe!

HOOPOE: What is it?

CHORUS LEADER: Take them in and give them a good lunch. But, please! do send out your sweet little nightingale, who sings so divinely, and let her stay here and join us in our music-making.

PEISTHETAERUS: Oh, yes, do fetch her out, so that we can see her too.

HOOPOE: Very well, if you wish it. Procne! Come out here, my dear, and show yourself to the visitors.

   [PROCNE, *who like her husband has retained her human shape except for the bird-mask, comes out.*]

PEISTHETAERUS: Oh, what a pretty birdie! How soft and delicate! And what a lovely white skin!

EUELPIDES: Do you know, I wouldn't mind going to bed with her.

176

PEISTHETAERUS: What a lot of gold she's wearing, like a young bride.

EUELPIDES: I've a good mind to give her a kiss.

PEISTHETAERUS: She's got a beak, you fool – it'd be like kissing a couple of skewers.

EUELPIDES: Oh, that's all right. It's like eating an egg: you have to take the top off first. [*He lifts her mask, but gets slapped for his pains.*]

HOOPOE: Let's go in, shall we?

PEISTHETAERUS: Right; you lead the way.

[*They mount to the nest.* PROCNE *remains below with the* CHORUS.]

CHORUS:

> Nightingale, we all adore thee,
> Russet-coated,
> Vibrant-throated,
> Song-devoted, tremulous bird!
> Chief musician of the woodland,
> Sweetly fluting,
> Spring-saluting,
> Seldom seen though often heard.
> Many a time you've fluted for us
> And accompanied our chorus:
> Now at last you stand before us –
> How we love you, darling bird!
> Nightingale, we're mad about you –
> And we can't begin without you:
> Let your silver notes be heard!

[*Flute music.*]

CHORUS: Listen, you men down there in the half-light! Shadowy, impalpable, dreamlike phantoms: feeble, wingless, ephemeral creatures of clay, dragging out your painful lives till you wither like the leaves and crumble again to dust! Pay attention to us, the immortals; to us, the eternal, the airborne, the un-ageing, the imperishable; and hear from us the whole truth about what lies around and above you! We will explain to you the nature of birds, the birth of the gods, the genealogy of the rivers, the origin of Erebus and Chaos – and when you have learnt the truth you can pay off old Prodicus,[14] with our compliments. – In the beginning there existed only Chaos, Night, Black Erebus and Dreary Tartarus: there was no

Earth, no Air, no Sky. It was in the boundless womb of Erebus that the first egg was laid by black-winged Night; and from this egg, in due season, sprang Eros the deeply-desired, Eros the bright, the golden-winged. And it was he, mingling in Tartarus with murky Chaos, who begot our race and hatched us out and led us up to the light.

There was no race of immortal gods till Eros brought the elements together in love: only then did the Sky, the Ocean and the Earth come into being, and the deathless race of all the blessed gods.

So you see we are much older than any of the gods.

And that we are the children of Eros is plain by many tokens.

Like him, we fly.

Like him, we are associated with love.

Why, many a bashful beloved, in the prime of beauty and youth, has been won over, thanks to us: the gift of a quail, a goose or a cockerel at the critical moment has been known to work wonders.

It is from us, the birds, that Man receives all his greatest blessings. From us he learns of the coming of spring, of winter, of autumn. The cry of the crane as it flies back to Libya tells him it is the season for sowing; the shipmaster knows that he can hang up his rudder and enjoy a good night's rest; Orestes[15] weaves himself a warm winter cloak – no point in freezing to death while he's on his way to steal someone else's. But when the kite appears, another season is at hand. Time for the sheepshearing! Spring is here! Then comes the swallow: time to sell those warm woollen clothes and buy something more summery.

We are your oracles too: your Ammon, your Dodona; your Delphi, your Phoebus Apollo. Whatever you are going to do, whether it's a matter of trade, or feeding the family, or getting married, you always consult the birds. Why, you even use the word bird for anything that brings good luck or bad luck: whether it's a chance remark, a sneeze, an unexpected meeting, a noise, a servant or a donkey, you call it a bird! So you see we really are the oracle you depend on most!

> So let us be your gods
> And your Muses prophetic!
> To all your requests
> We'll be most sympathetic.

We won't put on airs
Like the gods you've been used to,
Or skulk in the clouds
As Apollo and Zeus do;

We'll always be present
To aid and defend you;
There's really no end
To the blessings we'll send you:

Long life and good fortune,
Peace, happiness, wealth,
Youth, laughter, and dancing,
Good cheer and good health.

[*Song, with flute accompaniment:*]
                Come, woodland Muse,
                Tio, tio, tio, tiotinx,
With changeful melodies inspire me as of old,
                Tio, tio, tio, tiotinx,
                When, perched on leafy ash
Down in the vale, or high on yonder hill,
                Tio, tio, tio, tiotinx,
                From quivering throat I poured
                A holy hymn to Pan,
Or solemn dances for dread Cybelē;
                Tŏ tŏtŏ–tŏtŏ tŏtŏ tŏtŏtinx;
                    And Phrynichus,
Flitting from song to song, culled like a honey-bee
Ambrosial music for his choruses.
                Tio, tio, tio, tiotinx.

CHORUS LEADER: How would you like to come and live with the
birds? Do come and join us, we can promise you a very happy life.
You know, lots of things that are looked down on where you come
from, or even forbidden by your laws, are regarded by us as perfectly right and proper. Among you, it's a crime for a son to strike
his father: but if a young fighting-cock struts up to his father and
says 'Come on, raise your spur and fight', it's the most natural
thing in the world. We admire his spirit. Have you been branded as

a runaway? It won't show – lots of us are speckled and banded; and a jailbird's as good a bird as any. If you're a Phrygian, like Spintharus, we'll call you Phrygilus, the finch, a bird of impeccable ancestry. If you're a slave, and a Carian one at that, like Execestides,[16] never mind: we'll soon find you a family tree to nest in. Come and hatch yourself some ancestors! If the son of Peisias wants to let in the rebels, as his father did, *we* won't call him a traitor -- merely a chick of the old cock. Nothing wrong in feathering your own nest, from a bird's point of view.

CHORUS [*Song, continued*]:

> Ev'n thus the swans,
> Tio, tio, tio, tiotinx,
> Hieing to Hebrus' banks on slowly beating wing,
> Tio, tio, tio, tiotinx,
> Once sang Apollo's praise,
> And to the airy clouds their cry arose:
> Tio, tio, tio, tiotinx.
> The beasts of earth fell dumb,
> All waveless lay the sea,
> While high Olympus echoed to their hymn:
> To toto–toto toto tototinx!
> The imperious gods
> With wonder stood transfix'd, and all the heavenly Graces
> Joined in the singing, and the Muses too:
> Tio, tio, tio, tiotinx!

CHORUS LEADER: Have you ever thought how useful a pair of wings would be in the theatre? No need to sit through all those tragic choruses, getting hungrier and hungrier: just fly home whenever you feel like it, have a good lunch, and get back to your seat in time for our comedy. And if ever you're caught unawares and want to leave in a hurry, how convenient! Simply fly off somewhere, find a secluded spot, and fly back to your seat without a stain on your – clothes. Or suppose you're having an affair with a married lady, and you see her husband down there in the front row, firmly wedged into his official seat. What an opportunity, if you've let us fit you out with a pair of wings. All you have to do is fly to his house, have it off with the lady, and be back in your seat before the end of the play. Oh, wings are splendid things, make no mistake: they really help you rise in the world. Look at Diitrephēs:[17] what a meteoric career, and *his* wings are only made of wicker. First they made him a captain; then a colonel; and look at him now – Lord High Admiral of the Hobby-Horse Marines!

[PEISTHETAERUS *and* EUELPIDES *re-enter, each wearing a large pair of wings.*]

PEISTHETAERUS: Well, that's that, then.

EUELPIDES: My God, you do look funny. I never saw anything so ridiculous.

PEISTHETAERUS: What's so funny about me?

EUELPIDES: Those mighty pinions of yours. You know what you look like with wings on?

PEISTHETAERUS: *You* look as though someone had started to paint a goose and then run out of paint.

EUELPIDES: Well, *you* look like a blackbird with a pudding-basin haircut.

PEISTHETAERUS: We'd better drop these comparisons, or we'll be like the eagle in Aeschylus, 'slain by an arrow winged with his own feathers'.

EUELPIDES: What do we do next?

PEISTHETAERUS: First we must give our city a fine, high-sounding name, and then we must offer a sacrifice.

EUELPIDES: That sounds very sensible. Now, what name are we going to give it?

PEISTHETAERUS: How do you like the great Lacedaemonian name of 'Sparta'?

EUELPIDES: Not for my city, thank you. I hate the name so much I wouldn't even use esparto for a mattress. I'd rather sleep on the straps.

PEISTHETAERUS: What shall we call it, then?

EUELPIDES: We want something more ethereal – you know, something to do with skies and clouds and things.

PEISTHETAERUS: Yes [*He ponders.*] What about 'Much Cuckoo in the Clouds'?

CHORUS LEADER: Oh, marvellous! That's a fine big name, and no mistake.

EUELPIDES: 'In the clouds'! Where Theagenes keeps all that money he talks about, and Aeschines[18] keeps his – well, everything.

PEISTHETAERUS: The famous battlefield, where the gods beat the giants – at the game of boasting.

EUELPIDES: Oh, what a splendid city it'll be! Who's going to be its guardian deity? For whom do we weave the sacred scarf?

PEISTHETAERUS: What's wrong with Athene?

EUELPIDES: Oh, no. You can't expect a well-run city if you've got a female goddess standing up there in full armour, while Cleisthenes gets on with his knitting.

PEISTHETAERUS: Well, someone's got to guard the citadel.

CHORUS LEADER: We have among us no less a warrior than the Cock. Of Persian birth: the war-god's most illustrious chick.

EUELPIDES: O mighty chick! And just the right god to perch up there on the rock.

PEISTHETAERUS: Now, Euelpides, you'd better get up into the air and give a hand with the wall-building. Collect a barrowload of rubble: take your coat off and get down to mixing the mortar; carry the hods up the ladder, fall off, tell the watchmen what to do, keep the fires covered, rush round ringing a bell, fall asleep on the job – you know, make yourself thoroughly useful. Oh, yes, and send off a couple of messengers – one to tell the gods, and one to tell the men on earth; and then they can report back here to me.

EUELPIDES: And *you* can – get stuffed! Why should I do all the running about?

PEISTHETAERUS: Get along now, go where I tell you: none of those things'll get done if you're not there.

[EUELPIDES *climbs a few steps up the cliffside and is wafted away.*]
Now, if I'm going to sacrifice to the new gods, I must find a priest to conduct the ceremony. [*To* XANTHIAS] Boy! Take up the basket and the holy water.

[PEISTHETAERUS *goes off in search of a priest.* XANTHIAS *and* MANES *proceed to the altar with the basket and water-jar.*]

CHORUS:
> Agreed, agreed!
> With solemn odes
> The gods must be addressed –
> You're right about that.
> And to ensure their favour

Some kind of sacrifice
Is quite essential.

CHORUS LEADER:

Fling wide your beaks
And raise the holy cry;
And Chaeris the piper
Will play the accompaniment.

[*The* CHORUS *break out into a cacophonous parody of the cries of ecstatic worshippers, while a* PIPER *masked as a raven provides a painful obbligato. He is still playing when* PEISTHETAERUS *returns, carrying the sacrificial 'victim' and followed by a* PRIEST.]

PEISTHETAERUS [*to the* PIPER]: Stop that wheezing, for goodness' sake!

[*The* PIPER *retires.*]

Well, I've seen some odd things in my life, but a raven playing the oboe just about beats the band. [*To* PRIEST] Now, sir, do your stuff. Perform the sacrifice to the new gods. [*He hands him the victim.*]

PRIEST: Very well: where is your basket bearer, is he ready?

[PRIEST *and* PEISTHETAERUS *proceed to the altar and a small procession is formed, led by* XANTHIAS *and* MANES *with the basket and water-jar.*]

PRIEST [*as they march round the altar*]: Pray to the birds' equivalent of Hestia, to the Stork who guards your hearth, and to all the Olympian cock gods and hen gods –

PEISTHETAERUS: O Stork who stalkest over Sunium, all hail!

PRIEST: – and to the Pythian and Delian Swan, and Leto the Quail-Mother; Artemis and Bunting –

PEISTHETAERUS: I think she's gone a-hunting.

PRIEST: – and to the Phrygian Finch, and Ostrich the great Mother of gods and men –

PEISTHETAERUS: Ostrich the mother of Cleocritus! [*He imitates the walk of a well-known citizen.*]

PRIEST: – to grant health and safety to the people of Much Cuckoo in the Clouds, and likewise to their faithful allies in Chios.

PEISTHETAERUS: I love the way *they* always get dragged in.

PRIEST: And to the hero-birds and their descendants: the Purple Coot, the Pelican, the Shag; the Eagle and the Grouse; the Peacock and

the Sedge-warbler; the Tern and the Teal; the Heron and the
Gannet; the Blackcap and the Tufted Tit –

PEISTHETAERUS: Whoa there, stop, stop, that's quite enough –
what are you doing inviting all these ospreys and vultures? Look at
the size of what we're sacrificing – a single kite could carry it off.
Get away, go to the crows, you and your garlands – go on, beat it.
I'll do the sacrifice myself. [*He chases the* PRIEST *away*.]

CHORUS:
> Once again, oh once again
> We must chant a holy strain:
> Cancel what we said before,
> Call to one god and no more;
> As you see, our sacrifice
> For more than one will not suffice –
> It's nothing but the beard and horns.

PEISTHETAERUS [*raising the sacrificial knife*]: As we sacrifice this victim, let us pray to the feathered gods – oh dear, who's this?

[*Enter a ragged* POET, *shivering with cold*.]

POET:
> Come, come, my Muse, and we will s-sing
> A merry, merry roundelay
> For M-much – Cuckoo – In – the Clouds,
> The happy town that's born today!

PEISTHETAERUS: What's all this in aid of? Who on earth are you?

POET: A fount of honeyed words, of sweetest song; a bard; a nimble
servant of the Muse, as Homer puts it.

PEISTHETAERUS: A servant, with hair that long?

POET: No, no, you misapprehend me: we poets are all nimble servants
of the Muse, as Homer puts it.

PEISTHETAERUS: Did Homer put those holes in your shirt, as well?

POET: I've composed dozens of poems in honour of your noble city,
Much Cuckoo in the Clouds: dithyrambs, of the finest quality,
any number of them; songs for female voices, lyrics in the style of
Simonides –

PEISTHETAERUS: When did you write all these? How long ago did
you start?

POET: Oh, for as long as I can remember I've been praising your city
in my poems.

PEISTHETAERUS: Well, that's a very odd thing, because I'm only just carrying out the naming ceremony at this moment.

POET:

> Did not the Muses whisper in my ear,
> Wafting their message on the crystal breeze,
> Swift as the glancing flash of horses' feet?
> And now, O noble founder of this state,
> Whose name (I quote from Pindar) calls to mind
> The holy fire that on the altar burns,
> What contribution would you care to make?

PEISTHETAERUS: We'll never get rid of the blighter at this rate, unless we give him something. [*To* XANTHIAS] Hey, you've got a jerkin on over your tunic: off with it, and give it to the learned poet.

[XANTHIAS *reluctantly obeys.*]

There you are, you can have the jerkin. Not that it'll do much for that frigid poetry of yours. Brrr! [*He shivers.*]

POET:

> Far from unpleased is the Muse,
> And graciously she doth accept thy gift;
> But let me quote from Pindar once again –

PEISTHETAERUS: Some people just can't see when they're not wanted.

POET:

> Wand'ring with the Scythian nomads
>   How shall Straton fare
> If he hath no woven garment
>   Next his skin to wear?
>
> Of thy bounty, gracious sovereign,
>   I will gladly sing;
> But a jerkin with no tunic –
>   Is that quite the thing?

You perceive the allusion?

PEISTHETAERUS: I perceive that you want the tunic as well. [*To* XANTHIAS] Come on, we can't deny a poet.

[XANTHIAS, *with a sigh, removes his tunic and hands it to the poet.*]

There, take it and go.

POET: I go; and as I speed homewards I will compose something. How about this?

> Lord, on thy golden throne,
> Sing of the shimmering, shivering
> Tremulous city – ah, I have visited
> The fruitful snowfields,
> Alalae!

[PEISTHETAERUS *makes a threatening gesture, and the* POET *leaves hastily.*]

PEISTHETAERUS: There he goes again, shivering in the snowfields, even in that nice warm tunic. Well, that was a nuisance I hadn't bargained for: however did he find out about the city so quickly? – Right, pick up the jar and let's get on with the ceremony.

[*Before they can resume their positions at the altar, the* ORACLE MAN *enters, carrying a tray of scrolls.*]

ORACLE MAN: Psst! Don't start the sacrifice yet!

PEISTHETAERUS: Who are you?

ORACLE MAN: Who am I? The oracle man.

PEISTHETAERUS: Well, get to hell out of here.

ORACLE MAN: Here, here, this won't never do. Scoffing at things divine? Look at this now – I've got an oracle here, guaranteed genuine, it's by Bakis himself. All about this here city of Much Cuckoo in the Clouds. Couldn't be plainer.

PEISTHETAERUS: Then why didn't you come out with it before I founded the city?

ORACLE MAN: Oh, come, sir – I couldn't do that, sir, not with my respect for religion I couldn't.

PEISTHETAERUS: Well, let's hear it – I'm dying to know what it says.

ORACLE MAN [*reading*]: 'But when the wolf and the grey crow do build their home together in the region that lieth between Corinth and Sicyon –'

PEISTHETAERUS: Corinth? What's all this got to do with me?

ORACLE MAN: Sssh! It's an oracle, don't you see? Bakis means *the air.* [*Reading*] '– in that day shalt thou sacrifice a white ram to Pandora; and upon him that first bringeth thee my words, thou shalt bestow a cloak without spot or blemish, and with new sandals shall he be shod –'

186

PEISTHETAERUS: Sandals too? Does it really say all that?

ORACLE MAN: Take the book and see for yourself. [*Reading*] 'And a bowl of wine shall be given unto him, and of the cooked meats of the sacrifice, yea, even so much as his hands can hold.'

PEISTHETAERUS: Is that bit in it too? About the cooked meat?

ORACLE MAN: Take the book and see for yourself. [*Reading*] 'And if thou doest these things according to my command, thou shalt be as an eagle that soareth in the clouds; but if thou doest them not, and givest not the gifts, verily thou shalt not be as an eagle, nay, nor a turtledove, nor so much as a lesser spotted woodpecker.'

PEISTHETAERUS: Hold on! Does it really say all that?

ORACLE MAN: Take the book and see for yourself.

PEISTHETAERUS [*surreptitiously taking a heavy scroll from the tray*]: Funny, your oracle isn't a bit like the one I got from the temple of Apollo: I wrote it down – listen! [*Unrolling the scroll and pretending to read from it*] 'But when an impudent scoundrel cometh uninvited and maketh himself a bloody nuisance to them that do carry out the sacrifice, and asketh for a share of the cooked meats, then shalt thou sock him hard between the ribs.'

ORACLE MAN: It doesn't say that.

PEISTHETAERUS: Take the book and see for yourself. [*He bangs him on the head with the scroll.*] And get out! Go and soothsay somewhere else.

[*The* ORACLE MAN *flees, scattering his stock, which* PEISTHETAERUS *flings after him. Meanwhile* METON *enters from the other side.*]

METON: I have come among you –

PEISTHETAERUS: Oh, no, not another! [*Imitating an actor in tragedy.*] How purposed, sir, / Do you thus visit us on buskin'd foot? / What grave intention, what inspir'd design / Counsels your journey? What's the big idea?

METON: I propose to survey the air for you: it will have to be marked out in acres.

PEISTHETAERUS: Good lord, who do you think you are?

METON: Who am I? Why, Meton. *The* Meton. Famous throughout the Hellenic world – you must have heard of my hydraulic clock at Colonus?

PEISTHETAERUS [*eyeing* METON's *instruments*]: And what are those for?

METON: Ah, these are my special rods for measuring the air. You see, the air is shaped, how shall I put it? – like a sort of extinguisher; so all I have to do is to attach this flexible rod at the upper extremity, take the compasses, insert the point here, and – you see what I mean?

PEISTHETAERUS: No.

METON: Well, I now apply the straight rod – so – thus squaring the circle; and there you are. In the centre you have your market place: straight streets leading into it, from here, from here, from here. Very much the same principle, really, as the rays of a star: the star itself is circular, but it sends out straight rays in every direction.

PEISTHETAERUS: Brilliant – the man's a genius. But – Meton!

METON: Yes?

PEISTHETAERUS: Speaking as a friend [*he lowers his voice*] I think you'd be wise to slip away now.

METON: Why, what's the danger?

PEISTHETAERUS: The people here are like the Lacedaemonians, they don't like strangers. And feeling's running rather high just at the moment.

METON: Party differences?

PEISTHETAERUS: Oh no, far from it: they're quite unanimous.

METON: What's happening, then?

PEISTHETAERUS: There's to be a purge of pretentious humbugs: they're all going to get beaten up. You know what I mean: like this. [*He begins to demonstrate.*]

METON: Perhaps I'd better be going.

PEISTHETAERUS: I'm not sure you're going to get away in time. [*His blows get progressively harder: meanwhile the* CHORUS *advances menacingly.*] Something tells me that someone's going to get beaten up quite soon!

[METON *hastily gathers up his instruments and makes for the exit, pursued by the* CHORUS.]

I warned you! Go and measure how far it is to somewhere else.

[*As* METON *leaves, the* INSPECTOR *enters from the other side. He is dressed in impressive official robes, and carries two ballot-boxes, one marked 'Ayes' and the other 'Noes'.*]

INSPECTOR: Where are the consular representatives?

PEISTHETAERUS: Blimey, who's this? Sardanapalus?

INSPECTOR: I have been appointed by lot to carry out an inspection of Much Cuckoo in the Clouds.

PEISTHETAERUS: An inspector? Who sent you?

INSPECTOR [*producing his credentials*]: Proposed by Teleas. Damned nuisance, really.

PEISTHETAERUS: I see, and you just want to draw your fee, do nothing and go back home, is that it?

INSPECTOR [*who doesn't like it being put quite so bluntly*]: Well, the fact is, I *am* rather anxious not to miss the Assembly today: there's a little matter coming up that I've had something to do with, about talks with the Persians.

PEISTHETAERUS [*kicking him from behind*]: Well, here's your fee. Take it and clear out.

INSPECTOR: What do you think you're doing? What's the meaning of this?

PEISTHETAERUS: Ask your Persian friends.

INSPECTOR: You can't kick an inspector! I'll have you prosecuted.

PEISTHETAERUS: Oh, go away. Shoo.
      [*The* INSPECTOR *goes off indignantly in search of a witness.*]
And take your ballot-boxes with you. [*To the audience*] Would you believe it? Before we've even got through the dedication ceremony, they send us inspectors!
      [*A* STATUTE-SELLER *enters from the other side.*]

STATUTE-SELLER [*reading from a scroll*]: 'But if an offence be committed by a Much Cuckoovian against an Athenian –'

PEISTHETAERUS: What, more sinister documents?

STATUTE-SELLER: Buy my lovely by-laws! Statutes, regulations, decrees! Come on, sir, you'll be wanting new laws here – I've got just what you want.

PEISTHETAERUS: What's that?

STATUTE-SELLER [*reading*]: 'Article 6. Furthermore, the weights, measures and currency of the Much Cuckoovians shall be identical with those of the Olophyxians.'

PEISTHETAERUS: I'll Olophyx you if you don't clear off. [*He knocks the scroll from his hand.*]

STATUTE-SELLER: Here, what are you doing?

PEISTHETAERUS: Take your laws away and be quick about it, or I'll give you some laws you won't care for.

[*The* INSPECTOR *re-enters.*]

INSPECTOR [*seeing* STATUTE-SELLER]: Ah, good, a witness. Take
note that I hereby charge Peisthetaerus with assault and summon
him to appear at the April sessions.

PEISTHETAERUS: What, are *you* still here?

[INSPECTOR *is chased away.*]

STATUTE-SELLER [*reading*]: 'Article 44. For the offence of chasing
away a legally appointed official and refusing to accept his authority,
the penalty shall be –'

PEISTHETAERUS: Oh, for pity's sake, are *you* still here too?

[STATUTE-SELLER *is chased off.*]

INSPECTOR [*returning*]: You shall suffer for this! I'll see that you get
the maximum penalty. A fine of ten thousand drachmas!

PEISTHETAERUS: And *I'm* going to upset your precious ballot-boxes.
[*He kicks them across the stage, and the* INSPECTOR *rushes to retrieve
them.*]

STATUTE-SELLER [*returning*]: I happen to know that one evening you
were seen relieving yourself on hallowed ground, to wit, against a
sacred pillar.

PEISTHETAERUS: Catch that man, somebody!

[STATUTE-SELLER *is caught and belaboured: the* INSPECTOR
prudently makes off.]

PEISTHETAERUS [*to* INSPECTOR]: What, aren't you staying?

[STATUTE-SELLER *escapes.*]

PEISTHETAERUS [*to the* SLAVES, *with a sigh of relief*]: Let's go inside,
quickly, and finish the sacrifice indoors.

[*They carry the goat and the sacred vessels into the kitchen, the rock
closes behind them, and the* CHORUS *is left in possession of the stage.*]

CHORUS:

> All mortals from now on
> Are going to sacrifice to us,
> Say prayers to us,
> The birds, all-seeing and all-ruling.
> For we see the whole earth,
> We preserve the thriving crops,
> We kill the multitudinous creatures
> That sit in the trees
> And with voracious jaws

Feed upon the fruit as it grows:
We kill the destroyers of sweet-smelling gardens,
The ravishers of plants,
And everything that creeps and stings,
We slay them all, they cower at our approach.

CHORUS LEADER: Today I heard a public announcement: To him that kills Diagoras the Melian, a reward of one talent; to him that kills one of the tyrants, likewise a reward of one talent[19] – and this struck me as odd, seeing that the tyrants were killed years and years ago. Well, we wish now to make an announcement ourselves. To anyone who kills Philocrates the bird-merchant we will pay one talent: to anyone who brings him here alive we will pay four. And why? Because he strings chaffinches together and sells them at seven for an obol. Because he inflicts indignities on thrushes, inflating them by blowing through a tube, and then puts them on show. Because he sticks feathers up the blackbird's nostrils. Because he catches pigeons and keeps them caged, ties them up in a net and uses them as decoys. Such is our proclamation. And if anyone has got any birds caged up at home, we strongly advise you to set them free. Because if you don't, you'll be caught by the birds and tied up and used as decoys.

CHORUS:
Happy race of feathered fowls,
Who in winter
Are not muffled up in blankets,
And in summer
Live enfolded in the grass of flowery meadows,
Unscorched by rays of stifling heat,
While the divine cicada, mad for the sun,
Shouts his shrill song in the blazing heat of noon.
We winter in hollow caves,
Playing with the mountain nymphs:
In spring we feed on the virginal white-growing myrtles
And the herbs of the Graces.

CHORUS LEADER: We'd like to say something to the judges, about the good things we shall give them all if they award the prize to us: far finer gifts than Paris got for a similar task. Firstly, what every judge desires most of all: owls from Laurion – an inexhaustible supply. They shall nest in your homes and breed in your purses, hatching little coinlings, jingle jingle jingle. And your houses will be like temples, with eagles perching on the roof. And if a little official job falls to your lot, we'll give you a keen-eyed falcon to swoop down on the pickings. And if you're dining out anywhere we'll send you appetites like ours. But if we don't get the prize, you'll have to wear metal haloes, like the ones they put on statues. And if you're out for a walk in your best party cloak, and you're not wearing your halo – we'll be there! And I think we'll get our own back somehow.

PEISTHETAERUS: Well, birds, the sacrifice went off all right – omens very good. But I'm a bit worried we haven't had a messenger from the wall yet, I'd like to know how things are going up there. Ah, here he comes – panting like an Olympic sprinter.

[*Enter* FIRST MESSENGER, *out of breath.*]

FIRST MESSENGER: Where's – huff – where's – huff – where's – huff – President Peisthe – huff – taerus?

PEISTHETAERUS: Here I am.

FIRST MESSENGER: Your wall's built.

PEISTHETAERUS: Good.

FIRST MESSENGER: And a very fine structure it is. Most impressive. Wide enough for – two chariots – to pass on the top. Even if one belonged to – Theagenes and the other to Proxenides[20] the Boastmaster. With horses bigger than the – wooden horse of Troy.

PEISTHETAERUS: Fantastic.

FIRST MESSENGER: The height I measured myself. Six hundred feet.

PEISTHETAERUS: Who ever managed to build it up to that height?

FIRST MESSENGER: Birds, just birds. No outside help. No Egyptian bricklayers, no masons, no carpenters: just the birds, with their own hands. I was amazed. Thirty thousand cranes arrived from Libya, with foundation stones in their crops. The corncrakes shaped the stones with their beaks. Ten thousand storks carried the bricks, and the water was brought up by the plovers, and other river birds.

PEISTHETAERUS: Who carried the mortar for them?

FIRST MESSENGER: The herons brought it, in pans.

PEISTHETAERUS: How did they get the mortar into the pans?

FIRST MESSENGER: Oh, that was most ingenious: the geese put it in for them. They used their feet as shovels.

PEISTHETAERUS: Quite a feat!

FIRST MESSENGER: The ducks had their aprons, of course, so they did the bricklaying; and the swallows fluttered above, with their little trowels behind them, carrying the mud in their beaks.

PEISTHETAERUS: Who's going to bother to hire a team of workmen, after this? But go on – what about the wooden parts of the wall, who coped with those?

FIRST MESSENGER: Oh, there were bird carpenters too – the wood-peckers, naturally. Very skilful the way they split the timber for the gates with their beaks; and what a noise they made with their hacking and hewing – it sounded just like a shipyard. And now the gates are all in position: a guard's been set all around – sentries posted everywhere, regular tours of inspection, bell signals laid on, beacons on all the towers. I must go and wash. I've done my job, you can get on with yours. [*Exit.*]

CHORUS LEADER [*to* PEISTHETAERUS *who is gazing upwards in a puzzled way*]: What's bothering you? Are you surprised the wall's been built so quickly?

PEISTHETAERUS: Well, yes, it sounds a tall story – but look at this: there's a fellow on his way down here in a deuce of a hurry. One of the sentries. Looks as if he's on the warpath, too.

[*Enter* SECOND MESSENGER.]

SECOND MESSENGER: Sir! Sir! Sir! Sir! Sir!

PEISTHETAERUS: Now then, what's all this about?

SECOND MESSENGER: Oh, sir, terrible news. One of the gods has just violated our air space: flew in through one of the gates. One of Zeus's lot. The jackdaws were on guard but he slipped through, sir.

PEISTHETAERUS: The dirty dog! How dare he? Which of the gods was it?

SECOND MESSENGER: We don't know, sir. But he's got wings, we do know that.

PEISTHETAERUS: You should have sent out a pursuit force straight away.

SECOND MESSENGER: We have, sir: thirty thousand mobile archers of the Hover and Swoop Corps: every bird with curved talons is on the wing – kestrels, buzzards, vultures, owls and eagles. Listen, you can hear the whirring of their wings, filling the air with thunder – he must be somewhere quite near.

PEISTHETAERUS: We'd better arm ourselves with bows and slings.
Stand forward, bodyguard! Give me a sling, somebody.

[*The* CHORUS *take up defensive positions.*]

CHORUS:

> The war is on!
> War unutterable!
> War with the gods!
>
> Scan, scan the cloud-filled sky,
> Born of black Erebus!
> Let no god pass unseen!
> Quick, in a ring!
> Keep watch on every side.
>
> Listen, the whirr of the wings
> Of the airborne god
> Draws closer!
> He's here!

[*The whirring sound resolves itself into the wheezing and creaking of the cumbrous stage machinery, with the aid of which* IRIS, *petite and pretty, but with enormous rainbow wings and headdress, now flies into view.* PEISTHETAERUS *seizes her by one foot as she sails over his head, and pulls her down closer to the stage.*]

PEISTHETAERUS: Here, where do you think you're flying to? Stop!
Keep still! Stay where you are! Halt! Who are you? Where do you come from? Come on, speak up!

IRIS [*outraged*]: I am on an errand for the Olympian gods.

PEISTHETAERUS: What are you supposed to be, a ship in full sail?
What do they call you?

IRIS: Iris the fleet.

PEISTHETAERUS: I'm not surprised.

IRIS: What *is* going on, please? [*She flies upwards again.*]

PEISTHETAERUS: Quickly, one of you buzzards, fly up and arrest her.

IRIS: Arrest *me*? What is this tomfoolery, I should like to know?

PEISTHETAERUS: You're going to get it hot.

IRIS: Absolutely unheard of.

PEISTHETAERUS [*catching her foot and pulling her down*]: Now then,
you saucy trollop, which gate did you come in by?

IRIS: Gate? How should I know which gate?

PEISTHETAERUS: Hear that? She won't give a straight answer. – Did
you report to the jackdaws at Immigration? You didn't? Did you
get an entry visa from the storks?

IRIS: What kind of nonsense is this?

PEISTHETAERUS: You didn't, is that right?

IRIS: You can't be in your right mind.

PEISTHETAERUS: Have you been properly entered by one of the
ornitharchs?

IRIS: Certainly not! What a suggestion!

PEISTHETAERUS: So you just thought you'd take a flight through
space and cross our city on the quiet, did you? Don't you realize this
is foreign territory?

IRIS: What other route is there for the gods to fly by?

PEISTHETAERUS: I've no idea, but they certainly can't use this one.
You're breaking the law at this moment. Don't you realize you
could be arrested and put to death? And rightly too, Iris or no Iris.

IRIS: But I'm immortal.

PEISTHETAERUS: You'd be put to death just the same. A fine thing
it'll be, if everyone else obeys us but you gods still don't realize
that we're the stronger power. Now tell me, where are you sailing
to on those wings of yours?

IRIS: I'm bound for Earth, with orders from my father: men are to
sacrifice to the Olympian gods, slay sheep on the sacrificial altars,
and fill the streets with the savour of burnt offerings.

PEISTHETAERUS: I beg your pardon: to *what* gods, did you say?

IRIS: To what gods? To us, of course – the gods in heaven.

PEISTHETAERUS: Oh, you're gods, are you? That's interesting.

IRIS: What other gods can there be?

PEISTHETAERUS: Birds are now the gods as far as mankind is concerned, and it's to the birds that men must sacrifice, not to Zeus, by
Zeus.

IRIS [*mustering all her divine dignity*]: O fool, fool! Tempt not the awful
anger of the gods! Take heed, or Justice, armed with the pickaxe of
Zeus, will uproot your whole miserable race, and the fiery smoke of
the Licymnian bolt will char your body and consume your house.

PEISTHETAERUS: Now listen, you. Stop fulminating. And [*grabbing
her as she begins to fly off*] stay where you are! Do you take me for a
Lydian or a Phrygian? Do you really expect to scare me with that

kind of talk? Now get this into your head: if I have any more trouble from Zeus. I shall launch a squadron of fire-bearing eagles and burn down his palace. I'll send a whole troop of porphyrions up to heaven to attack him – more than six hundred of them, all in leopard skins. He found one Porphyrion more than enough on a previous occasion, I seem to remember.[21] And as for you, messenger girl, if I have any more nonsense from you – Iris or no Iris, I shall force open these legs of yours, and you'll get a big surprise, I promise you. A very big surprise, considering my advanced age.

IRIS [*flying out of reach*]: Lightning, flash forth! Strike the blasphemer dead!

[*Nothing happens.*]

PEISTHETAERUS: Off with you now! Quickly! Shoo! Beat it!

IRIS [*dissolving into tears*]: Just wait till my father hears about this: he'll soon put a stop to your insults.

PEISTHETAERUS: Oh, for pity's sake, fly away. Go and incinerate someone a bit younger.

[IRIS *flies away.*]

CHORUS:

> Never again
> Through my domain
> Shall a god presume to stray;
> The birds are on guard,
> The gates are barred,
> Not one shall pass this way!

> Never again
> Through my domain
> Shall the smoke from the altars rise;
> In vain they'll sniff
> For the faintest whiff:
> We've cut off their supplies!

PEISTHETAERUS: Now, what's happened to that messenger I sent off to Earth? Isn't he ever coming back, I wonder?

[*Enter* THIRD MESSENGER.]

THIRD MESSENGER [*with great solemnity*]: Hail, Peisthetaerus! Hail, Blessed One, hail, Wisest of the Wise! Hail, Illustrious Hero, hail, Wisest of the Wise – oh, I've said that. Hail, Subtlest of the Subtle, hail, Thrice Blessed – oh, do say something, I'm running out.

PEISTHETAERUS [*noticing him for the first time*]: Eh? What's that you say?

THIRD MESSENGER: All the nations revere and honour you for your great wisdom. In token of which I bring you this golden crown.

PEISTHETAERUS [*accepting it and putting it on*]: Thanks. Why do they all think so highly of me, these nations?

THIRD MESSENGER: Why, because you have founded this noble city in the skies. Don't you realize how much men admire you, how many enthusiasts there are for this city of yours? You see, until you founded Much Cuckoo, Sparta was all the rage. People grew their hair long, they starved themselves, they stopped having baths (like Socrates), they all carried walking sticks. But now there's been a complete change, they're all bird-mad. They're so enraptured, they model themselves on the birds and do everything that birds do. Up with the lark in the morning, and then all day long they're busy with their bills – bills of impeachment, mostly. They flock together – to the courts; they brood – on their grievances; and, believe me, they're always hatching something. It's really got a hold on them, this bird mania; they've even started naming each other after birds. There's a tavern-keeper, for example, fellow with a game leg – they call him the Grouse. Then there's the Swallow – that's Menippus, of course; Opuntius is the One-Eyed Raven; Philocles is the Crested Lark; Theagenes the Ruddy Shelduck; Lycurgus the Sacred Ibis; Chaerephon the Nighthawk, and Syracosius the Popinjay. As for Meidias, they call him the Quail – he winces when he's spoken to, just like a quail that's been flipped on the head.[22] It's spread to their songs too: no one can write a song these days without working in a swallow or a duck or a goose or a dove, or wings, or a feather or two at least. And I'll tell you another thing – they'll soon be here in their thousands, clamouring for wings, hooked talons and other avian accessories. So you'd better have a supply of wings handy: there's going to be a run on them.

PEISTHETAERUS: There's no time to be lost, then; we must get busy. Xanthias, fill all the baskets and boxes you can find with wings; and Manes, you bring them out as they're filled. I shall have to stay out here to receive the visitors.

[XANTHIAS *and* MANES *hurry into the building. During the singing of the chorus which follows,* MANES *staggers out with a large basket full of wings.*]

CHORUS:
> It looks as if our city state
> Will not take long to populate!

PEISTHETAERUS:
> If Fate approves, so be it!

CHORUS:
> The new republic in the clouds
> Is all the rage, and eager crowds
> > Are flocking here to see it.
> Where could they find a dwelling-place
> Fitter than this, where Wisdom, Grace
> > And Love pervade the scene?
> A tranquil sweetness fills the air –

PEISTHETAERUS:
> Now Manēs, get a move on there:
> > How very slow you've been!

CHORUS:
> Yes, hurry, do, the time is short;
> And fetch more wings of every sort.

PEISTHETAERUS:
> Move faster, Manes, faster!

CHORUS:
> We need another basket yet:
> Look lively now, or you will get
> > A drubbing from your master.
[*To* PEISTHETAERUS.]
> While there's still time, it would be wise
> To sort them out by shape and size,
> > On each a label tying;
> Then all can get the wings they need –
> The wings of song; sea-wings for speed;
> > Or wings for prophesying.
[REBELLIOUS YOUTH *enters, singing.*]
REBELLIOUS YOUTH [*sings*]:
> Gonna fly high!
> Gonna fly high!

Gonna spread them wings and sweep, sweep, sweep
Over the waves of the boundless deep,
   Gonna fly like an eagle in the sky!

PEISTHETAERUS: Looks as if that messenger was right: there's someone arriving already and he's singing about eagles.

REBELLIOUS YOUTH: Wow! Flying's the answer, man, you can't beat it. And I like the sound of those laws of yours, I really do. Honestly, I've gone bird crazy, you should see me fly! And those laws – I'm coming here to live, I really am.

PEISTHETAERUS: What laws do you mean? The birds have a good many, you know.

REBELLIOUS YOUTH: All of them. Especially the one about – you know, about it being all right for birds to throttle their fathers and bite them and all that.

PEISTHETAERUS: Ah, well, admittedly, if a young chick strikes his father we birds do call this *manly* behaviour . . .

REBELLIOUS YOUTH: Yeah, well, that's why I've moved house and come here. I want to do the old man in and get all his money.

PEISTHETAERUS: But the birds have another law, a very old one – you can see it written up on the Stork Law tablets: that when the parent stork has brought up his fledglings and sent them out into the world, then it's their turn to support him.

REBELLIOUS YOUTH: Oh no! After I've come all this way you calmly tell me I've got to support my father as well as myself?

PEISTHETAERUS: Never mind, you came here in a friendly spirit, so I'll fit you out like a real War Orphan bird. And I'll give you a bit of useful advice, young man: I had to learn the same lesson myself when I was a boy. If you feel like hitting your father – don't. Here you are, lad, take this wing in one hand and this spur in the other [PEISTHETAERUS *arms him with these as though they were a shield and a spear respectively*] . . . put on this crest . . . and there you are, a real fighting cock, ready for battle.

   [REBELLIOUS YOUTH *at once adopts a soldierly stance and is already a changed character.*]

Off you go, then, man the defences, march into battle, live on your pay and leave your father in peace. If it's a fight you want, take wing for the Thracian front and do your fighting there.

REBELLIOUS YOUTH: By all the gods of Thrace, I think you're right. I'll do it.

PEISTHETAERUS: A very sensible decision.

[REBELLIOUS YOUTH *marches off, full of manly determination. The next visitor is the poet* CINESIAS, *who now enters, pirouetting in circles and singing to his own accompaniment on the lyre.*]

CINESIAS [*sings*]:

> See, see, to Olympus I rise:
> > On gossamer wing
> > > I float where I will,
> > And ever I sing
> As I flit through the skies,
> > Now hither,
> > Now thither . . .

PEISTHETAERUS: We'll need a barrowload of wings for this one.

CINESIAS [*sings*]:

> On, on, ever fearless
> > In body and mind
> > > I plough through the ether,
> > > Now heether, now theether,
> > New themes for my peerless
> > Creations to find.

PEISTHETAERUS: Why, it's Cinesias, the walking withy. What brings you spinning in this direction, on those wobbly pins of yours?

CINESIAS [*sings*]:

> Fain would I be a singing bird,
> A shrill-voiced nightingale.

PEISTHETAERUS: Don't sing it – just say it.

CINESIAS: Give me wings, and then I can soar high in the air, visit the clouds and seek new odes – high-flying, snow-capped dithyrambs.

PEISTHETAERUS: I didn't know that was where they came from.

CINESIAS: Ah, but indeed it is: our whole art derives from the clouds. Where else can you find all the ingredients of a perfect ode: the airy vapour, the obscurity, the purple patch, the ecstasy of whirling motion? Let me illustrate.

PEISTHETAERUS: No, please don't bother.

CINESIAS: Ah, but I must: no trouble at all. I'll just take you on a quick run through the whole firmament.

[*sings*]   Ah, the fair shapes
    Of the sky-borne, slender-necked birds ...

PEISTHETAERUS: Whoa there!

CINESIAS [*sings*]:
    Bounding above the wavetops
    I skip with the breeze ...

PEISTHETAERUS: I'll soon put an end to your breezes. [*He selects a large wing from the basket and starts to pursue* CINESIAS *as he prances around, flipping him with the wing.*]

CINESIAS [*sings*]:
    A southerly course I pursue,
    But anon to the northward I turn:
    Oh, straight is the furrow I carve
    Through the harbourless air –

oh, I say you know, a joke's a joke, but really, old chap –

PEISTHETAERUS: Why, don't you care for the ecstasy of whirling motion?

CINESIAS: This is no way to treat an artist of my calibre: in Athens, let me tell you, I'm in such demand as a chorus trainer that they positively fight for my services.

PEISTHETAERUS: Why not stay here and train a chorus of flying birds for Leotrophides? For solo corncrake and Quail Voice Choir.

CINESIAS: You're making fun of me, that's obvious. [PEISTHETAERUS *flaps the wing at him until he is forced to run off the stage.*] But you mark my words, I shan't rest till I can fly through the air, with wings on. [*Exit.*]

  [*Enter* INFORMER.]

INFORMER [*sings*]:
    Oh swallow, dear swallow, I hang on your words:
    Who *are* these strange creatures? They seem to be birds
    Of every conceivable colour and sort
    And without any visible means of support.

PEISTHETAERUS: This business is getting beyond a joke: here comes another of them, caterwauling like the rest.

INFORMER [*sings*]:
    Oh swallow, dear swallow, I ask you again –

PEISTHETAERUS: He'll need more than one swallow before he feels warm in *that* cloak.

INFORMER [*furtively*]: Where's this fellow who hands out wings to new arrivals here?

PEISTHETAERUS: Here I am, but what exactly do you want?

INFORMER: Wings, wings, of course: do I have to keep telling you?

PEISTHETAERUS: Are you thinking of flying straight to Pellene,[23] for a new cloak?

INFORMER: No, no, I need them for my job. I'm a summoner: an informer, you know. I work the islands.

PEISTHETAERUS: A noble profession: I congratulate you.

INFORMER: Rigging up prosecutions and so on. Well now, if I had wings I could really put the wind up those islanders – fly round and summon the whole lot.

PEISTHETAERUS: You mean you can summon them more efficiently if you're on the wing?

INFORMER: No, but I can avoid the pirates. I can fly back home with the cranes, with a cropful of lawsuits for ballast.

PEISTHETAERUS: And this is how you earn your living? A young man like you, with nothing better to do than go round laying information against foreigners?

INFORMER: What else can I do? I'm no good at digging.

PEISTHETAERUS: There are lots of respectable jobs a man like you could do. You could earn an honest living instead of hanging round the lawcourts all the time.

INFORMER: My dear good man, don't start lecturing me. Just give me wings.

PEISTHETAERUS: That's exactly what I am doing, by talking to you like this.

INFORMER: How can words give a man wings?

PEISTHETAERUS: Words can give everybody wings.

INFORMER: Everybody?

PEISTHETAERUS: Wings to their spirit, their imagination. Haven't you heard the way fathers talk to their friends in the barber's shops: 'Ever since that fellow Diitrephes[24] started talking to him about chariot-racing, that boy of mine has been living in the clouds.' 'With my son, it's the theatre,' says another: 'a tragedy sends him right up in the air.'

INFORMER: All done by words, eh?

PEISTHETAERUS: Words can uplift a man's spirit and raise him up to higher things: that's why I'm talking to you now – I want *my* words to give you the wings you need, to make you turn to a more honest trade.

INFORMER: But I don't want to.

PEISTHETAERUS: What's your idea, then?

INFORMER: I can't let the family down like that: my father was an informer, and his father before him. Now if you can fit me out with a nice light pair of wings – kestrel or sparrowhawk for preference – I can summon the islanders to court, give evidence against them on the mainland, and fly back to the islands –

PEISTHETAERUS: So that the case will be all settled and the fine imposed before the defendant can even arrive: I understand.

INFORMER: You've got it exactly.

PEISTHETAERUS: And while he's still on his way to Athens you're already back on the island, distraining on his goods. [*Both laugh heartily at the idea.*]

INFORMER [*through his laughter*]: I shall have to whizz back and forth like a top!

PEISTHETAERUS [*through his laughter*]: Like a top! [*In a changed tone*] Like a top – that gives me an idea. Yes, I think I've got a pair of wings here that'll set you spinning all right. [*He takes a whip from the basket.*]

INFORMER: But that's a whip you've got there!

PEISTHETAERUS: Yes. For a whipping-top. I'll give you wings! [*He whips the ground close to* INFORMER'*s ankles.*]

INFORMER: O! O! Help! [*He leaps away, and continues to skip and revolve as* PEISTHETAERUS *chases him round the stage, aiming whip-strokes at his ankles.*]

PEISTHETAERUS: Bzz! Bzz! I'll make you whizz, you nasty little twister, you! Go on! Fly! Right away from here! And I hope this'll teach you a lesson.

[*Exit* INFORMER.]

Ah, well, let's collect up the wings and go.

[MANES *helps* PEISTHETAERUS *put the wings back in the basket, and they carry it back inside.*]

CHORUS:
    We have flown to distant countries, over land and over sea,
        And seen strange sights beyond the blue horizon;

For instance we could tell you of a certain monstrous tree,
The ugliest we ever clapped our eyes on.

It serves no useful purpose, it is rotten to the core,
It gives no shade, no wholesome fruit it yields:
It blossoms in the spring, when the courts are in full swing,
And in the fall it sheds a shower of – shields.

If the riddle isn't plain you must rack your brains again,
For our tree can hardly hope to stay anonymous:
It is by no means small, and it has no heart at all,
And its name (ah yes, you've guessed it) is *Cleonymus*.[25]

A visit to the Lampless Lands
 Is pleasant in fine weather;
There men and heroes can converse,
 Or even eat together.

But not at night! For legend tells
 That if, when shadows thicken,
You meet a hero, down one side
 With pains you will be stricken.

'Tis true, for here *Orestes*[26] prowls:
 Ye mortals, heed my warning!
Or in a ditch, without a stitch,
 They'll find you in the morning.

[*Enter* PROMETHEUS, *enveloped from head to foot in a blanket and carrying an umbrella.*]

PROMETHEUS: Phew! I hope to goodness Zeus won't spot me. Where's Peisthetaerus?

PEISTHETAERUS: Hallo, what have we here? Who's this muffled figure, I wonder?

PROMETHEUS [*indistinctly, through the blanket*]: There isn't a god following me, is there?

PEISTHETAERUS: Not that I can see. Why? Who are you?

PROMETHEUS [*unable to hear a word*]: What time of day is it?

PEISTHETAERUS: What time of day? Early afternoon. But [*louder*] who are you?

PROMETHEUS: How dark is it, then?

PEISTHETAERUS [*to test his deafness*]: You disgust me!

PROMETHEUS: And what's the weather like? Is old Zeus piling up clouds or scattering them?

PEISTHETAERUS [*shouting*]: You stink!

PROMETHEUS: Oh, good. Well, in that case perhaps I can unwrap. [*He uncovers his face.*]

PEISTHETAERUS: Prometheus, my dear fellow!

PROMETHEUS: Ssh! Keep your voice down!

PEISTHETAERUS: Why, whatever's the matter.

PROMETHEUS: Quiet! And whatever you do, don't shout my name all over the place. If Zeus sees me here, I'm done for. Here, you hold up this umbrella so the gods can't see me, and then I can tell you all about what's going on up there.

PEISTHETAERUS [*taking the umbrella and holding it over* PROMETHEUS *and himself*]: That's a brilliant idea. Truly Promethean. Come along under, then, and tell me all.

PROMETHEUS: Well now, listen.

PEISTHETAERUS: I'm all ears.

PROMETHEUS: Zeus is finished.

PEISTHETAERUS: Oh? Since when?

PROMETHEUS: Ever since you people started your aerial colony. The earth-dwellers have stopped sacrificing to the gods: not so much as a whiff of burnt mutton fat has reached our nostrils from that day to this. We're having to fast, like the women on Thesmophoria Day. And the barbarian gods upstairs are squawking like Illyrians – they're absolutely ravenous, and they're threatening to come down and attack Zeus if he doesn't get the trade routes opened up again: they're getting really worried about their shredded offal imports.

PEISTHETAERUS: D'you mean to say there's another lot of gods living up above you – are there really such things as barbarian gods?

PROMETHEUS: Of course there are. Even Execestides²⁷ has to have a patron god somewhere, hasn't he?

PEISTHETAERUS: And what are they called, these barbarian gods?

PROMETHEUS: Triballians.

PEISTHETAERUS: Can't make a pun on that – too bally difficult.

PROMETHEUS: One thing I can tell you for certain: there's a delegation on its way here, from Zeus and these Triballians, to talk about a peace settlement. But don't you agree to anything, except on two conditions: A, Zeus must hand the sceptre back to the birds, and B, *you* must be granted the hand of Sovereignty in marriage.

PEISTHETAERUS: Sovereignty? Who's she?

PROMETHEUS: She's the very beautiful girl who looks after Zeus's thunderbolts for him. She also holds the key of the Gifts to Mankind department, where Zeus keeps all the blessings of civilization: good government, wise policies, law and order, dockyards, endless slanging matches, public assistance officers and the half-drachma they pay out for a day's jury service.

PEISTHETAERUS: She seems to control everything.

PROMETHEUS: You name it, she can give it to you. Get her from Zeus, and you've got the lot. I came here specially to tip you off – I always have been a friend of Man, as you know.[28]

PEISTHETAERUS: You certainly have. If it hadn't been for you there'd have been no grilled sardines.

PROMETHEUS: And I hate that other lot, up there.

PEISTHETAERUS: Yes, you always have been at odds with the gods.

PROMETHEUS: When it comes to a chip on the shoulder, Timon isn't in it. Well, I'd better be running along. Hand me the umbrella, and then if Zeus looks down and sees me he'll think I'm part of the Panathenaic procession.

PEISTHETAERUS: Carry this stool as well, and he'll take you for one of the attendant virgins.

[*Exit* PROMETHEUS. PEISTHETAERUS *and his slaves fetch a brazier from the kitchen and begin to make preparations for a meal.*]

CHORUS:

> The Skiapods, or Ombripeds
> Are most engaging fellers:
> They hold their feet above their heads
> And use them as umbrellas.
>
> They live beside a stagnant lake,
> Where Socrates – just fancy! –
> Instructs his half-starved pupils in
> The art of necromancy.
>
> Peisander saw him work the trick
> And said 'Oh, please repeat it!

I lost *my* spirit long ago;
  I'd dearly love to meet it.'

'Then slay,' the unwashed sage replied,
  'A lamb – but no, a lamb'll
Be much too small a sacrifice;
  You'd better slay a camel.'

And now, to suck the victim's blood,
  What grisly spectre rises?
'Tis Chaerephon,[29] the human bat!
  You do get some surprises!

[POSEIDON, HERACLES *and the* GOD OF THE TRIBALLIANS *enter, with attendants carrying their baggage and their ceremonial togas.*]

POSEIDON: Ah! I see we have arrived at our destination, gentlemen: the city of Much Cuckoo lies before us, and the delegation can proceed to business.

[*The attendants hand them their togas, which they put on. The* TRIBALLIAN, *unfamiliar with the garment, does his best to copy the movements of the other two. They move forward and are about to approach* PEISTHETAERUS, *when* POSEIDON, *glancing at the* TRIBALLIAN, *exclaims in horror.*]

Good heavens man, what are you thinking of? Do you realize you're improperly dressed? Dammit sir, you might at least wear it over the right shoulder. Who do you think you are, Laespodias[30] or somebody?

[*The* TRIBALLIAN *transfers the tail of his toga to his left shoulder, and then, in perplexity, back to the right.*]

That's not the right shoulder, idiot, it's the *wrong* shoulder. The right shoulder is the *left* shoulder – here, let me do it for you. So much for democracy – where's it going to lead us, if this is the kind of fellow the *gods* elect? STAND STILL, CAN'T YOU? Oh, be damned to you. [*He gives it up.*] I've met some barbarian gods in my time, but nothing quite as barbarous as this. Well, Heracles, how do we go about things?

HERACLES: I've told you my views already. Just let me get at this fellow who's walled off the gods, whoever he is, and I'll strangle him for you.

POSEIDON: My dear Heracles, we've been sent here to initiate peace talks.

HERACLES: All the more reason to strangle him, I say.

PEISTHETAERUS: Pass me the cheese-grater, somebody. And the silphium. And the cheese, please. Fan up the fire a bit, will you?

POSEIDON: H'm!

[PEISTHETAERUS *does not look up.*]

H'm! H'm!

[PEISTHETAERUS *begins to grate cheese and silphium over the birds.*]

Hail, mortal! Oh behalf of my two divine colleagues and myself, I –

PEISTHETAERUS: Hold on a minute, I'm grating silphium.

HERACLES: Hullo, hullo, what's this you're roasting?

PEISTHETAERUS [*still without looking up*]: Conservatives. Just a few birds that have been found guilty of opposing the Democratic Party.

HERACLES: I notice you grate the silphium over them *before* putting them on the spit.

PEISTHETAERUS [*looking up at last*]: Why, Heracles, I do declare! Welcome, welcome! What brings you here?

POSEIDON: We have been sent as a delegation by the gods to discuss terms for ending the war.

XANTHIAS: There's no olive oil left in the bottle.

HERACLES: Oh, that's a pity. I always say poultry should be served absolutely glistening with oil.

POSEIDON: After all, we gods have nothing to gain by being at war; and, from your point of view, well, with the gods on your side you birds could be assured of, well, er, a constant supply of rain-water in the puddles and, well, er, permanent halcyon days, what? We are fully authorized, I may say, to negotiate with you over all that kind of thing.

PEISTHETAERUS: We never started this war: we're quite ready to agree to an armistice here and now – so long as you're prepared to grant us our rights. In other words, Zeus must hand back the sceptre to the birds. If that is agreed [*he glances at* HERACLES] I shall be happy to invite the delegation to lunch.

HERACLES: Sounds fair enough. I vote we accept their terms.

POSEIDON: What, you gluttonous nincompoop? Are you going to deprive your father of his sovereignty?

PEISTHETAERUS: On the contrary, don't you see that the gods will be even *more* powerful, if the birds are in charge down below? As things are now, men can easily swear false oaths by you and get away with it. You never even notice; all they've got to do is wait till a cloud comes along. Whereas if you have the birds as your allies, and a man has to swear, not just 'by Zeus', but '*by the Raven* and by Zeus' – then if he breaks his oath, at least the *raven* can do something about it: he can fly down quietly and peck the fellow's eyes out.

POSEIDON: By Poseidon, you've got a point there!

HERACLES: I couldn't agree more.

POSEIDON [*turning to the* TRIBALLIAN]: What's your opinion, sir?

TRIBALLIAN: Nabaisatreu.

PEISTHETAERUS: Well, there you are, you see: he thinks so too. Incidentally I'll tell you another useful thing we can do for you. Suppose a man vows an offering to one of you gods, and then, when the time comes – well, you know how it is, one excuse or another: 'the gods are patient', he'll say, to quiet his conscience – the miserly rascal. *We'll* make him pay up.

POSEIDON: How can you do that?

PEISTHETAERUS: When he's counting out his money, or lying in his bath, a kite can swoop down, snatch up the price of a couple of sheep, and bring it back to the god concerned.

HERACLES: I vote in favour of giving the sceptre back to the birds.

POSEIDON: You'd better ask the Triballian what he thinks.

HERACLES: Hey, you! Wake up there! Do you want a bashing?

TRIBALLIAN: Saunaka baktarikrousa.

HERACLES: There you are! He says I'm absolutely right.

POSEIDON: Well, if you're both in favour of the proposal, I won't oppose it.

HERACLES [*to* PEISTHETAERUS, *who is still busy with his cooking*]: Hi! About that sceptre – we accept your terms.

PEISTHETAERUS: Oh, there's just one other thing, I nearly forgot. Zeus can keep Hera, but the girl, Sovereignty, must obviously become *my* wife, so he'll have to hand her over, I'm afraid.

POSEIDON: You obviously don't *want* a peace treaty; [*to his colleagues*] come on, let's get back home.

PEISTHETAERUS: Go, by all means, if you want to. Now, cook, mind you make the sauce really tasty.

HERACLES: Here, I say, Poseidon, where are you off to? Good god, man – I mean good man, god – we're not going to fight a war over a woman, are we?

POSEIDON: What else can we do?

HERACLES: What can we do? We can make peace.

POSEIDON: You poor fool, can't you see you're being swindled? You're acting against your own interests. If Zeus were to die, after handing over Sovereignty to these birds, you'd be reduced to penury. Don't you realize you inherit all his property when he dies?

PEISTHETAERUS: Don't listen to him, he's trying to confuse you. Come over here a minute and I'll tell you something. Your uncle's deceiving you. As the law stands, you won't get a penny out of your father's estate: you don't count as a pure-bred god.

HERACLES: Are you calling me a mongrel?

PEISTHETAERUS: Your mother was an alien, in other words a mortal. Do you think Athene would be addressed as 'Heiress of Zeus', if she had legitimate brothers?

HERACLES: Ah, but suppose my father leaves me the property in his will?

PEISTHETAERUS: He can't, it's against the law. And you can be quite sure that if you laid any claim to your father's estate, Poseidon would dispute it. What he's telling you now is just to stir up your feelings. When the time comes he'll be the first to point out his racial purity. Solon's law makes it quite clear: 'Where there are pure-bred off-spring, the children of alien wives have no right of inheritance; if there are no pure-bred offspring, the property is to be shared between the nearest relatives.'

HERACLES: Do you mean to say that I don't get anything at all?

PEISTHETAERUS: Not a penny. Did your father ever take you along to the phratry[31] and have you enrolled?

HERACLES: No, he never did. I've always thought that was a bit odd. Why, the old –! [He shakes his fist heavenwards.]

PEISTHETAERUS: No use scowling and shaking your fist at Heaven. But listen, if you come over to us I'll make a prince of you. You'll feed on peacock's milk.

HERACLES: Well now, as far as that girl is concerned – well, there again I think what you say is absolutely right. I'm in favour of handing her over.

PEISTHETAERUS [*to* POSEIDON]: And what do you say?

POSEIDON: I vote against it.

PEISTHETAERUS: Then the decision rests with the Triballian here. [*To* TRIBALLIAN] Well?

TRIBALLIAN [*with a tremendous effort to speak Greek*]: Plitty girly – Sowollinty – beeg hand over birdy, me.

HERACLES: There, he says hand her over.

POSEIDON: Nonsense, he's talking about swallows or something.

HERACLES: That's right – 'hand her over to the swallows'.

[TRIBALLIAN *nods vigorously.* POSEIDON *shrugs his shoulders.*]

POSEIDON: Well, if that's how you both feel about it, there's nothing more for me to say. You've accepted his terms and that's that.

HERACLES [*to* PEISTHETHAERUS]: We accept your terms. So if you'll just step up to Heaven with us, we can hand over the bride and all the rest of it.

PEISTHETAERUS: Lucky we've got these birds roasting here: they'll do nicely for the wedding feast.

HERACLES: I tell you what – supposing I stay behind and do the roasting for you while you're away?

PEISTHETAERUS: Do the tasting, more likely. No, I think you'd better come along with us.

HERACLES: Pity, I could have made a lovely job of it.

PEISTHETAERUS [*calling up to the* HOOPOE'*s nest*]: Anyone got a wedding outfit I could borrow?

[*A wedding robe is brought, and* PEISTHETAERUS *is helped into it. He and the three gods, with their attendants, set off in procession, heavenwards.*]

CHORUS:

> The Gastroglots are sleek and round,
>   Their tongues are long and supple,
> And lurking by the water-clock
>   You'll always find a couple.
> They use their tongues to plough and sow
>   And fleece their helpless neighbours,
> And gleefully they gather up
>   The fruit of these their labours.
> The name of one is Gorgias,
>   Another's called Philippus;

And they have come to Attica
With subtle tongues to trip us.
Let them beware, for in our ways
They seem to be unversed:
In Athens, when we sacrifice,
We cut the tongue out first!

[*Fanfares and processional music, over which is heard the voice of a* HEAVENLY HERALD.]

HEAVENLY HERALD: O feathered race of birds, O lordly ones! Thrice blest are ye this day: tongue cannot name, mind cannot conceive the grandeur and the bliss that now are yours. Receive your king, and bid him welcome to his happy realm. No golden gleaming star, no piercing ray of the sun ever shone with such splendour as he who now approaches; at his side a wife of unmatchable beauty; in his hand the winged thunder of Zeus. High into the deeps of heaven a delicious fragrance rises, as the coil of incense-smoke drifts on the breeze, a beautiful sight. Behold, he comes! Now raise your voices in songs of good omen, and let the Muse be heard.

[PEISTHETAERUS *and* SOVEREIGNTY *enter from above, he bearing the thunderbolt of Zeus in his right hand.*]

CHORUS LEADER:
He comes! Make way! Spread out! Get into line!
Fly round the blessed one and bid him welcome!

CHORUS:
How lovely she looks!
How fresh and how fair!
What a day of delight
For the birds of the air,
When Sovereignty comes
Among us to reside!
How blest are we all
In your choice of a bride!

CHORUS LEADER:
Rejoice, rejoice, good people all;
With eager voice on Hymen call.

CHORUS:
When Hera to great Zeus was wed,
The Fates stood by to bless their bed,

And made the halls of Heaven ring
With just the song we now do sing:
    Hymen, O Hymen,
    Hymen, Hymen, O.

Eros, with wing-tips glittering bright,
Played groomsman in the nuptial rite;
With practised skill he held the rein,
While all around them rose the strain: –
    Hymen, O Hymen,
    Hymen, Hymen, O.

PEISTHETAERUS:
    Your songs delight me, dearest birds;
    I like the tunes, I like the words.

CHORUS LEADER:
    Come, sing his power! All creatures now
        In awe before him stand;
    He bears the thunder on his brow
        And lightning in his hand.

CHORUS:
    Now the dreaded shaft of vengeance,
        Symbol once of Zeus divine,
    And his arsenal of thunder,
        And his handmaid, all are thine!

    Now by *thee* the earth is shaken,
        Seared with flame or drenched with showers:
    Sovereignty from Zeus is taken,
        And the future shall be ours.

    Hymen, O Hymen,
    Hymen, Hymen, O.

PEISTHETAERUS:
And now in gay procession move to Zeus's lordly hall,
For you, my feathered comrades, are invited one and all
To celebrate this happy day! Come, Sovereignty, my treasure,
Stretch out your hand and take my wing, and we will dance a
                                                        measure.

213

I'll lift you lightly off the ground, and skywards we will tread,
And music and rejoicing shall surround our marriage bed.

[*The procession moves off, to music, with much cheering, clucking, crowing and general rejoicing.*]

       Alalai!
       Twang twang for the conquering hero!
       Greatest of deities!
       Alalai!

The Assemblywomen

or

Women Seize the Reins

(Ecclesiazusae)

Translated by David Barrett

Introductory Note to *The Assemblywomen*

Of the plays written by Aristophanes after the end of the Peloponnesian war only two survive: *The Assemblywomen* (*c.* 393–391 B.C.)
and *Wealth* (388 B.C.). A gap of at least a dozen years separates *The
Assemblywomen* from *The Frogs*. The great war had ended in 405 with
the utter defeat of Athens and the loss of her Aegean empire. Under
the pro-Spartan oligarchs who then came to power in Athens, a reign
of terror ensued: in the course of the year 404 no fewer than 1,500
Athenian citizens were executed, and 5,000 were banished. A force
of exiled democrats was raised by Thrasybulus, and after some months
of civil war they re-entered the city and the democratic constitution
was restored (September, 403). Since then there had been a slow
recovery; but since 395, through her defensive alliance with Boeotia
and other Greek states, Athens had again been involved in inconclu-
sive hostilities with the Spartans. The state of war dragged on, a drain
on money and manpower: the future was obscure, the economy
shaky, counsels divided, and the glory of Athens (it seemed) a thing of
the past. It is difficult, particularly as the dating of the play is not
absolutely certain, to assess the exact situation at the time of its production: but the question asked at the end of *The Frogs* – what can be
done to save the city? – was again sufficiently relevant to serve as the
peg for a comedy. In this play the women of Athens have their own
solution to this problem: the government must be handed over to
them. Disguised as men, they pack the Assembly, which has met to
debate this very question, and their proposal is carried – on the
grounds that this is the only solution that has not yet been tried.

Once in power, the women introduce a series of measures which
bear a very strong resemblance to certain ideas put forward by Plato
in *The Republic*. In the opinion of most scholars, the resemblance is too
close to be a mere coincidence. Community of property and of wives
and children, communal dwellings and meals, and the abolition of
brothels, are all features of Plato's ideal state; and some of the ques-

217

tions and objections raised by Blepyrus and Chremes in the play (e.g., on the subject of children not recognizing their own fathers) are raised and dealt with by Plato in a very similar way. The two men were almost certainly well acquainted, and possibly close friends. Plato's *Symposium* contains a convincing portrayal of the poet; and the attribution to Plato of an admiring epitaph on Aristophanes implies at least a tradition that they were friends. *The Republic* is not believed to have circulated in its 'published' form until some years after the date of *The Assemblywomen*; but Plato may well have been working out some of his ideas for many years beforehand, and there seems no reason why they should not have been known to his friends and perhaps to wider circles as well. Aristophanes would not have been slow to see the comic possibilities of the Platonic Utopia.

But *The Assemblywomen* is a disappointing work. It begins promisingly enough, with a skilful opening scene very like that of *Lysistrata*. The 'rehearsal' is well handled, and the character of Praxagora better drawn and more interesting than that of Lysistrata in the earlier play: her encounter with her husband, when she has to bluff her way out of an awkward situation, gives her an extra comic dimension which Lysistrata lacks. Her specimen speech is very effective, as is Chremes' subsequent account of the proceedings in the Assembly. The long exposition of her proposals is broken up and kept amusing by the questions and interpolations of Blepyrus and Chremes. But the second part of the play lacks balance and cohesion. The conversation between Chremes and the cynical Citizen contains a few good satirical touches, but it goes on for at least twice as long as it should: we miss the economy and the brilliant timing of similar scenes in the earlier comedies. The Citizen departs, hinting that he has thought of a way of circumventing the rules; he is determined to enjoy the public banquet without surrendering his property, and we look forward to seeing his efforts frustrated. But he never appears again. The following scene, dealing with the operation of the new sex laws, can doubtless be made very funny in performance, but it completely lacks the wit and sparkle that one expects from Aristophanes. In structure it resembles no other scene in Old Comedy as we know it; with its singing match and love duet (involving three actors who must also be singers), it seems to belong to a different tradition altogether. The finale, which now follows abruptly, deals with a public banquet, but otherwise has no obvious connection with anything else in the play. The manuscripts give no firm identification of the identity of the speakers; and although, at a pinch, the errant husband can be identified as Blepyrus and the tipsy maid's mistress as Praxagora, the whole scene, as far as internal evidence goes, could just as easily have been lifted from an entirely different play.

The role of the Chorus in *The Assemblywomen* is curious too. In the opening scene (as in that of *Lysistrata*) they are incorporated in the action, arriving singly or in small groups to represent the women who are to disguise themselves under Praxagora's direction and take their places in the Assembly. After the rehearsal they march off, singing in chorus. On their return they remove their disguises to the accompaniment of instructions which are perhaps recited by the Chorus Leader alone. A few lines of encouragement, spoken in unison (or again, perhaps, by the Leader alone) precede Praxagora's exposition of her plans, at the end of which they leave with her for the Agora. They are not seen again until the finale. Apart from the marching song, the supper cantata and the short final chorus, they have no singing to do; and there is no indication that they do any dancing either. (The songs in the second part are provided by the characters; the dancing in the finale is executed by the 'Blepyrus' character and two or more dancing-girls specially introduced for the purpose.) One is reminded of the ending of *The Wasps*, a play produced at a time when so many men were absent on active service that only older men were available for the Chorus: here too the dancing was provided by one of the actors and a group of professionals, the 'sons of Carcinus'.

In *Wealth*, as we shall see, the part played by the Chorus is reduced still further: it is clear that in an impoverished City the lavishly costumed and expensively trained Choruses of earlier days had ceased to be a practical proposition. In the great days of Old Comedy the importance of the Chorus had been paramount: the whole structure and atmosphere of the play, and its relevance to a great national and religious festival, depended upon it. An important feature of the older plays had been the *parabasis*, in which the Chorus addressed the audience directly, clinching the mood (and message, if any) of the play. The disappearance of such conventions marks the transition to a new kind of comedy altogether. In *The Assemblywomen* we seem to observe this transition at its most uncomfortable moment: it is almost as though the author had begun his play in the belief that he was to have a Chorus of the old type, and then, discovering that he was not, handed it over to someone else to finish.

We do not know how the judges responded to the final appeal by the Chorus Leader (p. 262), but its suggestion of 'something for *almost* everybody' (wit and wisdom in the first half, knockabout fun in the second) strikes one as fair comment. The play has not lost its power to entertain, as recent productions have shown.

CHARACTERS

PRAXAGORA
FIRST WOMAN
SECOND WOMAN
CHORUS LEADER
CHORUS OF ATHENIAN WOMEN
* {MAID TO PRAXAGORA
GIRL CRIER
BLEPYRUS *husband to Praxagora*
CHREMES
* {NEXT-DOOR NEIGHBOUR *husband to First Woman*
CITIZEN
GIRL
YOUNG MAN
FIRST HAG
SECOND HAG
THIRD HAG

silent characters:
SICON
PARMENON } *slaves to Chremes*
GROUP OF DANCING GIRLS *for the finale*
CITIZENS, NEIGHBOURS

* The two parts can be doubled, or treated as a single character.

221

SCENE ONE

A street in Athens, somewhere between the Pnyx, where the Assembly meets (offstage and uphill, to the audience's left), and the Agora or Market Square (offstage and downhill, right). The doors of at least two houses, those of BLEPYRUS *(left) and his* NEXT-DOOR NEIGHBOUR *(right), open on to the street.*

It is still dark, but dawn is not far off. A cock crows. The faint glimmer of an oil lamp is seen as PRAXAGORA *stealthily lets herself out of* BLEPYRUS' *house, letting slip a muttered curse as the door-hinge creaks. Before closing the door she gathers up a number of articles from just inside: it is still too dark for us to see what they are, but they include her husband's cloak and shoes, a walking-stick, a false beard and a bundle of ceremonial head-wreaths. Her lamp is of the simple Greek type, a small earthenware vessel with a nozzle for the wick.*

PRAXAGORA:
    Hail, radiant orb (I'm talking to my lamp),
    Borne on swift wheel to light this world of ours –
    A more appropriate phrase than you might think,
    For in an invocation of this kind
    It is quite proper to describe the birth
    And other details of the god addressed,
    And you *were* born upon a (potter's) wheel,
    And from your nozzle spurts the sacred flame.
    Awake, and give the signal as agreed! [*She pulls up the wick.*]
    It's right that you should be the only one
    To overhear our plans, for, after all,
    You know so much about our private lives.
    You watch while in the ecstasies of love
    Our bodies twist and heave, and no one dreams
    Of putting you outside; your singeing flame
    Has penetrated many a hairy nook

And secret crevice of the female form;
You are at hand when furtive wives unlock
The storehouse door, or siphon off the wine –
And can be trusted not to tell the world.

So we shan't mind if you overhear the conference which is shortly
due to begin. It was all arranged at the Skira Festival.[1] But honestly,
this is really most annoying: none of them have turned up, and it's
nearly dawn. It'll soon be time for Assembly; and those of us who
are in on the plot – or 'in on the pot', as Phyromachus once put it[2]
– have got to get to our seats and settle our limbs without being
spotted. What's gone wrong, I wonder? [*Cock crows again.*]
Haven't they managed to finish sewing the beards they promised
to bring? Perhaps they're finding it difficult to pinch their husbands' clothes without being caught. Ah! I see a light moving this
way, there's somebody coming. I'd better step back a bit, it might
be a man.

[PRAXAGORA, *on the point of withdrawing, steps forward again as*
female voices are heard, and the CHORUS LEADER *hurries in (from*
right) with several other women (members of the CHORUS).]

CHORUS LEADER: We'll have to look sharp: did you hear our old
friend crowing for the second time, as we came up? 'Cock-a-
doodle-doo! Last call for Assembly!'

PRAXAGORA [*motioning them to make less noise*]: And here have I been
awake all night, waiting for you. Well, now I can give my neighbour here the signal to come out. I'll just tap lightly on the door:
we don't want to wake her husband. [*She goes over to the other house*
and gives the signal.]

[FIRST WOMAN, *carrying her husband's cloak, stick and shoes, comes*
out of the house and closes the door quietly behind her.]

FIRST WOMAN: I was just putting my shoes on, when I heard you
scratching at the door. I haven't slept a wink. That man of mine!
He comes from Salamis, do I need to say more? He's been at me all
night, I wonder the bedclothes aren't torn to shreds. I've only just
managed to pinch his cloak.[3]

PRAXAGORA: Ah, here comes Kleinarete and Sostrate – and here's
Philaenete.

[*The rest of the women forming the* CHORUS *are now beginning to*
arrive; among them are the wives of well-known individuals: most

*wear costumes or carry objects giving a clue to their husbands' identity
or trade; the tavern-keeper's wife has brought along the huge torch
which serves as a tavern sign.*]

CHORUS LEADER [*to the newcomers*]: Come along, hurry! Don't forget what Glyce said! She vowed that the last to arrive would pay a
forfeit to the rest: three gallons of wine and half a pound of
chickpeas.⁴

FIRST WOMAN: Oh, look at Smicythion's wife, Melistiche, trying to
hurry in those great shoes of his! I reckon she's the only one of us
who's had time to put them on. No problem for *her* to get out of
the house without her husband knowing!

PRAXAGORA: Aha, that must be Geusistrate, the tavern-keeper's
wife: over there, with the torch.

FIRST WOMAN: And here comes the wives of Philodoretus and
Khairetades, and lots of others – my dear, what a distinguished
gathering!

PRAXAGORA: Well, sit down, everybody. Now that you're all here
I'd first of all like to check whether you've done all the things we
decided on at the Festival.

[*The last to arrive is the* SECOND WOMAN.]

SECOND WOMAN: My dear, I had such a job to get away! My
husband had anchovies for supper, he's done nothing but cough
the whole night long.

PRAXAGORA: Well, sit down, everybody. Now that you're all here
I'd like first of all to check whether you've done all the things we
decided on at the Festival.

FIRST WOMAN: I have. I've grown an absolute forest under my
armpits, as per instructions. And every day, as soon as my husband
went out, I oiled myself all over and stood in the sun all day to get
brown.

SECOND WOMAN: So did I. The first thing I did was to throw away
my razor, so as to get hairy all over and not look like a woman at
all.

PRAXAGORA: And have you all got the beards I asked you to bring?

FIRST WOMAN: Mine's a beauty!

SECOND WOMAN: I've got one Epicrates would envy!

PRAXAGORA: And the rest of you?

[*They nod affirmatively.*]

FIRST WOMAN: Yes, we've all got them.

PRAXAGORA: And I see you've done the other things: you've all brought outdoor shoes and walking sticks and men's cloaks, as we agreed.

SECOND WOMAN: Look what I've brought! Lamias's staff! I pinched it while he was asleep.[5]

PRAXAGORA: My goodness, all that man needs is a sheepskin coat and you might mistake him for Argus. Well now, there's a lot more preparation to do before it gets light and we have to move off – Assembly starts at dawn, remember.

FIRST WOMAN: Yes, and you must make sure we get seats close to the speakers' platform, facing the praesidium.

SECOND WOMAN [showing a wool-comb and a basket of wool]: I've brought these along, I thought I might as well get on with a bit of wool-combing while the Assembly fills up.

PRAXAGORA: While it fills up? Why, you stupid idiot, don't you realize –

SECOND WOMAN: What's wrong with that? I can listen to you just as well while I'm doing my combing. My children are running about naked.

PRAXAGORA: If you think you're going to sit here combing wool till the Assembly fills up, you're very much mistaken. Don't you realize we mustn't let anyone see any part of our bodies? If we wait till it's full we'll have to clamber over all those men to get to our seats; fine thing if one of us had to hitch her clothes up to get by, and someone got a close-up view. No, if we get to our seats first we can settle down and no one will notice us; we'll have our cloaks well wrapped round us; and when we're sitting there, with our beards tied on, there'll be nothing to show that we're not men. After all, Agyrrhius[6] got away with it when he started wearing a beard – he must have borrowed it from Pronomus, he can't have grown it himself, because up till then he was so obviously a woman. And look at him now, one of the top men in Athens. Which in fact is why we women are embarking on this great venture of ours today: in the hope that *we* can take over the management of affairs and do a bit of good for the City. Because, as things are at present, the ship's adrift: we're not getting anywhere.

FIRST WOMAN: But how can we frail females expect to sway the Assembly?

PRAXAGORA: Nothing easier, I should think. It's well known that the most successful young orators are the ones who get laid most often. So we start off with certain natural advantages.

FIRST WOMAN: All the same, lack of experience will be a great handicap.

PRAXAGORA: So it's just as well that we're having this little meeting here; we can rehearse what we're going to say. [*To* FIRST WOMAN] Get that beard of yours tied on. And anyone else who's prepared to talk, please do the same.

FIRST WOMAN: Oh, we're all prepared to *talk*, I'm sure: what woman isn't?

PRAXAGORA: All right, then; put your beard on. From now on you're a man. I'll just put these head-wreaths down and tie my own beard on, in case I want to say something.

[PRAXAGORA, FIRST WOMAN, SECOND WOMAN, *and one or two others put on their home-made beards.*]

FIRST WOMAN: Oh, Praxagora dear, do look at us all! Isn't it just too absurd!

PRAXAGORA [*in a matter-of-fact masculine voice, pretending not to be amused*]: Absurd? Why, whatever do you mean?

FIRST WOMAN [*still convulsed*]: A lot of grilled cuttlefish with beards tied on!

PRAXAGORA [*in the role of Herald*]: Silence for the purification ceremony! [*To her* MAID, *who has just opened the door to let the cat out*] Officer, perform the lustral round, bearing the sacrificial – [*she snatches up the only animal in sight*] – cat![7]

[PRAXAGORA *hands the cat to the* MAID, *whc very solemnly 'consecrates' a section of the street by carrying the cat round it.*]

PRAXAGORA: Move forward into the lustral area! Ariphrades, stop talking! Come on, you, hurry up and sit down. Who wishes to speak?

FIRST WOMAN: I do.

[*The women are now seated in a semicircle.* PRAXAGORA *hands a wreath to* FIRST WOMAN.]

PRAXAGORA [*still acting the part of Herald*]: Assume the wreath, and may your words bring blessing.

[FIRST WOMAN *puts the wreath on her head and steps forward, uncertain what to do next.*]

FIRST WOMAN: Well? I've done that.

PRAXAGORA: Get on with your speech, then.

FIRST WOMAN: Don't we drink first?

PRAXAGORA: Drink!! Listen to her!

FIRST WOMAN: Why did I have to put a wreath on, then?[8]

PRAXAGORA: Oh, go and sit down. You'd have done this at the Assembly and made fools of us all.

FIRST WOMAN: Why, don't they drink there too?

PRAXAGORA: Drink – I ask you. Really!

FIRST WOMAN: They do, you know – and they don't water it either. You can't tell me they're stone cold sober when they pass those crazy resolutions. And they must have libations too: why do they have all those long prayers, if there's no wine? And the way they slang each other – it's quite obvious they're drunk the whole time. If they get too obstreperous the constables have to carry them out.

PRAXAGORA: Go back to your seat, you're hopeless.

FIRST WOMAN [*returning the wreath and sulkily removing her beard*]: If I'd known that wearing a beard meant dying of thirst . . . [*She sits down, and continues muttering to her neighbour.*]

PRAXAGORA: Perhaps somebody else would like to speak.

[SECOND WOMAN *stands up.*]

SECOND WOMAN: Yes, I would.

PRAXAGORA: Come on, then; put on the wreath – we must do everything properly.

[SECOND WOMAN *steps forward, takes the wreath and puts it on.*] Now let's have a manly, eloquent speech. Lean on your stick, that's it.

SECOND WOMAN: Er-hrrm! Unaccustomed as I am to public speaking, I would have preferred, gentlemen, to keep my seat and listen in silence while more, erm, experienced orators propounded their, erm, views. But I am utterly opposed to the obnoxious practice, adopted by so many tavern-keepers today, of installing water-tanks on their premises. I feel most strongly about this, by Persephone I really do!

PRAXAGORA: By Persephone? You stupid idiot!

SECOND WOMAN: What have I done wrong? I didn't ask for a drink!

PRAXAGORA: No, but no man ever says 'by Persephone'! Otherwise your speech was quite good.

SECOND WOMAN: All right, then: by Apollo.

PRAXAGORA: That's better. But that's enough from you. [*She takes the wreath from* SECOND WOMAN, *who resumes her seat.*] I'm not going a step further in this business unless we can get things absolutely right.

FIRST WOMAN [*rising*]: Give me the wreath, I'd like to try again. I've thought it all out very carefully this time. [*She puts on the wreath and steps forward.*] It is my opinion, ladies –

PRAXAGORA [*icily*]: Do you really think members of the Assembly will appreciate being addressed as 'ladies'?

FIRST WOMAN [*pointing into the audience*]: Sorry, I caught sight of Epigonus over there, and I really thought for a moment –

PRAXAGORA [*snatching the wreath from her*]: You go and sit down too.
   [FIRST WOMAN *resumes her seat.*]
A fat lot of help I'm getting from you lot. It looks as though I shall have to do the speaking myself. Where did I put that wreath? [*She puts it on.*] I pray to the gods for success in bringing our plans to fruition. – Gentlemen, my interest in the welfare of this state is no less than yours; but I deeply deplore the way in which its affairs are being handled. The task of speaking for the people is invariably entrusted to crooks and rascals. For every one day they spend doing good they spend another ten doing irreparable harm. If you try somebody new, he turns out to be even worse than the last one. It's difficult to give advice to men so hard to please as yourselves: you're frightened of the people who really want to serve you, and you throw yourselves at the feet of those who don't and won't. There was a time when we didn't bother to come to Assembly at all, but in those days at least we knew that Agyrrhius was a scoundrel.[9] Now, thanks to him and his bright idea of payment for attendance, it's full to overflowing; and those who get in and get their money are full of his praises; while those who are turned away merely say that people who go just for the money ought to be executed.

FIRST WOMAN: Well said, by Aphrodite!

228

PRAXAGORA: *Not* by Aphrodite, stupid! Fine fools we'd look if you went and said that in the Assembly!

FIRST WOMAN: Oh, I wouldn't say it there.

PRAXAGORA: Well, don't say it here, then. You've got to get out of the habit. – Now, where were we? Ah, yes – when we were debating the plan for an Anti-Spartan Treaty Organization,[10] everyone said the city's very existence depended on it; yet when ASTO was finally set up, everyone grumbled, and the speaker who had originally proposed it was hounded out of the City. Someone proposes new ships for the navy: the poor say yes, the rich men and the farmers say no. You hate the Corinthians, and they hate you; suddenly they're good chaps and you fall over yourselves trying to be nice to them. At one moment you think the Argives are fools and Hieronymus has the right idea – to go right ahead and make peace at the first favourable opportunity. Yet when the chance does arise, and salvation lies within your grasp, what do you do? Instead of calling on the only man capable of pulling it off,[11] you send him off in a huff.

FIRST WOMAN: What an excellent speaker that fellow is!

PRAXAGORA: That's better, you've got it right at last. – And who is responsible for this state of affairs? You, the people of Athens. Now that you are paid out of public funds, you think of nothing but your own individual pockets, and the state is left to stagger on as best it can, like Aesimus on his way home from a party. But if you will only listen to me, the situation can yet be saved. I propose that we hand over the running of Athens to the women. They are, after all, the people to whom we look for the efficient management of our homes.

ALL [*applauding*]: Hear, hear! Bravo! Well done, young man! Go on!

PRAXAGORA: It will not take me long to demonstrate the superiority of their methods to ours. In the first place, they all, without exception, continue to use hot water when dyeing wool, as has always been the custom. I mean you won't find them experimenting with other methods, such as the use of cold water. Whereas, if the City had some institution that worked well, do you think *you'd* try to preserve it? You wouldn't rest, I tell you, till you'd thought up something different. Women still sit down to do the roasting, as they've always done. They carry things on their heads, as they've always done. They hold the Thesmophoria Festival, as they've always done. They bake cakes, as they've always done. They infuriate their husbands, as they've always done. They conceal lovers in the house, as they've always done. [*The other women begin to join in, with increasing gusto, when this phrase recurs.*] They buy themselves little extras on the side, as they've always done. They drink their wine neat, as they've always done. They enjoy a bit of sex, as they've always done. – And so, gentlemen, let us waste no time in fruitless debate, or in asking what they propose to do, but quite simply hand over the reins of government to them, and let them get on with the job. In doing so we need only remind ourselves, firstly, that as mothers they will naturally be concerned for the safety of our soldiers; and who is more likely than a mother to ensure them an adequate supply of food? Further, that a woman is a highly resourceful creature when it comes to ways of raising money; and certainly when in office she will never allow herself to be taken in – she knows all the tricks already. I need say no more: pass this measure and a happy life will be yours.

FIRST WOMAN: Oh, Praxagora my sweet, what a magnificent speech. How clever you are? Wherever did you learn to do it so well?

PRAXAGORA: When we had to take refuge inside the City, my husband and I lived up on the Pnyx; you could hear every word. I used to listen to the speakers and study their technique.

FIRST WOMAN: No wonder you're so good. – I propose we elect Praxagora here and now to the post of Generalissima: if her motion is passed, she takes command – agreed?

[*The others assent, with enthusiasm.*]

But suppose somebody like Cephalus[12] is rash enough to get up and heckle you, tell us how you're going to dispose of *him*.

PRAXAGORA: Cephalus? I shall say he's a deluded fool.

FIRST WOMAN: But everybody knows that already.

PRAXAGORA: I'll say he's a raving lunatic.

FIRST WOMAN: Everybody knows that too.

PRAXAGORA: I'll tell him that if he wants to make a mess of something he'd better stick to his pottery. And not potter with state affairs.

SECOND WOMAN: And supposing old Squinny-eyes attacks you?

PRAXAGORA: Neocleides? I shall tell him to go and squint up a – dog's behind.

SECOND WOMAN: And if some of the others try to get a rise out of you?

PRAXAGORA: Why shouldn't they, bless their little hearts. They can all get rises for all I care. I'm quite used to that.

FIRST WOMAN: Well, that covers pretty nearly everything, I think – unless the constables try to arrest you. What will you do then?

PRAXAGORA: Simply stick my elbows out like this, so that they can't get their hands round my waist.

CHORUS LEADER: If they do, *we'll* tell them to let go.¹³

PRAXAGORA: Thank you very much, that'll be most helpful, I'm sure.

FIRST WOMAN: So now we've settled everything, haven't we? Only – how on earth are we going to remember to raise our *hands*? We're more used to raising our legs.

PRAXAGORA: Good point. When we vote, we have to hold up one arm, like this, bare to the shoulder. – Now, hitch up your skirts and put those walking-shoes on, just as you've seen your husbands do when they're going to Assembly or down town somewhere. – And now if you've all got your shoes on properly, fix on your beards, and see that they're properly adjusted. Right, now put on your husbands' cloaks that you've so cleverly stolen, lean on your sticks – that's the way – and off you go. And on the way, sing one of the songs the old men sing when they come in from the country.¹⁴

CHORUS LEADER: Good idea.

PRAXAGORA: And we'll go on ahead. Because I think there'll be other women coming in from the villages, and they'll be going straight there. So don't be long, because people who're not there by daybreak miss their pay, and have to slink back home without so much as a clothes peg.

[PRAXAGORA, FIRST WOMAN *and* SECOND WOMAN *move off to left*]

CHORUS LEADER:
Time we were moving, gentlemen – and we must not forget
To use this title all the time, or there'll be trouble yet.
A bold and secret enterprise demands the utmost care,
And if we're caught, the game is up, so – gentlemen – beware!

CHORUS:
Then on to the Pnyx
                    With urgent tread:
A fearful threat
                    Hangs over our head.
If we fail to arrive
                    By the break of day,
All dusty and hungry
                    We'll get no pay.
For a frugal meal
                    We've had to stickle,
Contenting ourselves
                    With garlic pickle –
Which helps to explain
                    The sour expressions
So often observed
                    At Assembly sessions.
So keep up the pace
                    And watch what you're doin':
One false note
                    Will spell our ruin.
A ticket first
                    We must each procure,
Then sit together
                    To make quite sure
That we vote with our sisters –
                    Oh, what am I saying?
Our *brothers*, I mean!
                    My wits are straying.

But as for the mob
                    That arrives from town,
We must push them aside
                    If we want to sit down.
When attendance pay
                    Was a single groat,
Do you think they bothered
                    To come up and vote?

    No, they sat in the square
                And gossiped all day;
    But now that it's tripled
                They can't keep away.
    How different things were
                In Myronides' time![15]
    A citizen then
                Would have thought it a crime
    To suggest being paid
                To attend a debate;
    For his pride and his joy
                Lay in serving the state.
    With two heads of garlic,
                Some wine in a flask,
    A loaf, and three olives,
                What more could he ask?
    A fine public spirit
                Our voters had then –
    But now they want wages,
                Like wheelbarrow men.

[*The entire* CHORUS *now marches off, left. After they have gone,* BLEPYRUS *comes out of his house, dressed in* PRAXAGORA'*s yellow undergown and a pair of pretty Persian slippers.*]

BLEPYRUS: What's going on, and where on earth has my wife got to? It's nearly morning and there's no sign of her. I've been wanting to come out and have a crap, but could I find my shoes and cloak? I've been lying awake for hours, groping about in the dark: couldn't find them anywhere. It was getting urgent! In the end I just grabbed hold of whatever came to hand – this yellow slip of my wife's and a pair of her Persian slippers, I must look a sight! Now, where's a good place to squat? Somewhere not too public – oh, well, what does it matter, it's not light yet, no one'll see me. [*He squats down.*] What a bloody fool I was to get married at my time of life: I really deserve a good shaking, I must say. She's up to no good, I'm certain, leaving the house like this. Excuse me, I must concentrate on the business in hand.

[*His* NEXT-DOOR NEIGHBOUR *appears at a window of the other house.*]

NEXT-DOOR NEIGHBOUR: Who's that? Not my neighbour Blepyrus?

BLEPYRUS: Right first time.

NEXT-DOOR NEIGHBOUR: Excuse me asking, but – why are you looking so yellow? Has someone had an accident over you? Cinesias been flying over?[16]

BLEPYRUS: No, no, I just had to pop out for a minute, so I put on this yellow what's-it of my wife's.

NEXT-DOOR NEIGHBOUR: Where's your cloak, then?

BLEPYRUS: I wish I knew. It should have been on the bed, but I couldn't find it.

NEXT-DOOR NEIGHBOUR: Didn't you ask your wife where it was?

BLEPYRUS: No, I did not. For the simple reason that she's not there. She's gone off somewhere and given me the slip. And I'd very much like to know what mischief she's up to.

NEXT-DOOR NEIGHBOUR: Well, I'll be blowed – exactly the same thing's just happened to me. *My* wife has gone off somewhere, and taken *my* cloak. I don't mind that so much, but she's got my shoes as well. At least I think she has; I can't find them anywhere.

BLEPYRUS: I couldn't find mine either. But I simply had to come out, so I just shoved my feet into these. Didn't want to soil the blanket, you know; it's only just come back from the wash. Well, what's happened, I wonder? Has some woman friend asked her round to breakfast?

NEXT-DOOR NEIGHBOUR: I expect that's what it is. She's not immoral, so far as I know. You must be shitting a cable. Well, it's time I got off to Assembly, but I'll have to get that cloak back first, it's the only one I have.

BLEPYRUS: So must I, as soon as I've finished. I think I've got a blockage; must be a cucumber up there or something.

NEXT-DOOR NEIGHBOUR: Oh dear! Well, remember what Thrasybulus said to the Spartans: 'Nothing must be permitted to interfere with the free passage of food supplies.'[17] [*He withdraws from the window.*]

BLEPYRUS: Well, it's certainly holding things up. What am I going to do? This is bad enough, but what's going to happen when I eat another meal? How's *that* going to get out, with this big fellow in the way, barring the exit? I need an operation. Question is, who'll perform it? [*To the audience*] Hey, anyone out there with any experience of bottoms? My God, dozens of them. Amynon? No, I won't ask him; he's choosy these days, he might say no. Fetch Antisthenes, somebody, for goodness' sake; he's always grunting and groaning himself, he'll understand. Oh, Goddess of Childbirth, can you look on unmoved as I crouch here, bulging, but bunged up? It's just like a scene in some low comedy.

[*It is now light.* CHREMES *enters, coming from left.*]

CHREMES: Hullo, what are you doing? Having a shit?

BLEPYRUS: What, me? Just finished, actually.

CHREMES: Is that your wife's dress you're wearing?

BLEPYRUS: It was the only thing I could find, in the dark. Where are you coming from, anyway?

CHREMES: I've been to Assembly.

BLEPYRUS: What, is it over already?

CHREMES: It was over by daybreak, practically. They've had a regular field-day with the red paint,[18] you should have seen them scrambling!

BLEPYRUS: You got your pay all right?

CHREMES: No such luck. Got there too late, I'm ashamed to say.

BLEPYRUS: No need to apologize, old man. Except to your shopping basket. But how did that happen?

CHREMES: I've never seen such a crowd as there was this morning, swarming up to the Pnyx. We saw all these fellows and, honestly, we thought they must all be shoemakers, they looked so pale. The whole assembly was full of these white faces; I was too late to get any pay and so were a lot of others.

BLEPYRUS: I suppose I couldn't get mine if I went now?

CHREMES: You wouldn't have got it if you'd been there by second cockcrow.

BLEPYRUS: Just my luck. Three obols lost forever. Theirs is a happier life in realms unknown. While I, alas, am left to mourn alone.[19] But what was on the agenda, to attract such a crowd at that hour?

CHREMES: Don't you remember, today was the day for proposals on how to save Athens. The first speaker was Neocleides. He groped his way over to the rostrum, and everyone started yelling at him. 'You've got a nerve, standing up there making speeches. How can you cure *our* troubles? More sense if you cured your own!' He peered all round the audience and shouted back at them. 'All right,' he says, 'so I suffer from inflamed eyelids. How in heaven's name can I help that?'

BLEPYRUS: I'd have told him, if I'd been there. Pound up some garlic with a few drops of lemon-juice, add a bit of spurge for luck and apply to the eyelids nightly.

CHREMES: The next one to get up was Eudaeon. Very clever fellow: stood there stark naked, or that's what most of us thought. But no, he said, he was wearing a cloak, or what was left of one. And that's just the point, he says, if we're talking about saving the City I could do with a bit of salvation myself, about sixteen drachmas'-worth to be precise. You want my opinion, gentlemen, on how to save Athens and its citizens: well, I'll tell you. As soon as winter begins, the clothiers should issue warm cloaks to everyone who needs one. Then we wouldn't all get pleurisy. And people who haven't got proper beds or bedclothes should be allowed to sleep at the fur shop. They could have a wash first, of course. And anyone who shuts the door on them in winter time should be fined three sheepskin blankets.

BLEPYRUS: Good for him. He'd have had everybody's vote if he'd gone on to say that the corn merchants were to give every poor man three quarts of barley meal for a good dinner, on pain of a thrashing. That'd serve *our* corn-merchant right, whichever way it went.

CHREMES: Yes, but after that another chap jumped up – good-looking young man with a pale face, rather the Nicias type, if you know what I mean – and made a speech, and started telling us we ought to hand over the control of affairs to the women. And all these shoemakers began applauding like mad and shouting 'Hear, hear!' But the men from the country districts were all growling and muttering.

BLEPYRUS: I'm not surprised.

CHREMES: No, but they were in the minority. Anyway, he managed to shout them down, and went on and on, praising the women and slating you.

BLEPYRUS: Me? Why, what did he say?

CHREMES: He said you were a rogue.

BLEPYRUS: And what about you?

CHREMES: Don't interrupt. And a thief.

BLEPYRUS: Just me? No one else?

CHREMES: And a liar too.

BLEPYRUS: Only me?

CHREMES [*indicating the audience*]: And all this crowd here as well.

BLEPYRUS: Oh, well, no one's denying *that*.

CHREMES: But women, he says are creatures bursting with intelligence and darned good at making money. And they don't let out what happens at their secret festivals, the way you and I, when we're on the Council, leak state secrets right and left.

BLEPYRUS: By Hermes, he's right there!

CHREMES: And then, he says, there's another thing: when they lend things to each other – dresses, jewellery, money, drinking bowls, or anything else – it's just between themselves, it's a private matter: they don't insist on witnesses being present, and all that sort of nonsense; but the loans are always returned, they don't hang on to them, the way most of us do, so he says.

BLEPYRUS: True enough. Even when there are witnesses.

CHREMES: No informing, no prosecuting, no conspiring to overthrow the democracy – oh, he went on and on about women, it seems they have no vices at all, only virtues.

BLEPYRUS: And what was finally decided?

CHREMES: They voted to hand over control to the women. The general feeling was, that as this was the only method that hadn't yet been tried, they might as well try it.

BLEPYRUS: And this motion was actually carried?

CHREMES: Yes, I tell you.

BLEPYRUS: Does that mean that the women have now been given all the jobs that men used to do?

CHREMES: Just that.

BLEPYRUS: You mean my wife will have to sit on juries instead of me?

CHREMES: Yes, and she'll have to maintain the family, instead of you.

BLEPYRUS: And stagger out of bed in the early morning, instead of me?

CHREMES: That's right; those are going to be the women's jobs from now on. And you can sit on your arse at home and take things easy.

BLEPYRUS: But wait a minute, it's going to be a bit hard on some of

us older men, if they take advantage of, er, having the upper hand
to force us to –

CHREMES: Force us to what?

BLEPYRUS: Screw them. Supposing we can't – they won't give us
any breakfast.

CHREMES: You'd better eat your breakfast at the same time, and
make sure of it.

BLEPYRUS: I refuse to be raped.

CHREMES: If it benefits Athens, it's every man's patriotic duty.

BLEPYRUS: Well, in the old days they used to say: it doesn't matter
how foolishly and crazily we decide to act, everything works out
for our good in the end.

CHREMES: Ye gods and holy Athena, let's hope it will in this case!
Well, I must be getting along; bye bye for now.

BLEPYRUS: Bye bye, Chremes.

[CHREMES *goes off right, bound doubtless for the Agora, where there
will be plenty to gossip about this morning.* BLEPYRUS *re-enters his
house.*]

[*The* CHORUS *re-enter cautiously from left, glancing right and left as
they go. They are full of suppressed excitement, and there are signs
of slackening discipline: beards prematurely removed, sudden titters,
etc. The* CHORUS LEADER *calls them to order.*]

CHORUS LEADER: Come on, move along! Are you sure none of the
men are following us? Have a good look behind, there, be on your
guard and watch how you go. The wretches are everywhere
[*she points towards the audience*]; for all we know, they may be
admiring our figures from behind.

CHORUS:

So stamp your feet upon the ground, maintain a man-like pace;
If ever they should twig the truth, we'd all be in disgrace.
Gather your garments round you close, look carefully about,
Until we safely reach the spot from which we started out.
Why, here it is! – and that's the house where everything began,
For that was where Praxagora conceived her famous plan.
And now to get these beards off quick, for if we hang about
Some passer-by will see us, and the secret will be out.
So in the shadow of this wall, as swiftly as we can,
Let's all change back to what we were before this lark began.

Without a beard, the female chin feels nicer and looks neater. –
And look, our Leader has arrived; let's gather round and greet her.

[PRAXAGORA *enters from left, and starts to divest herself of her male clothing.*]

PRAXAGORA: Well, my dears, so far everything's gone according to plan. But now you must get those cloaks off quickly, before any of the men see you: shoes off and out of sight – untie those Spartan laces, throw away your sticks. [*To* CHORUS LEADER] I'll leave you to do the organizing; I must slip indoors before my husband catches me, and put his cloak back where I got it from, and the other things I took.

[*She lingers, however, to watch the* CHORUS *as they rid themselves of their beards, cloaks, shoes and sticks, which are collected and removed.*]

CHORUS LEADER: We've done as you said, and await your commands. We have full trust in your judgement, and, personally, I think you're the cleverest woman I've ever met.

[*The* CHORUS *assent, with cheers.*]

PRAXAGORA: Wait here, then, so that I can have you at hand as my advisers, as I take over the high office to which I have been elected. Up there, faced with all the uproar and all those clever opponents, you showed yourselves brave fighters.

[*She turns to go into the house, but at that moment* BLEPYRUS *comes out.*]

BLEPYRUS: Praxagora! And where have *you* been, I should like to know.

PRAXAGORA: What's that to you?

BLEPYRUS: What's that to me? There's manners for you.

PRAXAGORA: I suppose you think I've been with a lover.

BLEPYRUS: Several, I should think.

PRAXAGORA: There's a simple test that you could try.

BLEPYRUS: What's that?

PRAXAGORA: See if my hair smells of perfume.

BLEPYRUS: Can't a woman get screwed without perfume?

PRAXAGORA: Not in my case, I'm sorry to say.

BLEPYRUS: Than what *have* you been up to, sneaking out before dawn and taking my cloak?

PRAXAGORA: A friend of mine sent for me during the night. Her pains had come on.

BLEPYRUS: Couldn't you have told me you were going?

PRAXAGORA: And waste time chattering, with a childbirth to attend to?

BLEPYRUS: You should have told me first. There's something fishy about this.

PRAXAGORA: Honestly, I had to rush out straight away, just as I was. The girl who came to fetch me kept telling me to hurry.

BLEPYRUS: Well, you might at least have taken your own cloak. Instead of which, you rip mine off the bed, fling down your flimsy undergown in its place, and leave me lying there like a laid-out corpse. I wonder you forgot to deposit a wreath and a flask of oil.

PRAXAGORA: Well, it was very cold and you know how weak and delicate I am; so I put this on to keep me warm. After all, you had a nice warm bed to lie in, and *plenty* of bedclothes.

BLEPYRUS: And how did my walking-shoes come to accompany you on your travels? And my stick?

PRAXAGORA: Well, I didn't want to have your cloak snatched away by a thief, did I? I had to protect it. So I put on your shoes and imitated the way you walk, clumping along and banging the stones with your stick.

BLEPYRUS: Do you realize that you've lost me eight quarts of wheat, that I could have got with my pay, if I'd gone to Assembly?

PRAXAGORA: Never mind; it was a boy.

BLEPYRUS: What was? The Assembly?

PRAXAGORA: No, the baby, stupid. – Oh, did the Assembly meet?

BLEPYRUS: Yes, of course it did. I told you yesterday it was going to.

PRAXAGORA: Oh, yes, I remember now, so you did.

BLEPYRUS: So you don't know about the latest decisions?

PRAXAGORA: No, how should I?

BLEPYRUS: Well, sit down and take a deep breath. [*He gulps.*] They've decided to hand it all over to you women.

PRAXAGORA: What, all the weaving?

BLEPYRUS: No, they're putting you in full control.

PRAXAGORA: What of?

BLEPYRUS: Everything – the whole shooting-match: all the City's affairs.

PRAXAGORA: Then by Aphrodite, this is a great day for Athens. What a splendid piece of news!

BLEPYRUS: You can't mean it.

[CHREMES *re-enters from right, on his way back from the Agora. He joins the group and stays to listen.*]

PRAXAGORA: But I do mean it. This'll put a stop to all the mischief and skulduggery! No more faked evidence, no more informing!

BLEPYRUS: Steady on, don't abolish that! One's got to earn a living somehow!

CHREMES: Shut up, there's a good fellow, and let your wife speak.

PRAXAGORA: No more mugging in the streets, no more envy of the neighbours, no more rags and tatters, no more poverty, no more slander, no more harrying for debt.

[BLEPYRUS *shakes his head incredulously.*]

CHREMES: By Poseidon, that sounds fine, if it all comes true.

PRAXAGORA: It will, and I'm ready to prove it to him, and you can be my witness. He won't have a word to say in reply.

[*The* CHORUS *crowd round to hear* PRAXAGORA's *detailed proposals.*]

CHORUS:
          Now summon all your eloquence,
          Your shrewdness, wit and common sense!
          Yours is the skill: to you must fall
          The task of speaking for us all.
          For eloquence, if rightly used,
          With wisdom and good sense infused,
          A myriad blessings can bestow
          On citizens both high and low,
          Who, in their present sorry plight,
          Need a good plan to set them right.
          Go on, and tell them what to do,
          But make quite sure it's something new:
          They always find it such a bore
          If they have heard it all before.
          And now get cracking, right away.
          Pace is what matters in a play!

PRAXAGORA: Well, personally I'm convinced that my proposals are good ones. What worries me is whether the audience here will be ready to try out new methods instead of muddling along for ever with the old ones that we know only too well.

BLEPYRUS: As far as trying out new stunts is concerned, you needn't worry: we don't need a new government to persuade us to do that!

PRAXAGORA: I don't want any contradictions or interruptions until you've heard enough to get the hang of what I'm saying. And what I'm going to say is that everyone is to have an equal share in everything and live on that; we won't have one man rich while another lives in penury, one man farming hundreds of acres while another hasn't enough land to get buried in; one man with dozens of slaves and another with none at all. There will be one common stock of necessities for everybody, and these will be shared equally.

BLEPYRUS: Shared equally? How can they be?

PRAXAGORA: If we had turds for dinner, you'd still want the first helping.

BLEPYRUS: Are turds to be shared equally too?

PRAXAGORA: No, you idiot, all I meant was that you always insist on chipping in. Now where was I? Oh, yes – first of all I shall declare all land, all money, and all private possessions to be common property. And from this common stock it will be our job – the women's job – to feed you and manage your affairs sensibly and economically.

CHREMES: What about the people who don't own any land, but have all their wealth hidden away in silver or Persian gold?

PRAXAGORA: They must put it all into the common pool, and not try to hold on to it by committing perjury.

BLEPYRUS: Which is how they got it in the first place.

PRAXAGORA: But now it won't be any use to them in any case.

CHREMES: How do you make that out?

PRAXAGORA: No one will be motivated by need: everybody will have everything – loaves, cutlets, cakes, warm cloaks, wine, head-wreaths, chickpeas.[20] So what advantage will there be in hanging on to one's wealth? If you can think of any, it's more than I can.

CHREMES: Having these things doesn't stop people stealing more of them, even now.

PRAXAGORA: That was true under the old system; but now everything will be owned in common, so why hold on to anything?

BLEPYRUS: Suppose someone has his eye on a young girl and wants to go to bed with her, he can dip into his private store for something to give her; then he can sleep with her and have his share of the common goods as well.

PRAXAGORA: But he can sleep with her *for nothing*! I'm making girls common property too. Any man who wants to can sleep with them and have children by them.

BLEPYRUS: Won't the men all make for the prettiest one and want to sleep with *her*?

PRAXAGORA: The plain unattractive girls will sit with the pretty ones; anyone who wants a pretty girl will have to lay one of the plain ones first.

BLEPYRUS: Bit hard on some of us older men, isn't it? If we've got to screw an ugly one first, how are we going to make it with the popsie?

PRAXAGORA: Don't worry, they're not going to fight over *you*. Not for the privilege of sleeping with you, at any rate.

BLEPYRUS: For what, then?

PRAXAGORA: For the privilege of *not* sleeping with you. I dare say even you could rise to that.

BLEPYRUS: I'm beginning to see what you're after, you're making sure all the women can get their holes plugged whenever they feel like it. But what about the men? The girls will all run away from the ugly men and chase after the handsome ones.

PRAXAGORA: The less attractive men will escort the handsome ones when they go out after dinner, and stay with them in all public places; and the women won't be able to sleep with the tall handsome ones till they've obliged the little weedy ones.

BLEPYRUS: And Lysicrates's nose can hold itself as high as anybody else's?

PRAXAGORA: Indeed yes, it's a very democratic idea, and a lot of la-di-da young fellows with signet rings are going to look pretty foolish when a yob in working boots pushes past and says, 'Do you mind stepping aside and waiting your turn?'

CHREMES: But how are any of us ever going to recognize our own children?

PRAXAGORA: You won't need to. The children will regard all older men as fathers.

BLEPYRUS: In that case they'll go round throttling every older man they meet: that's how fathers are treated these days. Bad enough now, when they do know who you are; what'll it be like when they don't? They'll shit on us!

PRAXAGORA: The others won't let them. It might be *their* father. In the old days, if someone wanted to beat up his father, that was nobody's business but his own. But now, if it sounds as if someone's getting beaten up, they'll rush to help in case it's 'him'.

BLEPYRUS: Well, on the whole you're making out quite a good case. But supposing Epicurus or – or *Leucolophus* came up and started calling me 'Daddy'. I just couldn't take it.

CHREMES: I can think of an even worse fate.

BLEPYRUS: What would that be?

CHREMES: If Aristyllus said you were *his* father, and gave you a kiss!

BLEPYRUS [*horrified*]: By god, he'd regret it!

CHREMES: So would you, old man. You'd stink for weeks.

PRAXAGORA: Well, fortunately he was born before the date of this new law, so there's not much danger of his kissing you.

CHREMES: But now tell me, who's going to farm the land?

PRAXAGORA: The slaves. All you have to do is make sure you're smart and tidy when you go out to dinner, just before sunset.

CHREMES: Who'll provide us with clothes? We mustn't forget that, you know.

PRAXAGORA: You've got some to be going on with. And after that, we'll weave you some more.

CHREMES: One more question. If there's a court case and someone has to pay a fine, where's the money coming from? He can't very well take *that* out of the common pool, can he?

PRAXAGORA: But there won't *be* any court cases!

CHREMES: Phew, you really are sticking your neck out now: you'll never convince anybody of that.

BLEPYRUS: Just what I was thinking.

PRAXAGORA: But why should there be? What would they be about?

BLEPYRUS: Hang it, all kinds of things. Take one example: supposing a debtor refuses to pay up?

PRAXAGORA: And this fellow who lent him the money – how did he come to have it, when everything's owned in common? The man must be a thief.

CHREMES: Well, I'm jiggered! That's a good point.

BLEPYRUS: Well, just tell me this, one of you: supposing somebody has too much to drink at dinner, and starts knocking people about. How's he going to pay compensation? Eh? That's got you!

PRAXAGORA: It'll be stopped out of his food allowance. He'll think twice before committing assault again, once his stomach has had to suffer.

BLEPYRUS: And there won't be any thieves?

PRAXAGORA: How can anyone steal what he owns already?

BLEPYRUS: No footpads at night to tear the clothes off you?

PRAXAGORA: If you sleep at home there's no danger of that anyway. But now it won't happen even if you do stay out; everyone will have the necessities of life. If this fellow wants to take your cloak, give it to him. Why fight about it, when you can go to the common store and get a better one?

BLEPYRUS: Well, anyway, you'll never stop people dicing.

PRAXAGORA: Why not? No point in dicing for their own property.

BLEPYRUS: And what kind of a home life are we going to have?

PRAXAGORA: That'll be communal. I shall have all the party-walls pulled down between houses: the whole city will be just one big communal residence. You'll be able to walk in and out where you like.

BLEPYRUS: And where are we going to have our dinner?

PRAXAGORA: I shall have all the lawcourts and arcades converted into dining-halls.

BLEPYRUS: What will you use the speakers' platforms for?

PRAXAGORA: They'll make very good stands for the wine-jars and the mixing-bowls. And the children can get up there and recite poetry about the men who have fought bravely in the war. And about those who haven't, so that they'll be ashamed and stay away.

BLEPYRUS: What a brilliant idea! And what will you use those lot-casting contraptions for?[21]

PRAXAGORA: I'll set them up in the Agora, and then I'll station myself by the statue of Harmodius and assign dinner-places to everybody, according to which letter they've drawn; and they'll all go off equally happy. There'll be an announcement: 'Will all those who have drawn the letter Beta please proceed to the Basileion; all Thetas to the Theseus Colonnade; all Kappas to the – oh, to Bakery Row.'

BLEPYRUS: For a capful of cake.

PRAXAGORA: No, for a capital dinner.

BLEPYRUS: And I suppose if you draw a blank you don't get in anywhere.

PRAXAGORA: No, no, we shan't have any blanks. There'll be enough of everything for everybody. You'll all come away well wined and dined, wreaths on your heads, torches in your hands; and at every street corner there'll be women waiting to waylay you, saying 'Come along to my place, there's such a pretty young girl there.' And then there'll be another voice, from an upper window: 'There's one up here, you never saw such a lovely creature; but you'll have to have me first!' And the less attractive men will be right on the heels of the handsome ones, and they'll shout 'Hey, not so fast, young fellow, you'll gain nothing by hurrying; they've got to let a snub-nosed man make love to them first, that's the new law! In the meantime you'll have to wait in the vestibule and abuse yourself as best you can.' – Now, tell me honestly, both of you, don't you like the sound of my scheme?

BLEPYRUS: It sounds fine to me.

PRAXAGORA: Good. Well, I must be off to the Agora to receive people's goods as they bring them in, and I must find a girl with a good strong voice to act as Crier. I'm the one who must do all this, because I've been elected Chief of State. And I must get on with the catering arrangements, to make sure you start off today with a really fine feast.

BLEPYRUS: A feast today? Already?

PRAXAGORA: Certainly. And then I intend to have all the brothels closed down.

BLEPYRUS: Whatever for?

PRAXAGORA: Well, obviously, so that these freeborn ladies can enjoy the young men's attentions, instead of letting dolled-up slave-girls snatch the pleasures of love from under their noses. Let slaves sleep with slaves, I say, and let their hair grow where it wants to.

BLEPYRUS: I think I'll come along too and stick around; then they'll all see me and say, 'Look, there's the Chief's husband, isn't he marvellous?'

CHREMES: Well, if I've got to take all my things to the Agora I'd better go and hold an inspection – get them all lined up.

[PRAXAGORA *and* BLEPYRUS *move off towards the Agora* (right), *and* CHREMES *goes to his house (just out of sight, left). The* CHORUS, *after a short dance, move off (right).*]

SCENE TWO

Outside CHREMES's *house.*

[*The door of the house is open, and* CHREMES, *assisted by his two slave-boys* PARMENON *and* SICON, *is carrying out his 'inspection'. However, his efforts to give the proceedings a military flavour are not very successful: he decides, instead, to turn his 'troops' (a miscellaneous jumble of household effects) into a ritual procession – the Panathenaic procession, no less. A parasol, a basket, and various pieces of drapery, are among the lucky finds which are now put to good use.*]

CHREMES: Come here, my pretty sieve, you shall be first in my procession: we'll make you Basket-Bearer. You're well powdered anyway, what with all the bags of flour I've put through you. Next comes the Litter-Bearer: cooking-pot, this way! You're black enough, in all conscience; if you'd been used by Lysicrates for boiling his hair-dye you could hardly be blacker. Stand here, by her. Now the Tiring-Maid! [*This item, when suitably draped, is given a parasol to hold over the first two.*] And next the Water-Carrier: bring that jar over here – that's right. [*A suitably-sized object is found and draped, and given the jar to 'carry'.*] And now, Musician, out you come! [*A cock, in a cage, is brought out.*] Ah, you rascal, many's the time you've been too early with your morning call, and sent me rushing off to Assembly in the middle of the night! Next, the man with the bowl of honeycombs; then the olive-branches; then come the tripods and the oil-flask. And finally you can send out all the little pots and pans and oddments, to bring up the rear.

[*While the final touches are being put to the 'procession',* CITIZEN *strolls in from right. He walks up and down, deep in thought.*]

CITIZEN [*aside*]: Hand over my property? You won't catch me doing that in a hurry. I wouldn't be such a fool. I'll have to think the

whole thing over very carefully. Why should I hand over what
I've sweated and slaved for, just because somebody says so? It's just
damned silly. I want to know what it's all about first. [*To*
CHREMES] Hey, what's all this stuff you've got lined up out here?
Are you moving house or something? Or are you going to pawn
it?

CHREMES: No, of course I'm not.

CITIZEN: Then why have you got it all lined up like this? Are you
taking it in procession to the auctioneer's?

CHREMES: No, I'm taking it to the Agora to hand it in to the state,
as I have to under the new law.

CITIZEN: You really intend to hand it in?

CHREMES: Certainly.

CITIZEN: Then heaven help you. You'll be ruined.

CHREMES: How?

CITIZEN: Only too easily.

CHREMES: Why? We have to obey the laws, don't we?

CITIZEN: What laws, you poor twit?

CHREMES: The ones that have just been passed.

CITIZEN: Oh, those! You must be very simple!

CHREMES: Simple?

CITIZEN: Not so much simple as stark raving mad. It's the craziest
thing I ever heard of.

CHREMES: What, obeying orders?

CITIZEN: You think obeying orders is a sign of good sense?

CHREMES: Yes, I certainly do.

CITIZEN: It's a sign of crass idiocy, if you ask me.

CHREMES: And you're really not going to hand your stuff in?

CITIZEN: I shall take jolly good care not to hand it in – until I see
what other people decide to do.

CHREMES: Well, they're all preparing to give theirs in, I'm quite sure.

CITIZEN: I'll believe it when I see it.

CHREMES: Anyway, I've heard them talking in the streets –

CITIZEN: Can't stop people talking.

CHREMES: And saying they're going to fetch their things –

CITIZEN: Can't stop people *saying* so.

CHREMES: Blast it, you disbelieve everything I say!

CITIZEN: Can't stop people disbelieving.

CHREMES: Oh, go and stuff yourself!

CITIZEN: Can't stop people stuffing themselves – no, but I mean, do you really believe that any single one of them, that's got any sense, will take his goods along? It's not the Athenian way. Grabbing, not giving, is what comes natural to us. And to the gods themselves, for that matter; you can tell from their statues – the hands especially. All the time we're praying to them to give us the good things in life, there they stand with their hands outstretched – palm upwards!

CHREMES: Well now, if you don't mind, sir, I'll get on with what I have to do. These things have got to be tied up. Where's that strap got to?

CITIZEN: You're really going to hand it all in?

CHREMES: Yes, I am. I'm tying up these two tripods, as you see.

CITIZEN: Oh, what folly, not to wait and see what other people are going to do, and then –

CHREMES: And then what?

CITIZEN: Wait a little longer, and even then, don't act at once.

CHREMES: I don't follow you. Why?

CITIZEN: Well, suppose there was an earthquake, or a flash of lightning, or a cat²² crossed the road, they'd stop taking their goods along, wouldn't they, you nincompoop?

CHREMES: Fine thing it would be if there wasn't any room left for my contribution, by the time I got there.

CITIZEN: No room for it? Is that what you're afraid of? Don't you worry, you'll find room for it all right – even if you put it off till the day after tomorrow.

CHREMES: How do you make that out?

CITIZEN: I know these citizens: they'll vote for anything on the spur of the moment – and then refuse to carry out what they've voted for.

CHREMES: They'll deposit their goods all right.

CITIZEN: Suppose they don't, what then?

CHREMES: They will, don't worry.

CITIZEN: Suppose they don't, I say, what then?

CHREMES: Then we'll fight them.

CITIZEN: Suppose they're bigger than you, what then?

CHREMES: In that case I'll leave them alone, and clear off.

CITIZEN: Suppose they won't let you, what then?

CHREMES: Oh, drop dead.

CITIZEN: Suppose I do, what then?

CHREMES: It'll make my day.

CITIZEN: You really *want* to hand it over?

CHREMES: Yes, I do. And look, there go my neighbours, taking theirs along.

CITIZEN: With Antisthenes in the lead, I have no doubt. Not on your life – he'd rather sit straining in the bog for three months.

CHREMES: Shut up!

CITIZEN: And Callimachus the chorus-trainer, do you think *he'll* bring anything in?

CHREMES: More than Callias, I dare say.

CITIZEN: Chucking away everything you possess, that's what you're doing.

CHREMES: You shouldn't talk like that, it's not right.

CITIZEN: Not right? Don't you understand, they're always passing resolutions like this. Remember the one about the salt?

CHREMES: I do, yes.

CITIZEN: And the one we passed about the copper coinage?

CHREMES: Oh yes, I remember that one all right. Very awkward that turned out, for me. I'd just sold my grapes for a whole heap of copper coins; shoved them in my mouth – easiest way to carry them – and went to the market to buy some barley-meal. I was just holding out my sack for it when the Crier made the announcement. 'No more copper coins to be accepted: silver only!' I nearly swallowed the lot.

CITIZEN: And then, just lately, that two and a half per cent tax proposed by Euripides: weren't we all swearing that it would bring in three million drachmas? And Euripides was a very fine fellow, worth his weight in gold. And then when we looked into it and found, as usual, that the idea wouldn't work, everyone started slanging Euripides again.

CHREMES: Yes, but that was different. That was when *we* were in charge. Now the women are running things.

CITIZEN: Well, I'm going to take very good care they don't land *me* in the shit.

CHREMES: I don't know what you're talking about. [*To his slaves*]

Come on, then, hoist up this bundle. [CHREMES *and the two slaves pick up the goods, which they have by now strapped into bundles, and help each other to hoist them on to their shoulders.*]

[*The young woman selected by* PRAXAGORA *for the role of* CRIER *enters, right.*]

CRIER: Calling all citizens, yes, I said *all* citizens, that's the way we do things now, *all* citizens to make haste and present themselves before Her Excellency the General, so that lots can be drawn and she can tell each of you where to go for your dinner. The feast awaits you, the tables are loaded with all kinds of good things, the couches are piled high with cushions and rugs, the drinks are ready for pouring, the perfumers are standing by; the stoves are aglow, waiting to grill your fish; the meat is on the spit, the cakes in the oven; the wreaths are being twined and the savouries are crackling in the pan. The youngest girls are preparing the pea soup in great cauldrons; Smoius is with them of course, in full riding kit, looking for something to lick. And Geron[23] is on his way too, looking very smart in a swagger-cloak and party shoes, laughing and chatting with another young fellow: he's flung away his tattered old coat and clumsy boots. So hurry along, the barley loaves have been brought in. Come and feed your faces! [CRIER *continues on her way, going out left.*]

CITIZEN: Oh well, I'll be getting along, then. I mean, why hang around, when the City decrees otherwise?

CHREMES: Hullo, hullo, where are you off to, in such a hurry? You haven't handed in your property yet.

CITIZEN: To the dinner, of course.

CHREMES: Oh no, you're not! If those women have got any sense, you won't get any dinner till you've handed your stuff in.

CITIZEN: Oh, I'll hand it in, some time.

CHREMES: When?

CITIZEN: It won't matter about mine, particularly.

CHREMES: Why not?

CITIZEN: You mark my words! Mine won't be the last lot to be handed in, by a long chalk.

CHREMES: And you're going to turn up for dinner, just the same?

CITIZEN: What else can I do? After all, every decent citizen must do what he can to help the State.

CHREMES: Suppose they won't let you in, what then?

CITIZEN: I'll go for them, head down.

CHREMES: Suppose they have you flogged, what then?

CITIZEN: I'll prosecute them.

CHREMES: Suppose they laugh at you, what then?

CITIZEN: I'll stand by the entrance.

CHREMES: What for?

CITIZEN: To grab the food as they take it in.

CHREMES: In that case I must make sure of getting there before you do. Come on, Sicon, come along, Parmenon, get these goods and chattels hoisted up.

CITIZEN: Let me help you carry them.

CHREMES: No, no, I won't hear of it. [*Aside*] Otherwise, when they're handed in to Her Excellency, the General, you'll pretend they're yours.

[CHREMES *and his* SLAVES *stagger off with their burdens, right.*]

CITIZEN [*to himself*]: Hang it, I must find some way of keeping what I've got without losing my share of all this public feasting! – Ah, yes, I think I know what to do.[24] I must hurry straight to the dinner, there's no time to be lost. [*Hurries out, right.*]

SCENE THREE

Evening. Another street in Athens, with three houses visible. Their occupants are FIRST HAG (*left*), GIRL (*centre*) *and* SECOND HAG (*right*).

[FIRST HAG *appears in her doorway and peers up and down the street.*]

FIRST HAG: Why don't the men come? They should have started arriving long ago. I've plastered my face with white lead, and put on my prettiest yellow gown, and now there's nothing to do but stand here and wait. Perhaps I'll croon a little song to myself and dance a few steps: that'll be the way to catch one of them on his way past. I must pray to the Muses to come and inspire me! Come, heavenly Muses! – and hurry up about it, I need you. Find me something catchy, one of those Ionian songs. [*She tries out a few trills.*]

GIRL [*appearing at her upstairs window*]: Oh, so you're flaunting yourself in the doorway, trying to cut me out, you mouldering antique,
you! Thought you'd steal a march on me, pick all the juiciest plums
for yourself, lure some man in with your singing. All right, then:
I can sing as well as you! We'll have a competition – that is, if it
won't be too much of a bore for the audience. You never know,
though; it's quite the fashion in comedy these days. They may even
like this kind of thing.

FIRST HAG [*hurling a fig at her*]: Talk to that, if you must talk, and get
back inside! Now come along, piper darling, pick up those pipes
and let's have a tune that's worthy of us both.

[*The tune is played:* FIRST HAG *listens, nods in time with the music,
and then begins to sing.*]

[*sings*]

> If love's ecstasy you seek,
> Come and sample my technique!
> No young girl could ever be
> As experienced as me.
>
> You'll be lucky if she stays
> True to you for seven days:
> Better far *my* love to try;
> I'll not leave you till I die.

GIRL [*sings*]:

> Much sooner for a young girl's love
>   Will men pour out their sighs;
> Rounded like apples are our breasts,
>   And smooth our tender thighs.
>
> Repulsive hag, in vain you flaunt
>   Your plucked and painted hide!
> Or are you hoping Death will come
>   And claim you as his bride?

FIRST HAG [*sings*]:

> When you are panting to receive
>   Your lover's hot embrace,
> O may those breasts and thighs dissolve
>   And leave an empty space!

When you stretch out your lustful hand
> His eager flesh to clasp
Beneath the bedclothes, may you find
> It is a *snake* you grasp!

GIRL [*sings*]:
> Oh why do you tarry, do you tarry, lover dear?
> Whatever shall I do, if you do not appear?
> My mother has gone out, and left me all alone –
> > I'm on fire with desire,
> > Need I say what I require?
> What a chance for you to make me all your own.
> – And as for you, Granny, you randy old cat,
> Get yourself a toy one, and enjoy yourself with that.

FIRST HAG [*sings*]:
> And what about yourself, you perverted little bitch?
> You've got what they call the Ionian itch.
> You're all twisted up like a great big S,
> And what that letter stands for, the audience can guess.

GIRL: Sing your head off if you want to, I don't care. Waddling up and down like a love-sick weasel!

FIRST HAG: I'm not letting anyone get to you first.

GIRL: Who'd want to get to you – except the undertaker? There, that's a new one on you. Isn't it, hag?

FIRST HAG: No, it isn't.

GIRL: Oh, no, of course, I forgot: 'to the old, nothing is new'.

FIRST HAG: It's not my *age* you have to worry about.

GIRL: No, it's all that rouge and white lead, I suppose.

FIRST HAG: There's no call to be insolent.

GIRL: There's no call to hover about in that doorway, either. What do you think you're doing?

FIRST HAG: Nothing, just singing quietly to myself. I'm making up a song to my boy-friend, if you must know. His name's Epigenes.

GIRL: Father Time, more like it, if you've got a boy-friend at all.

FIRST HAG: You'll see. He'll be here soon and he'll come straight to me.

[YOUNG MAN *enters stealthily, from right.*]

GIRL: Here he comes now, by the look of it.

FIRST HAG: He won't be needing anything from you, hussy!

GIRL: Won't he? We'll see about that. I'll draw back out of sight.

FIRST HAG: All right then, so will I. I have my pride, like anyone else. Never let it be said that I'm less of a lady than you are.

[FIRST HAG *and* GIRL *withdraw, but not before* YOUNG MAN *has seen them.*]

YOUNG MAN: Now the question is, how to sleep with the young one without having to lay that dreadful old bag first. Ugh! To a gentleman, the idea's intolerable.

FIRST HAG [*aside*]: Oh, so that's your little game, is it? Any tricks like that, and you're for it, my lad! This is a democracy, and laws are made to be kept! – I'll just have a peep and see what he's up to.

YOUNG MAN [*praying*]: Oh, gods above, let it be just the one – the pretty one! – The wine has made me desperate with desire.

GIRL [*looking out*]: Ha, that's tricked the old trout: she's gone, she thought I'd stay inside! – There he is! The same man!
[*sings*]

> Oh come, my heart's delight,
>> And share my bed to-night!
>> Strange, passionate desires
> Sweep through my body like a hundred fires;
>> My brain is in a whirl,
>> I love each single curl
> Upon your head, I want to be your girl.
>> This madness Eros sent:
>> O cruel god, relent
>> And set me free!
>> Delight not to torment:
>> Bring him to me!

YOUNG MAN [*sings*]:

> One detail you forget:
>> The door is bolted yet!
>> I lust with you to lie:
> Admit me soon or I shall surely die.
>> Nothing can ease my mind
>> Until I have entwined
> My limbs with yours and squeezed your plump behind.
>> This madness Eros sent:
>> O cruel god, relent

And set me free!
Delight not to torment:
   Bring her to me!

What I have sung so far
   Puts it quite mildly;
It's not too much to say
   I love you wildly.
Open the door, I beg,
   Child of the Graces!
Come, let me smother you
   In my embraces!

[YOUNG MAN *knocks at* GIRL'S *door.*]

FIRST HAG [*appearing at her own door*]: Yes, what is it? Oh – are you looking for me?

YOUNG MAN: Far from it.

FIRST HAG: Oh, but you must be; you were battering on my door.

YOUNG MAN: I'm damned if I was.

FIRST HAG: What do you want, then, coming here with a torch?

YOUNG MAN: I'm looking for a man with a limp.

FIRST HAG: With a limp what?

YOUNG MAN: He wouldn't do for you. You won't get what *you're* waiting for.

FIRST HAG: I will, by Aphrodite – whether you like it or not.

YOUNG MAN: I'm sorry, madam, we're not dealing with any cases more than sixty years old; we've put those off till later. Just now we're polishing off the under-twenties.

FIRST HAG: That was under the old rules, sweetheart: now you have to take us first – that's the law.

YOUNG MAN: It's optional. 'No player is obliged to take a piece unless he wishes to do so.'

FIRST HAG: You went to the dinner, though. You didn't say that was optional.

YOUNG MAN: I don't know what you're talking about. [*He knocks at* GIRL'S *door again.*] This is where I knock.

FIRST HAG: You've got a bit of knocking to do here first, love.

YOUNG MAN: Thanks, I've got a flour-bin already.

FIRST HAG: You like me really, I know you do. You're just embarrassed, meeting me out of doors like this. Come on, give me a kiss!

YOUNG MAN: Oh no! I'm frightened of your lover.

FIRST HAG: What lover?

YOUNG MAN: The great painter.

FIRST HAG: Who's he?

YOUNG MAN: The one who paints oil-flasks for funerals. Get inside quickly, you don't want him to catch you out of doors, do you?

FIRST HAG: I know what you're after! [*She grabs him by the wrist.*]

YOUNG MAN: And I know what you're after, by god.

FIRST HAG: By Aphrodite, my patron goddess, I won't let you go!

YOUNG MAN: You're out of your mind.

FIRST HAG: Not a bit of it. I'm going to take you to bed.

YOUNG MAN: I wonder why we use hooks to haul up our buckets! Just lower one of these old women into the tank and the job's done!

FIRST HAG: Don't you make fun of me, you naughty boy; just come this way.

YOUNG MAN [*struggling*]: But – you have no right – I'm not obliged to go with you. Not unless you've paid value-added tax on my – fixtures and fittings.

FIRST HAG: Oh yes, you are, by Aphrodite! I love sleeping with young men like you.

YOUNG MAN: And I hate sleeping with old women like you. And what's more, I'm not going to.

FIRST HAG [*producing a document*]: *This* will compel you to.

YOUNG MAN: What is it?

FIRST HAG: It's the law that says you must come with me.

YOUNG MAN: Read me what it says.

FIRST HAG: I was just going to. 'Be it known that the women hereby enact as follows: if a young man desire a young woman, it shall not be lawful for him to screw the same unless and until he has pleasured an old one; and if he refuses so to pleasure her in due priority it shall be lawful for the older woman to seize him by the tool and drag him away forthwith.'

YOUNG MAN: Yow! I'm in for a long-drawn-out evening, I can see that.

FIRST HAG: You have to obey *our* laws, now.

YOUNG MAN: Supposing I get a colleague or a friend to come and bail me out?

FIRST HAG: Contracts made by men no longer have legal force, except for amounts under one bushel.

YOUNG MAN: I'll swear an affidavit that I'm sick or something.

FIRST HAG: No, you can't wriggle out of this.

YOUNG MAN: I'll claim exemption, I'll say I'm engaged in essential trade.

FIRST HAG: You'll catch it hot if you do.

YOUNG MAN [*desperately*]: Oh, what am I to do?

FIRST HAG: Come to me.

YOUNG MAN: Must I?

FIRST HAG: You have no other choice.

YOUNG MAN: Then strew the floor with pungent herbs, break off four olive-twigs and set them down, bring out the oil-flasks, and place a pot of water at the door.

FIRST HAG [*thinking of weddings*]: And a garland – you'll buy me a garland too?

YOUNG MAN: Yes; made of wax – it's a *funeral* I'm talking about.
[FIRST HAG *begins to drag him into her house.*]
The moment we're inside, you'll fall to pieces!
[GIRL, *who has been watching from her window, hurriedly descends and comes out into the street.*]

GIRL: Hi! Where are you dragging that boy?

FIRST HAG: I'm taking him inside – he's mine!

GIRL: You're a fool, then. He's not old enough to sleep with you. You'd be more like a mother than a mistress. If people start doing this kind of thing we shall have little Oedipuses everywhere.
[FIRST HAG *splutters and almost swoons, relaxing her grip on* YOUNG MAN. *He and* GIRL *begin to push her backwards into her house.*]

FIRST HAG: You insolent minx, you're jealous, that's all it is. I'll pay you out for this!
[*They succeed in pushing* FIRST HAG *indoors, pull the door to and bolt it.*]

YOUNG MAN: Oh, thank heaven! And thank *you*, my sweetest, you really have done me a good turn, getting me away from that old dragon. You deserve a reward, and I'll see that you get it right away, this very night – a big fat reward.

[GIRL *takes his arm and is about to lead him into her own house.* SECOND HAG *comes out of the house on the right.*]

SECOND HAG: Now, then, you, where are you off to with that young man? Breaking the law, you are, I seen it written up. He's got to sleep with me first. It says so.

YOUNG MAN: Oh, help, this is a nightmare! Where did this one spring from? She's worse than the other!

SECOND HAG [*to* YOUNG MAN]: Come here! [*She pulls him away from the girl.*]

YOUNG MAN [*to* GIRL]: For pity's sake, don't stand there and let this one drag me off!

[GIRL *attempts to intervene, but* SECOND HAG, *with her free hand, pushes her into the house and bolts the door.*]

SECOND HAG: It's not me that's dragging you off, it's the *law.*

YOUNG MAN: It isn't, it's some kind of vampire, if you ask me. All swollen up with the blood of its victims.

SECOND HAG: Come along, my little chick! Hurry up, and don't argue.

YOUNG MAN: Oh – oh, I want to – er – sudden call of nature, you must excuse me a moment, I'll just step aside and – get my courage back. If I stay here another second there'll be an accident – I'm so scared.

SECOND HAG: Come along – this way; don't worry, you can do it when we get inside.

YOUNG MAN: I'll be doing a darn sight more than I want to, by the look of things. Look, I'll get two credit-worthy citizens to stand bail for me.

SECOND HAG: No, you won't, you'll just come along with me. [*She forces his head under her arm and starts to drag him towards her own house.*]

[*Enter* THIRD HAG, *from left.*]

THIRD HAG [*to* YOUNG MAN]: Here, where are you going with that woman?

YOUNG MAN [*unable to see her*]: I'm not going anywhere with her, I'm being dragged. But whoever you are, bless you for coming to my rescue; I was in a dreadful predic— [*He frees himself and turns to face his rescuer.*] Gods, goats and grandmothers, of all the ghastly apparitions! This is the worst yet, by far! What *is* this spectral shape, tell me, somebody, please! An ape, with white-lead all over it? A ghost, come back from the dead?

THIRD HAG: Don't mock me, just come over here. [*She seizes one of his arms.*]

SECOND HAG: No, you're to come over here, to *me*. [*She seizes his other arm.*]

THIRD HAG: I'll never let you go.

SECOND HAG: Nor will I.

YOUNG MAN: Help! You're tearing me apart, you loathsome creatures.

SECOND HAG: I'm the one you had to come with, it said so in the law.

THIRD HAG [*cackling*]: Not if an even uglier doth lay claim!

YOUNG MAN: How am I ever going to get to that pretty girl in there if you two harpies maul me to death first?

SECOND HAG: That's *your* problem. You've got your duty to do, first.

YOUNG MAN: Nothing for it: I'd better get it over, I suppose, or I'll never get away. Ugh! which shall I poke first?

SECOND HAG: Me, of course, dearie.

YOUNG MAN [*to* THIRD HAG]: Right, did you hear? Let me go to her.

THIRD HAG: No, you're coming this way, with me.

YOUNG MAN: I can't, she won't let go.

SECOND HAG: And I'm not going to, either.

THIRD HAG: Well, *I'm* not going to.

YOUNG MAN: Lucky you two don't work on the ferries.

SECOND HAG: Why?

YOUNG MAN: You'd pull the passengers in pieces between you.

SECOND HAG: Don't try to be funny. Just come along in with me.

THIRD HAG: You're coming with *me*, I say.

YOUNG MAN: This is worse than being in the dock, handcuffed to two screws. At least you don't have to screw *them*! Look, you two – I can't dip my paddle on two sides at once.

SECOND HAG: Oh, you'll manage all right: all you need is a plateful of tulip bulbs.

YOUNG MAN: Help, she's dragged me nearly to the door.

[*They have reached the door of* SECOND HAG's *house.* THIRD HAG *shows no signs of relaxing her grip.*]

THIRD HAG [*to* SECOND HAG]: You won't shake me off that way: I'll force my way in with you.

YOUNG MAN: Oh no, for pity's sake: one at a time is bad enough!

THIRD HAG: Whether you like it or not!

YOUNG MAN: Oh, what a fate! To have to spend all day and half the night rogering a toothless old crone, and then to find *this* ghastly apparition still waiting to have its turn before they lug it back to the graveyard. Zeus help me, it's no joke – the very thought of being shut up with these two ravening beasts! However, I suppose I must do my best to sail safely through these treacherous waters. And if I founder in the attempt, which seems only too bloody likely with these two strumpets at the helm, bury me right at the harbour mouth; and to mark the spot, take this one [*he indicates* THIRD HAG], if she doesn't die on you first, and tar the top half all over, pour molten lead round her ankles, stick her up on end, and you'll have a very fine imitation of a funeral oil-flask.

[*The two women haul him into* SECOND HAG's *house and the door is slammed shut.*]

SCENE FOUR

A lively street scene, somewhere in Athens. The public banquet is nearly over and many citizens (arriving from right) have already come away from it, in festive mood; they carry torches and seek female company, which is easily found. There is music and dancing. The CHORUS *mingle with the throng.*

[*Praxagora's* MAID *enters from right.*]

MAID: You happy people! And I'm happy too, and my mistress happiest of all. And all of you here at your doors, neighbours and citizens! And me too, in my humble capacity, what a time I'm having! I've had my hair done. Can you smell the perfume, isn't it marvellous? And the best thing of all, that Thasian wine, it's super, it really knocks you. Jars and jars of it. It goes to your head, you know. And it stays there. The effect doesn't wear off like it does with those other wines – oh, it's much the best, by golly it's good stuff. Drunk neat of course. Choose the wine with the best bouquet, I always say, and you'll stay in a good mood all night. – Excuse me, ladies, but do you happen to know where my master is? My mistress's husband, I should say.

CHORUS LEADER: I think you'll probably find him if you stay right here.

[BLEPYRUS *enters from left, with a group of* DANCING-GIRLS.]

MAID: You're dead right, here he comes, on his way to the feast. What a lucky man, what an in-credibly lucky man you are, sir.

BLEPYRUS: Me?

MAID: Yes, you. Luckier than anybody. Do you realize you're the only citizen, out of thirty thousand or more, who still has his dinner to look forward to?

CHORUS LEADER: A truly enviable situation.

MAID: *Now* where are you off to?

BLEPYRUS: I'm on my way to the banquet.

MAID: And high time too, by Aphrodite; you'll be the last to arrive, easily. But your wife has sent me to fetch you and bring you in, and the girls too. There's some Chian wine left, and lots of other good things too. So hurry up. And anyone in the audience who's enjoyed the play, and anyone in the judges' enclosure who isn't looking the other way, can come along too, you're welcome to everything.

BLEPYRUS: No, don't let's have any exceptions: invite them all, freely and generously: old men, striplings and boys. There's a dinner waiting for everybody – *at home*! I'm off to have mine now; and as you see, I have my torch with me [*he kisses one of the girls*], which is just as it should be.

CHORUS LEADER: Don't waste any more time, then, but take the girls along. And while you're on your way, we'll sing you a Supper Cantata. [*Turning to face the audience*] Just a word to the judges: are there any intellectuals among you? Judge our play by its wit and wisdom. Do you enjoy a good laugh? Judge us by the fun we've given you. – That should ensure top marks from *almost* all of you.

Oh, and don't let it make any difference that we were put on first; that's just how the lot fell out,²⁵ and you'll have to remember it all, and keep your oath, always to judge the choruses fairly, and not be like the sort of girl who can only remember the fellow she slept with last. [*To* CHORUS] And now, my dears, if we're going to sing them an appetizer, we'd better get on with it. And you [*to* BLE- PYRUS] can give us a dance, in the good old Cretan style.

BLEPYRUS: I will.

CHORUS LEADER [*to the* DANCING GIRLS]: And now come on, you nimble-footed nymphs, beat out the rhythm and – off we go!

[BLEPYRUS *and the* DANCING GIRLS *perform a wild dance, during which the* CHORUS *sing their 'supper cantata' at breakneck speed.*]

CHORUS: For –
                    there'll –
                    be –
        Mussels and whelks and slices of anchovy
        Octopus tunnyfish dogfish and skate
        Savoury chutney and sauce with a zing in it
        Lashings of pickle to pile on your plate
        Next come the birds with a glorious glaze on 'em
        Done on the spit what a pleasure to gaze on 'em
        Basted with honey and swimming in fat –
        Thrushes and blackbirds and wagtails and shagtails and
        Chicken and widgeon and skylark and pigeon and
        Duck, and a hare that's been cooked in red wine and a
        Gristly-winged Gramphus – and that's about that.

CHORUS LEADER [*to* BLEPYRUS]: Well, now that you've heard the menu, hurry up and get a plate and help yourself to porridge, in case you still feel hungry when you've finished.

[BLEPYRUS *and the* DANCING GIRLS *dance off, right, on their way to the banquet.*]

                    For –
                    they'll –
                    be –
        Stuffing themselves like mad, like mad
        And stuffing themselves like mad;
        Oh why on earth do we linger here
        When there's good food to be had?

March out, march out, with a lusty shout
And loud victorious cries,
For a play that ends with a good blow-out
Is sure to win first prize.
[CHORUS *march out, right, following* BLEPYRUS *and the* GIRLS.]

Wealth

Translated by Alan H. Sommerstein

Introductory Note to *Wealth*

Wealth was produced in 388 B.C., when Aristophanes was close to sixty. It stands in sharp contrast to all his other surviving plays, except, to some extent, *The Assemblywomen* (*c.* 391). The author's gift for fantasy is undiminished; but both the structure of the comedy itself, and the social situation that it presupposes, have undergone great changes.

The assumption of the young Aristophanes is that the world is all right at bottom, and its ills, notably war, are due to a combination of human wickedness and human stupidity, represented in *The Knights*, for instance, in the persons of the Paphlagonian and Thepeople. End the war, or get rid of Cleon, or revive the old standards of morality and public service, and all will be well. This optimistic philosophy has begun to be modified in *The Birds* (414), but it is still very strong in *The Frogs* (405), where both Euripides and Aeschylus are made to present simple, practicable recipes 'to save the City'. The hope is always for a return to normal, to a settled agricultural life where 'everything we needed we produced ourselves' (*The Acharnians*, line 36) under the benevolent protection of the gods.

Now Attica had returned to normal; for though there was again a state of war with Sparta, at least there were no invasions: Corinth, through whose territory any invasion would have had to pass, was now in alliance with Athens. But what disappointment! At home, Athens had suffered catastrophic losses in population and in agricultural resources; there was little exportable surplus either of rural or of urban products, and the farmer in particular was hard pressed even to support his family. Abroad, too, Athens' economic position had been much weakened by her loss of political supremacy; her currency reserves were low, and the war of 395–387 was fought largely from hand to mouth. Most people were poorer than they had been; and this time, there was nobody to blame. Those who had been responsible for the defeat of 404 were long dead. Of living politicians, some were good, some bad, none could improve the situation in any fundamental way. That situation was no man's fault; must it not, then, be the fault of the gods? Once again Aristophanes returns to the theme 'if we do this, all will be well'; but this time the necessary action is something which has no real-world counterpart at all.

The effect of Wealth's cure is felt in two stages, though the poet does not make the order of events very clear. First he arranges that virtue shall always bring prosperity and vice ... versa. To this stage belong the Good Man – Informer scene and the Old Woman – Young Man scene. But then it is to be expected that vice, deprived of its rewards, will disappear; and if Wealth is true to his principles, he must then make the whole population rich. And he does; with the result illustrated in the last two scenes.

It is to this second stage of the revolution that the *agon* looks forward. It is striking that we still have an *agon*; it is also striking how clumsily it is worked into the play. Poverty arrives from nowhere and goes off nowhere; and though she officially loses the debate, she is given powerful arguments to which Chremylus and Blepsidemus can find no adequate answer, as they themselves admit ('You won't persuade us, even if you do'). Normally Aristophanes encourages us to ignore the disastrous consequences that would ensue if his comic fantasy were acted out in real life; or rather, he occupies us so much with more interesting things that it does not occur to us to think of these consequences. Here he spells out the consequences in the plainest manner – and then continues with his fantasy as though nothing had happened. I cannot regard this as a very felicitous decision.

Already in *The Assemblywomen* Aristophanes had very much reduced the role of the Chorus and the lyric element generally. This seems to have been to conform to current trends rather than because his powers in lyric were failing; it is noteworthy that the longest lyric section (lines 893 ff.) is introduced by an apology ('This may bore the audience a bit, but it is quite amusing and comic'). In *Wealth* this development goes further, and after the *parodos* our Greek text gives the Chorus nothing but a few odd lines. Between scenes, however, manuscripts often have the note *chorou*, literally 'of the Chorus'. It has been disputed exactly what the nature of these choral performances was; I incline to the view that they consisted, as in earlier days, of both song and dance, and one passage in *Wealth* seems to support this (see the beginning of Act Two, Scene Two, with note 37). Be that as it may, these performances must now have been regarded merely as interludes, not as part of the play proper, and even if their words were written by the poet they were not included in the text that went into circulation. The use even of non-lyric metres other than the ordinary spoken iambic is also much reduced, with the result that *Wealth*, though one of Aristophanes' shortest plays, has more spoken iambic lines than any other of his surviving works. All these tendencies are indications that the transition to New Comedy is in progress, though *Wealth* remains essentially an Old Comedy: Aristophanes never made the assumption, basic to New Comedy, that the laws of nature and of human nature must always be respected.

There are in the play some signs that the poet was a tired man. In particular his agility with words is much diminished: throughout there is less sparkle and more logic. But the comic idea is as brilliant as ever, and often we can recognize the old Aristophanes, as in the vigorous *parodos* with its skit on a popular cantata by Philoxenus, or in Hermes' sudden transformation from blustering minion of the tyrant Zeus to beggar at the door.

The temple of Asclepius, where Wealth is cured, is most probably meant to be that at Zea, a district of the Peiraeus; but Aristophanes leaves the matter quite vague. The cure itself, including the appearance of the god with his attendants and the snakes, is similar to a number of cases described on a temple inscription from Epidaurus.

About twenty years previously Aristophanes had written another play with the same title. The two have occasionally been confused both in ancient and modern times, for which there was really no excuse. We know virtually nothing further about the earlier play.

CHARACTERS

CARION *a slave*
CHREMYLUS *his master, an elderly farmer*
WEALTH *a blind god*
CHORUS OF FARMERS
BLEPSIDEMUS *a friend of Chremylus*
POVERTY *a horrific goddess*
WIFE *to Chremylus*
GOOD MAN
INFORMER
OLD WOMAN
YOUNG MAN *formerly her lover*
HERMES *messenger of the gods*
PRIEST *of Zeus the Saviour*

SLAVE *to the Good Man*
WITNESS *brought by the Informer*
OTHER CITIZENS AND SLAVES

ACT ONE

SCENE: *A street in Athens; in the background the house of* CHREMYLUS.

[*There enters a blind old man, meanly clothed, who will prove to be* WEALTH. *Behind him, wearing the laurel wreaths that show they have just come from the Delphic oracle, come an elderly man and a youngish slave; these are* CHREMYLUS *and* CARION. CHREMYLUS *is evidently dogging the blind man's footsteps, but* CARION *is not very interested, and soon turns to the audience and gives vent to his feelings.*]

CARION: Zeus, but it's hard being a slave when your master's out of his mind! You can give the best advice in the world, but if your owner disagrees, *you* have to take the consequences of *his* actions! Fate's made your body not your own – it belongs to the man who buys you. Well, enough of that. But I've a complaint against Apollo too, yes, Apollo, him with the golden tripod. He claims to be a healer and a prophet. But now here's my master, just come away from his oracle, and look what a mood's come over him! Following in the footsteps of a blind man – it's directly contrary to nature! Normally the seeing guide the blind. Not master. He lets a blind man lead *him* around and forces me to come with him, and that although the man won't say a syllable to him. Well, even if he keeps quiet, I won't. [*He goes up to* CHREMYLUS.] Master, I insist on your telling me why we're following that man. If you don't I'll just keep on asking and asking and asking. You can't hit me, you know; I've got a sacred wreath on.

CHREMYLUS: If you go on pestering I'll take it off you, and it'll hurt you even more.

CARION: You just dare! I assure you, I won't stop asking till you've told me who he is. Aren't I always completely faithful to you?

CHREMYLUS: Well, I won't keep it from you. After all, you're the most reliable man and the best thief in all my household. The thing is, I consider myself a pious and upright person, but I've not done well in life. I'm a poor man.

CARION: I know.

CHREMYLUS: While temple-robbers, politicians, informers, wicked men of all kinds, have become very rich.

CARION: True.

CHREMYLUS: So this was what I went to Delphi to ask the god. As far as I was concerned, I reckoned I'd shot my bolt in life. But for my son – the only one I've got – I wanted to know if he ought to change his ways and become a criminal, a villain, a no-good – because that seemed to be the only way to get on in life.

CARION: And what did Phoebus' laurel wreaths shriek forth?[1]

CHREMYLUS: I'll tell you. Apollo said this. The first person I met on coming out of the temple, he said I should never on any account let him go, but I should persuade him to come home with me.

CARION: And who was the first person you met?

CHREMYLUS [pointing to the blind man]: Him.

CARION: And you mean you don't understand, you clot, what the god was trying to tell you? He was saying your son ought to follow the current fashion.

CHREMYLUS: What makes you think that?

CARION: Because even a blind man can see that it's much more profitable, in this age we're living in, to be a no-good.

CHREMYLUS: It's inconceivable that the oracle should mean that. It's something much bigger. Now if only this man would tell us who he is and why he's come here and what he wants, then we might find out what the oracle does mean.

CARION [going up to WEALTH and raising his fist]: Here, tell us who you are, or I'll give you one! Quick, out with it!

WEALTH: Go to blazes!

CARION [to CHREMYLUS]: That's a funny name.

CHREMYLUS: That's what he says to you, because you asked him in such a brusque and unrefined way. Now watch me. [To WEALTH] Sir, if you like men who keep their word, tell me, please, who you are.

WEALTH: Go to hell!

CARION: Oh, sir, it's an omen! You will go there – taking him with you!

CHREMYLUS [*to* WEALTH]: I swear, my man, you'll regret this.

CARION: Yes, tell us your name, or I'll do you!

WEALTH: Sir, please leave me alone.

CHREMYLUS: Not a hope.

CARION: I think what I said was best, master: I should do him. I can stand him on top of a cliff and just leave him there so he'll fall and break his neck.

CHREMYLUS: All right. Take his feet! [*They take hold of* WEALTH.]

WEALTH: No, stop, stop!

CHREMYLUS: You're going to tell us, then?

WEALTH: But if I tell you, I know you'll ill-treat me and refuse to let me go.

CHREMYLUS: I swear we will let you go if you want.

WEALTH: Then first of all, unhand me. [*They do so.*]

CHREMYLUS: There you are.

WEALTH: Now listen. I was going to keep my identity a secret, but it seems I've no choice but to reveal it. My name is Wealth.

CARION: You swine, you're Wealth and you kept quiet about it?

CHREMYLUS: Wealth, in such a squalid get-up? Apollo, Zeus and all the gods! do you mean you're really him?

WEALTH: I am.

CHREMYLUS: Wealth himself?

WEALTH: His very self.

CHREMYLUS: But so dirty! Where have you come from?

WEALTH: I've been staying with Patrocles, and *he's* never washed in all his born days.

CHREMYLUS: But how did you come to suffer from – your present affliction?

WEALTH: It was Zeus did this to me, out of spite against mankind. In my youth I used to say I would only visit the upright and wise and modest. So he made me blind so I couldn't know who they were. That just shows how much ill-will he bears against decent people.

CHREMYLUS: And yet it's only the good and the upright who pay Zeus himself due honour.

WEALTH: Quite true.

CHREMYLUS: Tell me: if you got your sight back again, would you keep away from the wicked?

WEALTH: I would.

CHREMYLUS: And come to the righteous again?

WEALTH: With pleasure; it's such a long time since I've seen any of them.

CHREMYLUS [*taking a look round the audience*]: Not surprising; I've got my sight, and I've not seen any for a long time either.

WEALTH: Now may I go? You know all about me now.

CHREMYLUS: All the more reason to keep you. [*Blocks his way.*]

WEALTH: Didn't I *say* you were going to do me harm?

CHREMYLUS: No, do listen and don't leave us! I assure you, search as you will, you won't find a better man than me.

CARION: Because there isn't one – except me.

WEALTH: That's what they all say; but as soon as they get hold of me and become rich, why, they're worse than anyone.

CHREMYLUS: I know – but still, not everyone is bad.

WEALTH [*emphatically*]: Everyone!

CARION: You've got something coming to you for that!

CHREMYLUS: But really, just listen and let me tell you what a lot of good we can do for you if you stay with us. I think – I think – by the gods' grace – I can get you cured of this – this eye disease and make you see again.

WEALTH: No, you won't. I don't *want* to see again.

CHREMYLUS: What?!

CARION: This one's a right nut!

WEALTH: If Zeus got wind of it, he'd crush me completely!

CHREMYLUS: You clot, isn't that what he's doing anyway? Letting you wander homeless and stumble on every stone?

WEALTH: I don't know, but I'm terribly afraid of him.

CHREMYLUS: Well, really, what a coward of a god! Why, don't you realize, if you regained your sight even for a short time, the monarchy of Zeus and all his thunderbolts wouldn't be worth three obols!

WEALTH [*scandalized*]: Sh, you mustn't say that!

CHREMYLUS: Sh yourself. I can prove to you that you've got far more power than Zeus.

WEALTH: *You* can prove that *I've*—?

CHREMYLUS: I swear. Point one: why is Zeus king of the gods?

CARION: Because he's got the most money.

CHREMYLUS: And who provides him with the money?

CARION [*to* WEALTH]: *You* do.

CHREMYLUS: And why do people sacrifice to him? It's for Wealth, isn't it?

CARION: Why, yes; they even pray to be rich in so many words.

CHREMYLUS: Doesn't it follow, then, that Zeus owes his power to Wealth here, and that Wealth could overthrow him if he wanted to?

WEALTH: How do you mean?

CHREMYLUS: I mean that if you so chose you could stop all sacrifices – oxen, barley cakes, the lot.

WEALTH: How could I do that?

CHREMYLUS: Why, if you don't provide the money, nobody will be able to buy anything to sacrifice. So if Zeus makes any trouble, you can depose him single-handed.

WEALTH: I still don't get it. You mean they sacrifice to *him* for *my* sake?

CHREMYLUS: That's right. And what's more, whatever's bright and beautiful and joyful in human life comes through you. Everything in the world is controlled by wealth.

CARION: Look at me. I was a free man; I slip a bit into debt and – I'm a slave.

CHREMYLUS: They say that in Corinth the tarts there, when a customer comes in who's poor, they just ignore him, but a rich man gets instant admission – even by the back entrance!

CARION: Same with the boys: they turn down men who really love them and go where the gold is.

CHREMYLUS: Ah, that's only the young *pros*, not the young *gentlemen*. A young *gentleman* never asks for money.

CARION: Then what does he ask for?

CHREMYLUS: Well, maybe a thoroughbred horse or a pack of hounds.

CARION: That's probably because they're ashamed to ask right out for money, so they flavour their vice with a respectable name.

CHREMYLUS: Anyway, Wealth, every art and craft and invention in the whole world owes its existence to you. It's for your sake that A sits making shoes –

CARION: – that B works metal and C carpenters –

CHREMYLUS: – and D is a goldsmith – and his very raw material comes from you –

CARION: E steals clothes, F burgles houses –

CHREMYLUS: G is a fuller –

CARION: H washes blankets –

CHREMYLUS: J tans hides –

CARION: K sells onions –

CHREMYLUS: And when L gets caught with M's wife –

CARION: It's through you that he gets off with being plucked and singed![2]

WEALTH: Good heavens, I never knew that!

CHREMYLUS: The Great King of Persia owes his proud position to you – the Assembly owes its quorum to you[3] –

CARION: Our warships owe their crews to you –

CHREMYLUS: Corinth owes its Foreign Legion to you[4] –

CARION: And with any luck, Pamphilus[5] will owe his conviction to you.

CHREMYLUS: And his needle-selling friend along with him.

CARION: It's because of you that Agyrrhius farts so freely[6] –

CHREMYLUS: It's for you that Philepsius tells his short stories, it's for you that the Egyptians have become our allies[7] –

CARION: It's for your sake that Lais is in love with Philonides[8] – and as for Timotheus's Tower[9] –

CHREMYLUS: May it come down on *your* head! So, Wealth, everything that's done in the world is done because of you. You alone are responsible for everything, be it good or evil.

CARION: You can see when there's a war; whichever side Wealth comes down on always wins.

WEALTH: You mean I can achieve all this by myself?

CHREMYLUS: Yes, and much more besides. Nobody ever has his fill of you. Anything else one can have too much of – for example, love –

CARION: Or bread –

CHREMYLUS: Or culture –

CARION: Or dried fruit –

CHREMYLUS: Or honour –

CARION: Or cakes –

CHREMYLUS: Or valour –

CARION: Or figs –

CHREMYLUS: Or ambition –

CARION: Or barley buns –

CHREMYLUS: Or power –

CARION: Or soup –

CHREMYLUS: But no one ever has enough of you. If a man has eighty thousand drachmas, he's all the more set on getting a hundred thousand; and once he's got that, he says life's not worth living unless he makes a quarter of a million.

WEALTH: I think what you say is very true. But there's just one thing I'm worried about.

CHREMYLUS: Yes, what?

WEALTH: This power you say I have – how can I hope to exercise it?

CHREMYLUS: I see – then it's true what they all say: Wealth's a coward.

WEALTH: Certainly not. It's a lie started by some burglar or other. He broke into a house and found nothing he could take, because everything was locked up. Mere prudence on my part, but he called it cowardice.

CHREMYLUS: Well, anyway, don't let it bother you. Be a man, lend a willing hand in our plan, and I'll give you sharper eyes than a lynx[10]!

WEALTH: But how can a mere mortal like you do that?

CHREMYLUS: My hope stems from what Apollo himself told me as his Delphic bay-trees trembled.[11]

WEALTH: What, Apollo is in on the idea?

CHREMYLUS: Yes.

WEALTH: Be careful –

CHREMYLUS: Don't trouble yourself about it, man! I'll see to everything, I assure you, even if it costs me my life.

CARION: With my help, if you like.

CHREMYLUS: And we'll have plenty of other assistants as well – all the honest men who don't have bread to eat.

WEALTH: Not very useful allies, I'd have thought.

CHREMYLUS: Ah, but wait until they become rich again! Carion, will you run off –

CARION: And do what?

CHREMYLUS: Tell all my farming friends to come here. I expect you'll find them doing their own donkey work in the fields. I want them all to be here, so they can get their fair share of our dear Wealth.

CARION: All right, I'm off. [*Shouts into the house.*] Here, will someone come and take in my sacrificial meat?

CHREMYLUS: I'll see to that; you run off.

[*He takes the piece of meat which CARION has been carrying on a skewer; CARION departs.*]

And now, Wealth, greatest of all the gods, come inside and make your home with me. This is the house which it's now up to you to fill with good things, by fair means or foul.

WEALTH: Ah, but I tell you, I'm always very embarrassed when I come to stay with anyone – because it's never yet done me any good. If my host is a miser, he immediately buries me underground, and then if an honest friend of his comes asking for ever such a little bit of me, he vows he's never seen me in his life. On the other hand, if I go to live with some wild young man, he squanders me so fast on whoring and gambling that before you can bat an eyelid I'm out on my ear, naked, in the street!

CHREMYLUS: Because you've never hit the happy medium; and that, more or less, is what I'd call myself. I'm as thrifty as any man, but when the occasion's right, I like spending too. Let's go inside. I want you to meet my wife, and my only son, whom I love more than anything in the world – except you of course.

WEALTH: No doubt!

CHREMYLUS: After all, there's no point in lying to you!

[*They go into the house, still talking. Presently CARION reappears from the wings. He is addressing the CHORUS of elderly farmers, who have been following him some distance behind.*]

CARION:

> You who eat the humble thyme
>   Sharing with my master,
> You who love good honest work,
>   Hurry, hurry, faster!
> Friends and neighbours, come in haste,
>   Pray you, don't delay!
> Seize your opportunity –
>   Now's decision day!

[*The* CHORUS *are now entering, as fast as their uncertain legs can carry them.*]

CHORUS:

> Can't you see the haste we make,
> Can't your eyes behold
> We're as fast as we can be
> Now we're weak and old?
> Do you think we ought to run?
> We reply, No fear,
> Till you let us know just why
> Your master's called us here!

CARION: I told you that long ago, it was you that weren't listening. My master says that you will now be able to free yourselves from your old, cold, dissatisfied life and pass your days in happiness!

LEADER: How come? What's happened?

CARION: Why, he's just brought this man home – a very odd old man, bent, unwashed, miserable, wrinkled, bald, toothless, the lot. And I've a strong suspicion he's lost half his cock into the bargain!

LEADER: What? But this sounds marvellous. Tell me again. The man's obviously got heaps of money.

CARION: Heaps of age and misery, that's all I know.

LEADER: Come on, you're having us on! Don't think you'll get away with it! I do have a stick, you know! [*Threatens* CARION *with it.*]

CARION: Is that the sort of person you think I am? You fancy I'd tell you a string of lies, do you?

LEADER: Bold as brass, isn't he? Your legs, boy, are crying out loud for a pair of good tight fetters!

CARION: And *you've* been drawn for jury service in the Court of the Coffin.[12] Off you go! Charon's handing out the tickets now!

LEADER: Get lost, you teasing little monkey! You're just playing with us, you haven't told us a word yet. Why does your master want us here? We're very busy people, you know, we don't have much time to spare. We were so keen to get here, we didn't even stop to pick any thyme to eat.

CARION: All right, I'll tell you. My master, friends, has brought home – Wealth himself! And *he's* going to make you all wealthy.

LEADER: We can really all be rich?

CARION: You'll all be like King Midas, except for the ass's ears!

LEADER:
>   If this is true, why then – O joy! O bliss!
>   Come all, and let us gaily dance –

CARION: Like this!
[*He sings as he and the* CHORUS *enact in dance the Cyclops and Circe*
stories:]

> I'll be the Cyclops, tra-la-la, and you will be my flocks;
> As with my feet I caper, I'll lead you o'er the rocks;
> Now bleat, you lambs, and cry, you goats, whose smell the senses
>   shocks;
> Oh follow me (for it's breakfast time) and raise on high your cocks.

CHORUS [*as Odysseus and his men*]:

> We'll seek the Cyclops, tra-la-la, and we'll the Cyclops find,
> A beggar's pack upon his back with herbs of rustic kind,
> And while he sleeps beside his flocks (for he's been thoroughly
>   wined)
> We'll put out his eye with a burning stake, and leave the Cyclops
>   blind!

CARION:

> And now will I be Circe who the magic potions made;
> The comrades of Philonides[13] in Corinth she persuad-
> ed just like *boars* to eat the shit she kneaded and purveyed –
> 'Oh, follow your mother, pigs,' she said, and grunting they
>   obeyed.

CHORUS:

> Then we will capture Circe who our comrades did defile,
> And like Odysseus hang you by the balls in manner vile,
> And rub your goatlike nose in shit; and open-mouthed the while
> 'Oh, follow your mother, pigs,' you'll say, in Aristyllus style![14]

CARION:

> Well, that's enough of jesting now, for no more can I play;
> You dance some more, and I meantime will try and spirit away
> Some bread and meat from master's store, for I've not eaten today;
> So I'll bite and munch till I've had my lunch, and then back to the
>   fray.

[CARION *goes into the house, while the* CHORUS *perform another*
dance. Then CHREMYLUS *comes out.*]

CHREMYLUS: I'd say 'good morning', friends, only that's rather antiquated and *passé* these days; so – blessings on you all! Thank you for coming so readily and strenuously and effortfully. Be my allies, and you will earn the name of Saviours of a God.

LEADER: Have no fear; I'll look as daggers as you could wish. After all it would be ridiculous, when we push and shove every Assembly day for the sake of a mere three obols,[15] if we were to stand aside while Wealth himself was lost to us.

CHREMYLUS: Ah, here's Blepsidemus coming, and pretty fast too! He must have heard about what's happened.

BLEPSIDEMUS [*entering hurriedly and excitedly*]: What's it all about? How come Chremylus has got rich all of a sudden? I just don't believe it. But that was what they said – this tremendous rumour going round the barbers' shops – that he'd become wealthy overnight. And what really amazed me was, his reaction to this happy stroke of fortune was to send for all his friends. I mean, that's just not the Athenian way.

CHREMYLUS: Blepsidemus, I'll tell you the whole story. Today there has been an improvement in my fortunes, and I want you, as a friend, to share in it.

BLEPSIDEMUS: Then what they say is true? You've really got rich?

CHREMYLUS: No, but I will soon, the gods willing. There is – there is – an element of risk about the matter.

BLEPSIDEMUS: What kind of risk?

CHREMYLUS: Sort of –

BLEPSIDEMUS: Come on, let's hear it.

CHREMYLUS: If we succeed, it means lasting, permanent prosperity. But if we fail, utter destruction.

BLEPSIDEMUS: This has the look of a suspicious package. I don't like it. To be all of a sudden so enormously rich, and at the same time afraid – it's the behaviour of a person whose hands are not clean.

CHREMYLUS [*indignant*]: What do you mean, not clean?

BLEPSIDEMUS: For example, if you've stolen some gold or silver from the god of Delphi, and been seized by a fit of repentance –

CHREMYLUS: So may Apollo protect me, I have not!

BLEPSIDEMUS: Now, none of that rot! I see it very well.

CHREMYLUS: You needn't suspect me of anything of the kind –

BLEPSIDEMUS: Ah, there's no honesty in the world! We're all the slaves of Gain!

CHREMYLUS: I think you're off your rocker.

BLEPSIDEMUS [*sentimentally shaking his head*]: How unlike his old ways!

CHREMYLUS: Bad case of the black bile,[16] if you ask me.

BLEPSIDEMUS: And look how shifty-eyed he's gone! His very face proclaims him a villain.

CHREMYLUS: Ah, I get what you're croaking on about! You think I've stolen something, and you want your whack.

BLEPSIDEMUS [*on his guard*]: My whack? What of?

CHREMYLUS: But that's not what it is; it's something quite different.

BLEPSIDEMUS: It isn't theft? You don't mean to say it was armed robbery?

CHREMYLUS: You're stark staring bonkers.

BLEPSIDEMUS: Then – oh, surely not embezzlement!

CHREMYLUS: Certainly not.

BLEPSIDEMUS: Really, in Heracles' name, what can one do? He just will not tell the truth.

CHREMYLUS: Look, you're accusing me before you know what's happened.

BLEPSIDEMUS: Tell you what, man; I can put everything in order at a very low cost, before the whole City gets to know of this. I only have to stop the prosecutors' mouths with a bit of silver.[17]

CHREMYLUS: I bet. You'll be a real friend to me – spend three hundred drachmas and bill me twelve hundred.

BLEPSIDEMUS: I can see a man sitting in the dock with a suppliant's olive branch, his wife and children beside him, for all the world like the Children of Heracles in Pamphilus' picture![18]

CHREMYLUS: No, stupid. I'm going to make you all rich right away – all the honest and wise and virtuous people – but nobody else.[19]

BLEPSIDEMUS: All at one go? You must have stolen a lot!

CHREMYLUS: You'll be the death of me!

BLEPSIDEMUS: You'll be your own, as far as I can see.[20]

CHREMYLUS: No, I won't, you idiot; I've got Wealth.

BLEPSIDEMUS: What kind of wealth?

CHREMYLUS: Wealth himself. The god.

BLEPSIDEMUS [*with a complete change of attitude*]: Where is he, where is he?

CHREMYLUS: Inside.

BLEPSIDEMUS: Inside where?

CHREMYLUS: Inside my house.

BLEPSIDEMUS: In your house?

CHREMYLUS: Exactly.

BLEPSIDEMUS: Go to hell, Wealth isn't in your house, is he?

CHREMYLUS: I swear he is.

BLEPSIDEMUS: Is that the truth?

CHREMYLUS: The truth.

BLEPSIDEMUS: At your family fireside?

CHREMYLUS: I swear it by Poseidon.

BLEPSIDEMUS: You do mean Poseidon the sea-god?

CHREMYLUS: If there's any other Poseidon, by him.

BLEPSIDEMUS: Then why don't you send this Wealth round to all your friends?

CHREMYLUS: I haven't got to that stage yet.

BLEPSIDEMUS: What do you mean? You haven't got to the stage of sharing him out, eh?

CHREMYLUS: That's right. First we've got to –

BLEPSIDEMUS: Yes?

CHREMYLUS: To cure his blindness.

BLEPSIDEMUS: Whose blindness?

CHREMYLUS: Wealth's. We've got to restore his sight, one way or another.

BLEPSIDEMUS: What, you mean he's really blind?

CHREMYLUS: He is indeed.

BLEPSIDEMUS: No wonder he never came to me.

CHREMYLUS: Well, now, the gods willing, he *is* going to come.

BLEPSIDEMUS: Oughtn't we to call a doctor right away?

CHREMYLUS: What doctor? There *are* no doctors in town. We've no pay to offer, so we've no practitioners.[21]

BLEPSIDEMUS: Let's have a look. [*He inspects the audience.*]

CHREMYLUS: I tell you there aren't any.

BLEPSIDEMUS: You're right, there isn't.

CHREMYLUS: No, my idea was to take him to the Temple of Asclepius and let him spend the night there. In fact I'm already making preparations.

BLEPSIDEMUS: First-rate! Don't let's wait then; let's get on with it. [*He makes to go into the house.*]

CHREMYLUS: I'm coming.

BLEPSIDEMUS: Hurry up!

CHREMYLUS: I am.

[*They are just about to go inside when* POVERTY *enters, a hideous old woman dressed all in black.*]

POVERTY [*pointing melodramatically at* CHREMYLUS *and* BLEPSI-DEMUS]: You miserable humanoids! You audacious perpetrators of lawless impiety! You monuments of temerity!

[*The two take to their heels.*]

Where do you think you are off to? Stay where you are!

[*They stop in their tracks, terrified.*]

BLEPSIDEMUS [*under his breath*]: Oh, Heracles!

POVERTY: I shall destroy you, as befits your evil schemes! You are venturing on an utterly intolerable course of action, such as no other man or god has ever dared before. You are doomed!

CHREMYLUS: And who may you be? You look like a bad case of anaemia.

BLEPSIDEMUS: A Fury escaped from a tragedy, perhaps. She has that wild tragic look in her eyes.

CHREMYLUS: She's not got any torch, though.[22]

BLEPSIDEMUS: Then she'd best look out!

POVERTY: What do you take me to be?

CHREMYLUS: An innkeeper, perhaps, or an omelette-vendor? Otherwise you wouldn't scream at us like that for doing you no harm at all.

POVERTY: No harm? You seek to expel me from the whole country, and you call it no harm?

CHREMYLUS: Not quite the whole country; we'll leave you a good high cliff to jump off. But out with it, straight away: who are you?

POVERTY: One who this very day will make you pay the penalty for conspiring to abolish me in this land.

BLEPSIDEMUS: She's not mine hostess from round the corner, is she, the one who never serves me a full half-pint?

POVERTY: No, I am Poverty, for many years your constant companion.

BLEPSIDEMUS: Apollo! Gods! Let's get out of here! [*He turns to flee.*]

CHREMYLUS: Here, what are you up to, you cowardly creature? Stay here!

BLEPSIDEMUS: Not on your life!

CHREMYLUS: Stop, stop! Do you want it said that two men fled in terror from one woman?

BLEPSIDEMUS: Woman? She's Poverty, fathead, the most vicious pest the world has ever bred.

CHREMYLUS: Stop, I beg you, stop!

BLEPSIDEMUS: I will not! [*He is about to disappear into the wings.*]

CHREMYLUS: Blepsidemus! Are we to be the greatest cowards in history? To desert the god we serve and run away without putting up a fight because we're scared of this – apparition?

BLEPSIDEMUS: But how *can* we fight? What weapons can we use? All the shields and breastplates we've got *she's* handed over, damn her, to the pawnbroker!

CHREMYLUS: Take courage! Wealth will handle her single-handed and beat her, be sure of that.

[BLEPSIDEMUS *slowly and fearfully returns.*]

POVERTY: How dare you utter a syllable, you scum, caught red-handed as you are in the act of committing such a foul crime?

CHREMYLUS: And how dare *you*, you swine, come here and insult us? What wrong have we done you?

POVERTY: Heavens above! You do not think you're wronging me in attempting to restore the sight of Wealth?

CHREMYLUS: That's not doing you any wrong: it's conferring a blessing on all mankind.

POVERTY: What is this blessing of yours?

CHREMYLUS: First and foremost, kicking you out of Greece.

POVERTY: Kicking me out? Don't you realize this is the greatest evil you could possibly do to mankind?

CHREMYLUS: Oh, I don't know. I can think of a greater one. Like *forgetting* to kick you out.

POVERTY: On that question I should like to explain my position right here and now. If I prove that I alone am responsible for everything good in the world, and that only because of me are you even alive – well, if I fail, you may do what you please.

CHREMYLUS: You dare to speak so, you infernal monster?

POVERTY: And I'd advise you to listen. I expect to prove with great ease that if you intend to make all honest men wealthy, you're making a great mistake.

BLEPSIDEMUS: Bludgeons and pilleries of the world, come to our aid!

POVERTY: Now, don't be childish and shout before you hear what I've got to say.

BLEPSIDEMUS: It's impossible *not* to scream when you hear such rubbish.

POVERTY: Only if you've no sense.

CHREMYLUS: Tell me, what penalty shall I name in your indictment, to be imposed if you are convicted?

POVERTY: Whatever you please.

CHREMYLUS: Excellent.

POVERTY: Provided that you will undergo the same penalty should you lose the case.

CHREMYLUS [*to* BLEPSIDEMUS]: What do you think? Will twenty deaths be enough?

BLEPSIDEMUS: For her, yes; *we'll* be quite satisfied with two.

POVERTY: Well, you might just as well die right now. There's nothing anyone could possibly find to say truthfully against me.

LEADER [*to* CHREMYLUS *and* BLEPSIDEMUS]:
Now find some clever things to say, your argument to clinch;
Whate'er you do, do not be soft and never give an inch.

CHREMYLUS: I think it is obvious to everybody that it is right that good men should be prosperous, while bad men who don't honour the gods should be just the opposite. This is what we have always wished for, and now, with great difficulty, we have found a way to bring it about, a splendid and noble plan, advantageous from every point of view. If Wealth now recovers his sight and ceases to wander about in darkness, he will visit only the good and never leave them, and keep well away from the wicked and impious; and that way everyone will be good and rich and pious too. Now what could anyone devise that would be better for mankind than that?

BLEPSIDEMUS: Nothing, I'll bear witness to that; don't bother to ask her.

CHREMYLUS: The present state of our human life can only be described as utter madness and lunacy. Many wicked men live in prosperity through their ill-gotten gains, while others of great virtue are poor and hungry and always accompanied by *you*. So I

say again that if Wealth recovers his sight and puts an end to all
this, this is the surest way to bring the greatest benefits to all men.
POVERTY: You two old men are certainly very easily persuaded to
lose your wits! You're real members of the Stuff and Nonsense
Club! If what you desire were to happen, it would by no means be
to your advantage. If Wealth were to see once more and divide
himself in fair shares to all, no one would pursue any trade or craft
any more. And with no trades or crafts, who'll do your metalwork?
Who'll build your ships? Who'll be your tailors, your turners, your
cobblers, your brickmakers, your launderers, your tanners?
Who'll break up the clods with his plough and harvest the fruits
of the Goddess of Corn, if it's open to him to forget about all that
and live in idleness?
CHREMYLUS: What rubbish you talk! All those things you mentioned, why, our slaves will do them for us.
POVERTY: And where will you get your slaves from?
CHREMYLUS: Buy them, of course.
POVERTY: But why should anyone sell them, if he's already got all
the money he wants?
CHREMYLUS: Oh, say a merchant coming from Thessaly, where all
the kidnappers are, to sell them at a profit.
POVERTY: But on the plan *you're* putting forward, there just won't
be any kidnappers. If a man's rich, why should he want to risk his
life doing something like that? So you see, you'll have to do all
your own ploughing and digging and all the other back-breaking
work. You'll have an even more miserable life than now.
CHREMYLUS: I hope *you* do!
POVERTY: You won't even have a bed to lie on: there won't be any.
No carpets: who's going to weave if he's not short of money? No
scents to perfume the bride with, no expensive richly-coloured
clothes to dress her in. And if you can't have any of these things,
what earthly point is there in being rich? Whereas with me you
have all your needs supplied in plenty. Every craftsman feels that
he is my slave: that I sit behind him, compelling him by sheer need
to seek a way of earning a livelihood.
CHREMYLUS: Huh! What do you ever give anyone? Blisters from
the bath-house stove?[23] A crowd of old women and starving little
children? Not to mention the innumerable lice and mosquitoes and

fleas that buzz around your head till they drive you mad, waking you up in the small hours as if to say 'Get on your feet, else you won't eat!' Rags to wear, instead of a proper coat. Nothing to lie on but a mattress stuffed with rushes, full of bugs, that would waken you even if you were asleep to begin with. A rotting rush-mat for a carpet. A dirty great stone for a pillow. And to eat! Shoots of mallow instead of bread. Withered radish leaves instead of buns. No chair to sit on, you have to use the top of a broken storage jar. No kneading-trough for your dough, only a broken rib from a cask. Have I adequately summarize' the incalculable blessings you bestow on mankind?

POVERTY: You're not talking about my kind of life at all; what you object to is the life of a pauper.

CHREMYLUS: Well, Poverty and Pauperism are sisters, aren't they?

POVERTY: Yes, you would say that – just as you say there's no dif-ference between Thrasybulus[24] and a dictator like Dionysius! The man who walks in my ways never has suffered and never will suffer the privations you speak of. You were talking about a pauper, who has absolutely nothing to live on. Poverty is quite different. It means living a thrifty life, sticking to your job, not having anything to spare but not having to go short either.

CHREMYLUS: A happy life, I must say! To toil and scrimp all your days, and then not to leave behind you enough to pay for your funeral!

POVERTY: You just want to jibe and poke fun at me. You're not interested in serious discussion. You don't realize that I give you better men than Wealth ever can, better in body and better in mind. He gives you all sorts of cripples: gout here, pot bellies there, dropsy in the calves, obesity beyond all bounds, while I give you lean, wiry, wasplike men, who are deadly to their enemies.

CHREMYLUS: Wasplike from starvation, no doubt.

POVERTY: Then on the subject of virtue, I can prove that all modesty and decency belong to me, while Wealth trains men to flout them.

CHREMYLUS: Oh, of course, thieving and burglary are *very* modest and decent!!

BLEPSIDEMUS: Well, they are, aren't they? The thief takes good care to be neither seen nor heard!

POVERTY: Then look at the politicians. Those who are poor always give the right advice to City and people; but as soon as they've enriched themselves at the public expense, they become criminals, conspire against the masses and make war on the community.

CHREMYLUS: You may have a poisoned tongue, but at least that's one true thing you've said! Don't wait for the applause, though; you'll still regret trying to convince us that poverty is better than wealth.

POVERTY: But you still haven't refuted me: you just flap your wings and talk nonsense.

CHREMYLUS: All right: tell us why everyone tries to avoid you.

POVERTY: Because I make them better people. Look at what happens with children. Their fathers love them, yet the children always try to avoid them. It's not at all easy to know what's good for you.

CHREMYLUS: According to you, then, even Zeus doesn't know what's good for him. He's got Wealth all right.

BLEPSIDEMUS: And sends Poverty down here!

POVERTY: You've got styes in your eyes and you're blind in the mind! Your stupidity is positively antediluvian! Zeus himself is poor, and I'll prove it to you. He founded the Olympic Games to bring the whole of Greece together every four years. Now if he was rich, would he, the founder, have arranged that when the winner of each event was named, he should be crowned with a wreath of *wild olive*? Surely he'd have made it gold!

CHREMYLUS: That only proves how much he likes Wealth. He's a miser and doesn't want to incur undue expense, so he fobs off the victors with trifles and keeps the real Wealth to himself.

POVERTY: You're accusing him of something far worse than poverty, if you say he's such a very mean and avaricious rich god.

CHREMYLUS: Oh, Zeus, give her a wreath of wild olive and send her to hell!

POVERTY: How can you have the audacity to deny that I, Poverty, am responsible for all the good things in life?

CHREMYLUS: Perhaps you should ask Hecate whether it's better to be rich or to starve. Do you know what she says? The *haves*, the rich, offer her a meal every month; but the poor whip it away before she even gets it.[25]

Get lost! not one more word we'll hear from you.
You won't persuade us, even if you do.

POVERTY:

       O Argive city, hear'st these words?[26]

CHREMYLUS:

       Best call for Pauson, he's your friend.[27]

POVERTY:

       What shall I do, what be my end?

CHREMYLUS:

       Get out of here and feed the birds!

POVERTY:

       Where on earth can I show my face?

CHREMYLUS:

       In the pillory, that's the place!
       Off you go and don't delay!

POVERTY [*departing*]:

       You'll beg to have me back one day.

CHREMYLUS:

       Then you'll come back, but meantime go!
       I'd rather be rich, I'd have you know:
         I'll take the pelf
       And you can go and stuff yourself!

[*Exit* POVERTY.]

BLEPSIDEMUS:

           Give me the rich man's life,
             In luxury's lap to dwell
           With happy kids and wife –
             Won't everything be swell!

           Anointed from the baths
             As homeward I depart,
          For *her* and all her crafts
             I'll give a rousing fart!

CHREMYLUS: That's got rid of that old creep! Now let's go straight
away and take Wealth off to spend the night in the Temple of
Asclepius.

BLEPSIDEMUS: Yes, don't let's wait. Someone else might come to
stop us getting on with the job.

CHREMYLUS [*calling into the house*]: Boy! Carion! Bring out our bedding! And bring Wealth with you, dressed for the ritual, and everything else we'll need. It's all ready for you in there.

[CARION *comes out, carrying baggage and leading* WEALTH, *who bears a suppliant's olive branch. All four go off.*]

CHORUS

ACT TWO

SCENE ONE: *The same (and so throughout the act). The next day.*

[*The* CHORUS *are present;* CARION *runs in in great excitement.*]

CARION: Friends! Friends who so often at the feasts of Theseus have
   had to eat your porridge with tiny tiny scraps of bread! What
   happiness is yours! What bliss for all who lead an honest life!
LEADER:

What is't, O best of thy co-servitors?[28]
I fancy thou hast some good news to tell.

CARION: It's worked! Master has done it! So has Wealth! He's blind
   no more, he has eyes again, his pupils shine as they used to;
   Asclepius the Healer has had mercy on him!
CHORUS:

At this we all rejoice
And high upraise our voice!

CARION: Yes, it's a time for joy, whether you like it or not!
CHORUS:

With joy shall I proclaim
Asclepius' holy name,
Head of a noble clan,[29]
Great Light of hope to man!'

[CHREMYLUS' WIFE *comes out of the house.*]

WIFE: What *is* all this shouting about? Is there some good news?
   I've been waiting impatiently for *you* for a long time.
CARION: Wine, mistress, bring wine quickly! You must celebrate
   too! [*Aside*] You'll be only too glad of the excuse,[30] [*Aloud*] I've
   brought you all the good news in the world!
WIFE: Where is it?
CARION: You'll soon hear.
WIFE: Well, go on, go on, can't you?

CARION: Then listen and I'll explain the matter from the beginning to the end for you.

WIFE: It had better *not* be the end for me, thank you very much!

CARION: What, you don't want to know about our new-found blessings?

WIFE: I thought you said something was the matter.[31]

CARION: Well then, we arrived at the temple, bringing with us a person who was then more wretched than any man alive, but now is supremely happy and blessed, and first of all we took him to the sea and gave him a bathe.

WIFE: Brrr, the cold! And at his age! Some happiness!

CARION: Then we entered the sacred precinct. We offered cakes and incense at the altar, 'sops for Hephaestus' flame' as the poet says, and then we put Wealth to bed in the proper manner and prepared rough-and-ready mattresses for ourselves.

WIFE: Were there any other patients there?

CARION: Yes, there was Neocleides,[32] the blind politician whom no sighted man can outdo in thieving; and there were a great many others with all kinds of diseases. Anyway, the temple servant put out all the lamps and told us to go to sleep, warning us to remain silent if we heard any noise. So we all lay there quietly; but I couldn't sleep. There was an old woman with a pot of wheat broth lying near her head, and I was very struck by this and I had a consuming desire to creep up on that pot. So I looked up, and what did I see but the priest taking the cheese-cakes and figs off the holy table; after which he went round all the altars seeing if anyone had left a cake there, and he consecrated all of them by putting them into his bag. Well, that assured me that what I intended to do was an act of the highest piety, so I got up and made for the pot of broth.

WIFE: Wretch, had you no fear of the god?

CARION: Indeed I had. I was afraid he might get to the pot first, coming with his holy garland on his head, as the priest had earlier told me he would do. What happened in fact was that the old girl heard me and put out her hand; whereupon I hissed, like one of the sacred snakes, and took it in my mouth. She drew her hand back like lightning, wrapped herself up very tight, and lay there in silent

terror, farting like a cat. Then I set to slurping down the soup, until
I was full, and then I stopped.

WIFE: And the god himself still hadn't come in?

CARION: Not yet, but he did right after. Then I did something really
funny. As he was approaching, I had an attack of wind and let out
an enormous fart.

WIFE: He must have been put to flight!

CARION: No, but his attendants! Iaso[33] blushed like anything, and
Panacea held her nose and turned away. My farts aren't exactly
incense and myrrh.

WIFE: And Asclepius himself?

CARION: He never even noticed it.

WIFE: What an earthy god!

CARION: Oh, I wouldn't say earthy; remember he tastes shit for a
living.[34]

WIFE: Really!!

CARION: Well, I was rather frightened after that and covered myself
up, while the god went round looking very carefully at all the
patients. Then a boy placed by his side a stone pestle and mortar
and medicine box.

WIFE: A stone one?!

CARION: Not the medicine box, silly.

WIFE: But, you lying scoundrel, how did you see all this? You'd
covered yourself up!

CARION: I saw it through my cloak; that had no shortage of holes!
Well, first of all he treated Neocleides. He prepared a plaster to
rub on his eyes: three heads of Tenian garlic, then he pounded in
some fig juice and sea onions, and finally soaked the lot with
vinegar from Sphettus. Then he turned up Neocleides' eyelids and
rubbed the mixture into them, so as to give the maximum pain. He
yelled and screamed, jumped up and ran off. Asclepius laughed
and said, 'That's got you good and plastered; no more moving the
previous question in the Assembly for you now!'[35]

WIFE: What a wise and public-spirited god!

CARION: Then he came to Wealth and sat at his side. He felt his head
and wiped his eyelids with a clean linen cloth, while Panacea spread
a red cloth all over his head and face. Then the god gave a clucking

sound, and at once two enormous snakes came out of the inner shrine.

WIFE: Gods save us!

CARION: They went under the red cloth and licked all round his eyelids, at least I think they did; and, mistress, before you could drink down ten cups of wine, Wealth was on his feet, and he could see. I clapped my hands for joy, and woke up master. At once the god disappeared, snakes and all, into the inner shrine. Well, you can imagine how the other patients congratulated Wealth. They were up all night until daybreak. And I praised Asclepius with all my heart – first, for so quickly restoring Wealth his sight; second, for making Neocleides' blindness worse.

WIFE: Lord Asclepius, how great is thy power! – But tell me, where's Wealth now?

CARION: He's on his way. And he's surrounded by a tremendous crowd. All the people who'd been living honest, decent lives for so long and yet been poor, they were delighted, all trying to greet him and shake his hand. Those who'd been rich and had a cushy life by dishonest means, they scowled at him and screwed up their faces. But the others all followed in his train, with garlands on their heads, laughter on their faces, and words of good omen in their mouths, to the resounding beat of the old men's rhythmic tread. Come on now, all of you together, dance and leap and celebrate! Never again when you come home will you hear the dread words, 'Dad, we've run out of barley'!

WIFE: By Hecate, you should have a crown for this good news! I'll get a string of fresh-baked loaves.

CARION: Best not waste time over that; they're nearly here.

WIFE: Then I'll go in and fetch the confetti,[36] to welcome his newly-acquired eyes. [She goes into the house.]

CARION: And I'll go to meet them. [He goes out.]

CHORUS[37]

SCENE TWO

[During the CHORUS's song WEALTH has entered, now with his sight restored. As they finish he reaches centre stage.]

WEALTH: I thank the gods indeed; and first I make obeisance to thee,

O holy Sun, and next to the far-famed Citadel of revered Athena
and to all the land of Attica that has received and welcomed me. I
am heartily ashamed of my previous experiences, thinking how I
unwittingly associated with wicked men, and ignorantly shunned
those who were worthy of my company. How wretched I was, to
be wrong in all I did! But now I will reverse my ways, and make
it plain to all men that if I formerly gave myself to the wicked, It
was against my desires.

[*Shouts heard in the wings. Enter* CHREMYLUS, *backwards, with
difficulty holding off a vast throng of well-wishers.*]

CHREMYLUS: Get out! Get lost! There's no worse pest than a fair-
weather friend!

[*The crowd gradually disappear.*]

Bruising your ribs and barking your shins – that's some way of
displaying goodwill! Was there anyone who didn't speak to me?
Was there any old man in the Market Square who didn't join the
encircling mob?

WIFE [*appearing at the door, with sweetmeats*]: Welcome, dearest, and
you too, dearest Wealth. Come, let's follow tradition and shower
you with these.

WEALTH: If you please, no. On my first entry into the house with
my sight restored, I should not be the cause of taking anything *out*
of the house; rather I should be bringing something *in*.

WIFE: Then where would you like to be showered?

WEALTH: Inside by the fireplace, as the custom is. That way we will
avoid any vulgarity. It ill becomes an author to bribe his audience
to laugh by throwing them figs and sweets.

WIFE: Quite right. Look, there's Dexinicus [*pointing to a member of the
audience*] already on his feet hoping to grab some.

[*All go into the house.*]

CHORUS

SCENE THREE
[CARION *comes out of the house.*]

CARION: Ah, friends, prosperity is a wonderful thing, especially
when it's achieved at no expense! We've been invaded by a heap of
blessings – and we haven't done a single bad thing to deserve it.

Our corn-store's full of beautiful white barley, our jars are full of fragrant dark wine. Every pot in the house is crammed with silver and gold – you'd be amazed. There's oil in our wells, perfume in our oil bottles, and our attic's full of figs. Every bowl, every plate and vinegar cruet, has turned to bronze, and all our rotting old fish dishes are solid silver. Even our lamps suddenly turned into ivory. We servants are playing odd-and-even with gold twenty-drachma pieces; and we no longer wipe our bottoms with stones – we're spoilt now, we always use garlic leaves. Master has garlanded himself and is making a sacrifice – a pig, a goat and a ram. I came out because of the smoke. I couldn't stay in there any more – it was biting my eyelids.

[*Enter a* GOOD MAN, *warmly and fashionably dressed, accompanied by a young* SLAVE *who carries his ragged old clothes.*]

GOOD MAN: Come on with me, boy; we must visit the god.

CARION: Hullo, who's this?

GOOD MAN: A man who has passed from misery to bliss.

CARION: An honest man, I imagine.

GOOD MAN: That's right.

CARION: What can we do for you?

GOOD MAN: I have come to thank Wealth for blessing me so. I inherited from my father an estate adequate for my needs, but I made a practice of helping my friends when they fell on bad times, because I thought that was wise policy.

CARION: I bet your money didn't last long.

GOOD MAN: Just so.

CARION: And so *you* fell on bad times.

GOOD MAN: Just so. And I thought that those who had benefited by my kindness when they were in need would be true friends in *my* hour of need; but they turned their backs and pretended not to see me.

CARION: And laughed at you, I'll warrant.

GOOD MAN: Just so. I was prostrated by monetary desiccation.

CARION: But not any more.

GOOD MAN: Just so; and so, as is only right, I've come here to offer my thankful prayers to the god.

CARION: But good heavens! what's that ragged old cloak that your boy's carrying?

298

GOOD MAN: I'm going to dedicate it to Wealth.

CARION: You don't mean that's the robe you wore for your initiation at the Mysteries?[38]

GOOD MAN: No, only the one I've been wearing these thirteen shivery winters.

CARION: And those old shoes?

GOOD MAN: They were my freezing companions too.

CARION: So you're going to dedicate them too?

GOOD MAN: Just so.

CARION: Agreeable gifts for Wealth, I must say!

[An INFORMER *storms in, seething with rage; he is accompanied by a* WITNESS.]

INFORMER [*who does not at first see the others*]: I am ruined! I am accursed! Thrice accursed, four, five, twelve, ten thousand times accursed! Help! I've been dropped into a concentrated solution of torture!

CARION [*aside to* GOOD MAN]: Apollo preserve us, what's happened to him?

INFORMER: I have suffered unheard-of indignity! This god has robbed me of everything in my house! I'll see him blind again yet; I still have my writs and summonses!

CARION [*aside to* GOOD MAN]: I think I've some idea what this is all about. He's in trouble. I fancy he's bad coin.

GOOD MAN [*aside to* CARION]: Good for *him*, then: well fallen!

INFORMER [*seeing* CARION]: Where is he? Where is he? That god who promised he would make us all rich if he got his sight back? There are some, I'd have you know, that he's utterly destroyed!

CARION: Who, for example?

INFORMER: ME!!!

CARION: Were you a criminal? A burglar, perhaps?

INFORMER [*waving his hands at the house*]: You're the criminals! I'll warrant you've got my property!

CARION: Holy Demeter, he's like a rushing mighty wind! Must have developed pathological hunger.

INFORMER: Off with you at once, boy, to the Market Square! We'll torture you there on the wheel, until you confess all your crimes.

CARION: You dare!

GOOD MAN: Oh Zeus, Lord and Saviour! Wealth has indeed proved a boon to Greece, if he's going to give the informers their just deserts at last.

INFORMER: Hang it, you're not in this too, are you, sneering at me? Here, where did you get that cloak from? I saw you yesterday wearing an old ragged one.

GOOD MAN: I'm not bothered about you. I've got a magic ring, see. I bought it from Eudamus for a drachma.

CARION [*examining the ring; in mock alarm*]: This is no good; it's not marked 'For informer-bites'.

INFORMER: This mockery is sheer Insulting Behaviour Liable to Cause a Breach of the Peace! And you haven't told me what you're doing here. Nothing good, I'll be bound.

CARION: Nothing for *your* good, anyway.

INFORMER: I should think not! You're about to dine on my money!

CARION: You and your witness can go and get stuffed – till you burst!

GOOD MAN: Yes – stuffed with nothing!

INFORMER: You deny it, do you, you villains? There's an enormous quantity of fish and roast meat in that house, you needn't try to fool me! [*Sniffing.*] Hn-hn, hn-hn, hn-hn, hn-hn, hn-hn, hn-hn.

CARION: Poor chap! Do you smell anything?

GOOD MAN: The cold, I expect.

INFORMER: This is bloody well intolerable! I'm being made an absolute laughing-stock! What a martyrdom it is to be a good and patriotic man!

CARION: *You're* good and patriotic?

INFORMER: More so than any other citizen.

CARION: Answer me this, then: are you a farmer?

INFORMER: D'you think I'm insane?

CARION: A merchant, then?

INFORMER: I claim to be, when necessary.³⁹

CARION: Then a craftsman of some kind?

INFORMER: I should think not!

CARION: Well, if you don't do *anything* how did you ever get a living?

INFORMER: I am unofficial superintendent of all public and private affairs.

CARION: What on earth do you mean?

INFORMER: I *desire*.⁴⁰

CARION: You burgling sneak! You think you're being a good citizen, do you, getting a foul reputation by busybodying into other people's affairs?

INFORMER: I don't busybody, you coot! All I do is seek to help my beloved City to the utmost of my ability.

CARION: That's your name, is it, for poking your nose in where it's not wanted?

INFORMER: It's my name for coming to the aid of the established laws and not letting anybody get away with violating them.

CARION: But isn't it for that express purpose that the City has set up the jury system?

INFORMER: Ah yes, but who's going to prosecute?

CARION: The law says, whoever desires.

INFORMER: And *I desire*. In other words, the whole City depends on me.

CARION: Some bloody protector we've got! Why don't you take a *desire* to live quietly for a change and leave us alone?

INFORMER: You're asking me to live like a sheep, with nothing in the world to occupy my time.

CARION: So you won't change your ways?

INFORMER: Not if you gave me Wealth in person, and all the silphium in Libya into the bargain.

CARION: Off with your cloak, you!

GOOD MAN [*to* INFORMER]: Hey, he's talking to *you*.

CARION: And your shoes.

GOOD MAN [*to* INFORMER, *who is still taking no notice*]: He's talking to *you*!

INFORMER: If anyone desires to take me on, let him just come and try!

CARION: Yes, I desire!

[*He rushes at the* INFORMER, *brings him to the ground and strips him; the* WITNESS *runs away.*]

INFORMER: Help! Help! I'm being stripped in broad daylight!

CARION: It was you chose to mind other people's business for a living.

INFORMER [*turning to where, a moment ago, his* WITNESS *had been*]: Do you see this? Assault! You be my witness!

CARION: You needn't look there, he's scarpered.

INFORMER: I am lost! Betrayed, deserted and taken!

CARION: Wailing now, eh?

INFORMER: Ah, woe is me!

CARION [*to* GOOD MAN]: Give me your old cloak and I'll put it on him.

GOOD MAN: I can't really; it's already sacred, I've vowed it to Wealth.

CARION: Then isn't this a good place to hang it, on this swine of a burglar? For Wealth's adornment we should reserve finer garments. [*He puts the tattered old cloak on the* INFORMER'*s shoulders.*]

GOOD MAN: And the shoes, what about them?

CARION: They really ought to be nailed up on an olive tree,⁴¹ but I'll use his forehead instead.

INFORMER [*already on his way off*]: I'm going, thank you very much. I know that by myself I'm no match for you; but just wait till I find a comrade whose *desires*⁴² match mine! I'll make this powerful god of yours pay for his crimes this very day. He is self-evidently guilty of attempting in an autocratic manner to subvert democracy, as is shown by the fact that he has failed to seek the consent of the People's Council or of the Assembly.

GOOD MAN: Now you're wearing my armour, why not trot off to the bath-house and take over my place there? It's the place of honour – the one nearest the fire.

CARION [*as the* INFORMER *departs*]: Why, the attendant will drag him out of the place at once by the scruff of the balls. He'll recognize as soon as he sets eyes on him that he's bad coin. But didn't you want to give thanks to Wealth? Let's go inside.

[*They and the* SLAVE *do so.*]

CHORUS

SCENE FOUR

[*Enter an* OLD WOMAN, *trying to look a quarter her age in a multi-coloured dress, accompanied by a* SLAVE *carrying a tray on which are sweet cakes, nuts, etc. She approaches the* CHORUS.]

OLD WOMAN: Could you tell me, my dears, hev we come to the home of this new god, or hev we taken ebsolutely the wrong turning?

LEADER: No, you're at just the right door, young lady – if I may make so bold as to guess your age from your manner of speaking.

OLD WOMAN: Let me see who's at home. [*She is about to knock at the door.*]

CHREMYLUS [*coming out of the house*]: It's all right, here I am. Could you tell me what brings you here?

OLD WOMAN: Darling, I have been treated most disgracefully and illegally. Since this god of yours got his saight back, he has made may layfe a total misery.

CHREMYLUS: What, you weren't an informeress too, spying among the women, were you?

OLD WOMAN: Heavens, no.

CHREMYLUS: Or was it that your letter hadn't come up and you went and sat in the boozer – the court – the boozer just the same?[43]

OLD WOMAN: You're making fun of me. [*Emotionally*] I have been wounded to the quick.

CHREMYLUS: Well, come on, tell us about your wound.

OLD WOMAN: Listen, then. There was this young led who was in love with me. He was quaite poor, but very good looking and very honest. And whenever I wanted anything, oh, he did it so beautifully and obligingly! And in return, I always gave him whatever *he* wanted.

CHREMYLUS: What did he mostly want?

OLD WOMAN: Not very much, you know, he respected me so tremendously. Only, say, twenty drachmas for a coat, or eight for shoes; or he'd ask me to buy dresses for his sisters or just a coat for his mother, or perhaps six bushels of wheat.

CHREMYLUS: Not very much, certainly! He had *some* respect!

OLD WOMAN: And he always said that he didn't ask for these things because he wanted them as such – it was out of love: he wanted to wear my coat so he'd always be reminded of me.

CHREMYLUS: Really head over heels in love, wasn't he?

OLD WOMAN: But now the young puppy has changed his maynd. Completely different person, he is. I sent him this cake here and all the sweets on that tray, with a message that I'd be coming round this evening, and he –

CHREMYLUS: What did he do?

OLD WOMAN [*sobbing*]: He sent them beck to me, and this cream cake in addition, and he said I was never to visit him again! And not only that, but he said – he said – 'Miletus' martial glory's past and gone!'[44]

CHREMYLUS [*aside to the audience*]: You see, he wasn't such an abandoned chap as you thought. Now he's rich he can afford to have taste – and he doesn't like pease porridge. When he was poor, before, he had to take what he could get.

OLD WOMAN: And until now he'd come to may door every day, by the Holy Twain[45] I swear he would!

CHREMYLUS: To see the coffin come out?

OLD WOMAN: No, to hear the sound of his loved one's voice.

CHREMYLUS: The chink of his loved one's silver, more like.

OLD WOMAN: And then if he thought I was the least little bit upset, he'd pet me and call me his little duckling and his lovey-dovey.

CHREMYLUS: And then ask you for the price of another pair of shoes.

OLD WOMAN: And when I went in my carriage to the Great Mysteries, if anyone so much as looked at me, this boy would beat me bleck and blue the rest of the day. Thet's how jealous he was.

CHREMYLUS: Didn't like handing round his sweets, eh?

OLD WOMAN: He said may hands were truly beautiful.

CHREMYLUS: Just as long as they had twenty drachmas in them.

OLD WOMAN: And that may skin was ebsolutely fragrant.

CHREMYLUS [*sniffing her face*]: Not surprising, if you made up with best Thasian wine!

OLD WOMAN: And that may eyes were soft and revishing.

CHREMYLUS [*aside*]: No fool either, you see? He knew just how to eat up a lovesick old woman's capital.

OLD WOMAN: So you see, darling, in may opinion this god of yours is breaking his promises. He said he'd always be`on the side of the victims of wrongdoing.

CHREMYLUS: What ought he to be doing? Speak, and it shall be done.

OLD WOMAN: I think, considering how much this boy's hed from me, he should at least compel him to repay me for it, or to forfeit his raight to wealth should he refuse.

CHREMYLUS: Come off it! He repaid you every night, didn't he?

OLD WOMAN: But he promised he'd never leave me as long as I lived.

CHREMYLUS: Fair enough; obviously now he reckons you're dead.

OLD WOMAN: Well, darling, I nearly *em* – melted away with grief.

CHREMYLUS: *Rotted* away, if you ask me.

OLD WOMAN: I've wasted so much, you could pass me through a ring.

CHREMYLUS: Well, yes, if you mean the kind of ring that goes on a round table.⁴⁶

OLD WOMAN: Ah, here he comes, the very person I've been complaining of. Looks as if he's planning to gatecrash some party or other.

CHREMYLUS: The garlands and the torch certainly point that way.
[*Enter a* YOUNG MAN, *crowned and carrying a torch. He is slightly drunk, and does not at first recognize the* OLD WOMAN.]

YOUNG MAN: Bleshings on you!

OLD WOMAN: What was thet?

YOUNG MAN: Oh, it'sh you, is it, old love? You've gone grey very fasht!

OLD WOMAN [*half to herself*]: Nothing but insults, insults right and left!

CHREMYLUS: Seems like a case of long time no see.

OLD WOMAN: Long time indeed! It's exectly twenty-four hours.

CHREMYLUS: Interesting abnormality, then: this fellow sees *clearer* when he's under the influence!

OLD WOMAN: Not a bit of it. He's a spoilt bret.

YOUNG MAN [*inspecting her closely, and waving his torch in her face*]: Poshcidon of the Sea! Godsh of Age and Decay! Never seen so many wrinklesh in my life!

OLD WOMAN: Here, here, get that torch away from me!

CHREMYLUS [*to* YOUNG MAN]: You'd better, you know. One spark and she'll go up like last year's olive branches.⁴⁷

YOUNG MAN [*to* OLD WOMAN]: Would you care to play a little game with me?

OLD WOMAN: We can't do it here, silly.

YOUNG MAN: Yes, we can. Take a few nuts there.

OLD WOMAN: I don't understand. What's the game?

YOUNG MAN: You know [*clenching his fist and holding it up*], 'how many have you got?' How many teeth, that is.[48]

CHREMYLUS: I know! Three.

[*The* YOUNG MAN *shakes his head.*]

Four?

YOUNG MAN: Pay up. She's exactly one molar.

OLD WOMAN: You detestable swayne! You're ebsolutely out of your maynd! How dare you treat me as a bit of dirt on a public ... stage?

YOUNG MAN: If only there were only *one* bit of dirt on you! You could do with a good wash.

CHREMYLUS: I shouldn't if I were you, not with the way she's tarted herself up. Wash off that white lead and prepare yourself to see the rags of a complexion!

OLD WOMAN: Hev *you* gone med in your old age too?

YOUNG MAN [*affecting surprise*]: You don't mean to say he's making advances to you and pawing you, do you, thinking I'm not looking?

OLD WOMAN: No, you filthy liar, he's not.

CHREMYLUS: I *would* be mad then, ducks![49] But really, my young friend, you ought not to be so ill-disposed towards the ... girl.

YOUNG MAN: Ill-disposed! I love her very much.

CHREMYLUS: And yet she's been complaining about you.

YOUNG MAN: Complaining? What of?

CHREMYLUS: She says you've been sneering at her, saying that 'Miletus' martial glory's past and gone'.

YOUNG MAN: Well, I won't fight you for her –

CHREMYLUS: What do you mean?

YOUNG MAN: You're older than me. I wouldn't have done this for just anybody, you know. The girl's yours; I wish you joy of her.

CHREMYLUS: I have a funny feeling you're trying to ditch her.

OLD WOMAN: For which you require permission which will *not* be forthcoming.

YOUNG MAN [*with dignity*]: I refushe to shpeak to a pershon debauched by the intimate attentionsh of thirteen thoushand ... years.

CHREMYLUS: Now, now; he who drinks the cup must drain the dregs!

YOUNG MAN: But such – pah! – such old and rotten dregs!

CHREMYLUS: You can work wonders with a straining-cloth, you know. [*Realizing the* YOUNG MAN *will not be persuaded*] Come along inside.

YOUNG MAN: Right, I will. I've got these garlands I want to dedicate to Wealth.

　　[*He and* CHREMYLUS *turn to enter the house.*]

OLD WOMAN [*hurrying after them*]: Yes, and I've got something to say to him.

YOUNG MAN: In that case I'm not going in.

CHREMYLUS: Don't be frightened, she won't explode.

YOUNG MAN: With the number of times I've plugged her leak she jolly well shouldn't.[50]

OLD WOMAN [*pushing* YOUNG MAN *towards the door*]: Go on in, I'm raight behind!

　　[*They go into the house.*]

CHREMYLUS: Lord Zeus, how she stuck to him, tight as a limpet!
　　[*He follows them inside.*]

CHORUS

SCENE FIVE

[*Enter the god* HERMES. *He knocks thunderously at the door, and then hides round the side of the house.*]

CARION [*coming to the door*]: Who's that knocking? [*Opens the door.*] What's this? Nobody here? You'll get one for that, door, creating such a racket for no reason at all.

HERMES [*reappearing*]: You, I say! Carion! Stay where you are!

CARION: Here, was it you that was bashing the door like that?

HERMES: Word of honour, no. I was just going to, but you opened it first. Now run quickly and fetch your master. Then his wife and children, and then the servants, the dog, yourself, and the pig.

CARION: Could you tell me what this is all about?

HERMES: Zeus, you villain, intends to mash up the whole lot of you in one dish and hurl you into oblivion!

CARION: I see, Hermes, we'd better remember to cut you a tongue out![51] – Why does Zeus want to do that?

HERMES: Because you have committed the most dreadful crime of all

307

time! Do you know that since Wealth regained his sight nobody has sacrificed a thing to us gods? No incense, no laurel, no barley-cakes, no animals, no nothing!

CARION: That's right. Nobody has and nobody will. When did you gods ever take proper care of us?

HERMES: It's not the *other* gods I'm so much concerned about – but what about *me*? My whole life's fallen apart!

CARION: Good for it!

HERMES: From break of day it used to be that the innkeepers would bring me all sorts of goodies: wine-cakes, honey, figs, all the things I might be expected to like. But now all I can do is put my feet up and starve.

CARION: No more than you deserve. People did you good, and you did them harm.

HERMES: Oh for the lovely cakes I used to get on the fourth of the month![52]

CARION: Thou seek'st what is not there, and cry'st in vain.

HERMES: Oh, for the ham I once guzzled!

CARION: You're giving a ham performance right now if ever I saw one![53]

HERMES: Oh, for the hot innards I used to love!

CARION: Got a pain in your own, have you, eh?

HERMES: Oh, for the wine mixed fifty-fifty!

CARION [*offering a bowl of dirty water*]: Here, have this to drink. Now be off.

HERMES: What, won't you help one of your own kind?

CARION [*in a more friendly tone*]: Well, if it's something I'm able to do.

HERMES: If you could get a well-baked loaf and let me have it, with a good honest slice of meat from that sacrifice you're making in there . . .

CARION: Sorry, it's strictly prohibited.

HERMES: Remember all the times you nicked your master's things? Didn't I make sure you didn't get caught?

CARION: On condition you got a share of the loot, you old villain. You always got a well-done fruit-and-nut cake.

HERMES: Which *you* promptly ate.

CARION: And when I did get caught, you made jolly sure you didn't get a share of my flogging!

HERMES: Look, you've won your war;⁵⁴ can't we have an amnesty? Please, I beg you, take me into your home.

CARION: You want to leave the gods and stay here with us?

HERMES: Well, of course; it's a much better life here.

CARION: You approve of deserting to the enemy, then?

HERMES: My country's where my comfort's best secured.⁵⁵

CARION: Very well. In what capacity could you serve us?

HERMES: I could stand by the door in my capacity as God of the Turning Hinge.

CARION: We've had enough of your turnings and twistings. No thanks.

HERMES: Or as God of the Market.

CARION: But we've got Wealth now; we don't need any stallholder gods any more.

HERMES: Then as the God of Trickery.

CARION: Trickery? Not on your nelly. Honesty and straightforwardness, that's what's required now.

HERMES: Or the Divine Guide.

CARION: But with Wealth's sight restored we've no opening for a guide now.

HERMES: I tell you what, I'll be the God of Competitions. That's got you! What could be more appropriate to Wealth than to sponsor competitions in sport and the arts?

CARION [to the audience]: Isn't it useful to have a lot of titles? He was bound to get himself a slot in the end. No wonder all the jurymen try to get themselves enrolled on several panels at once.⁵⁶

HERMES: Is it a deal, then? May I come in?

CARION: By all means. And you can start by going to the well and soaking our sausages. There was just one title you didn't mention. You're the Divine Servant. [He leads HERMES into the house.]

CHORUS

SCENE SIX
[Enter the PRIEST OF ZEUS, in considerable trepidation.]
PRIEST [to CHORUS]: Can anyone here tell me where I can find Chremylus?

CHREMYLUS [*coming out*]: Can I help you, sir?

PRIEST: You can't make things any worse! Now this Wealth's got his sight back, I'm nearly dead of starvation. I'm the Priest of Zeus the Saviour, and I've nothing to eat!

CHREMYLUS: Heavens, how come?

PRIEST: Nobody bothers to offer sacrifices any more.

CHREMYLUS: Why not?

PRIEST: Because they're all rich. In the old days, when they had nothing, you could count on a sacrifice from a merchant on his safe return from a voyage, or a defendant who had got off; or perhaps someone would have a grand sacrificial feast at home, and then naturally he'd invite me. But now nobody sacrifices at all. I never see a living soul, apart from a darn sight too many who think the temple is a gents' toilet.

CHREMYLUS: Well then, you get your share of the offerings they *deposit*, don't you?

PRIEST: Well, anyway, I've decided to say goodbye to Zeus the Saviour, and stay here with you.

CHREMYLUS: Don't be frightened about it, man! Everything will be all right, the gods willing. Zeus the Saviour's here himself; he had the same idea as you!

PRIEST: Thank heavens!

CHREMYLUS: Right, now we'll reinstall Wealth – [*To the* PRIEST, *who is rushing into the house*] Wait a moment! – reinstall Wealth in his old dwelling in the rear chamber of Athena's temple.⁵⁷ Lighted torches, somebody! [*Torches are brought.*] Take one, Priest, and lead the procession.

PRIEST: By all means.

[CITIZENS, SLAVES *and others are now forming a procession, many carrying torches, with the* PRIEST *at their head.*]

CHREMYLUS: Fetch out Wealth!

[*Two attendants lead* WEALTH *out of the house and enthrone him on a wheeled platform. Then the* OLD WOMAN *comes out of the house and beetles up to* CHREMYLUS.]

OLD WOMAN: Here, what about me?

CHREMYLUS: You can carry the dedication pots,⁵⁸ in solemn procession, on your head. You're already dressed for the occasion.

OLD WOMAN: But what about – what I came for?

CHREMYLUS: That'll all be seen to. He'll come round to your place
   tonight.
OLD WOMAN: If that's a cast-iron guarantee that he will – [CHRE-
   MYLUS *nods*], then I'll carry the pots.
   [*A platter is brought out, on which are the pots of vegetables. The* OLD
   WOMAN *puts it on her head and joins the procession.* CHREMYLUS
   falls in behind her, and the procession moves off.]
CHREMYLUS: Why are these pots different from all other pots? In
   all other pots the scum goes to the top; but in *these* pots the scum
   is beneath the pot!
CHORUS [*as they march out at the rear of the procession*]:
        No more must we dally, for now it is best
        With a song on our lips to depart with the rest.

Notes

NOTES

THE KNIGHTS

1. The reference is to Olympus, a half-legendary Asiatic flute-player of the seventh century.
2. This comes from Euripides' *Hippolytus* (line 345).
3. A reference to the evergreen legend about Euripides, that his mother sold vegetables in the market.
4. Beans were used as tokens when officials were elected by lot.
5. Meetings of the Assembly were held on the hill known as the Pnyx. In the Greek the old man's name is 'Demos', the regular word for 'the people'.
6. Legal cases were tried by large juries drawn from a panel of several thousands. Thus an offer of a paid half-holiday to the courts might sway votes in the Assembly. Three obols was a full day's pay for a juror.
7. See Introductory Note.
8. The Sibyl was a mythical prophetess. Books purporting to be collections of her oracles were circulating widely at this time.
9. In the Greek 'Chaonia', with a pun on *chaskein* 'to gape open'.
10. Themistocles, who had been largely responsible for the defeat of the Persians in 480–479, was later exiled from Athens, and eventually found refuge under Persian protection by giving vague undertakings to assist a future campaign against Greece. It was widely believed, without any evidence, that he had committed suicide to avoid having to fulfil these promises.
11. 'Pramnian' wine, whose original source appears to have been the Aegean island of Icarus, had been a prestigious type at least since Homeric times.
12. Many of the oracle-books circulating at Athens contained alleged utterances of the prophet Bakis.
13. An ancient commentator identifies this man as one Eucrates, but nothing is known of him. He is mentioned again on p. 45.
14. This was Lysicles (killed on active service 428/7), a leading politician shortly before and after the death of Pericles.
15. After his success at Pylos, Cleon was awarded various honours,

including the right to dine at the public expense in the Town Hall (the Prytaneum). The Sausage-Seller is to go one better.

16. Cf. p. 84, for talk of Athenian expeditions against this great and remote Power.

17. In the original there is a pun on another meaning of 'Demos', viz. 'animal fat'.

18. The Greek text says that the mask-makers were afraid to provide a portrait-mask (sc. of Cleon) for the actor. I have had to adapt with a view to a modern production without masks; my adaptation is intended to refer to the risk of a prosecution by Cleon such as Aristophanes had already had to face in 426.

19. The cities of Chalcidice, sited on three peninsulas in the north-west corner of the Aegean, were restive under Athenian rule. Later in 424 the Spartan general Brasidas induced most of them to defect from the Athenian alliance.

20. *Music:* the concluding *Allegro vivace* from the overture to Rossini's *William Tell.* (So also for the chorus on pp. 46–7.)

21. See note 13.

22. See note 6. Many retired people found jury-pay a useful 'pension', and of course they could not earn it without an ample supply of cases to try, in the ordinary way.

23. All magistrates, at the end of their term of office, had to pass an audit (*euthynai*) to show that they had not acted improperly or mis-used public funds.

24. The Gallipoli peninsula. There appears to be a reference to some recent prosecution, but we know nothing else about it.

25. This is the literal meaning of the Greek.

26. See note 15.

27. Each of the ten 'tribes' supplied fifty members to the Council, and each tribal delegation formed a committee which managed the business of Council and Assembly for one tenth of the year. I call this 'the Executive Committee'; in Greek its members were called the *prytaneis.*

28. From the subject allies of Athens.

29. Cleon is compared to a look-out who spies an approaching shoal of tunny, and calls to the fishermen to set their nets for it.

30. The Greek text refers to 'the son of Hippodamus'. This was Archeptolemus (mentioned again on p. 66), who had recently been involved in the abortive peace negotiations. Later he took a leading part in the oligarchic coup of 411, and on the overthrow of the oligarchy was executed for treason.

31. Miletus in Asia Minor was famous for the quality of its bass, and also, it would seem from p. 71, for a recent case of alleged bribery involving Cleon.

32. At Pylos; the 'ears' are, of course, the Spartan prisoners.

33. Cratinus, though now an old man, was still one of the leading comic poets. He was famous for his love of drinking, and in 423 won first prize with a satire on himself entitled *The Bottle*.

34. The tragedian Morsimus is frequently mentioned with disgust by Aristophanes (cf. *Peace*, p. 125; also *The Frogs*).

35. The quotation is from an ode by Simonides celebrating a chariot-racing victory.

36. This piece of popular wisdom appears to be quite accurate (with respect to stinging nettles, that is).

37. When in 429 the rebellious city of Potidaea, in Chalcidice, offered to submit to the Athenians, the Athenian generals did not insist on unconditional surrender. When such compromises were made, an accusation of bribery was inevitable.

38. The Alcmaeonid family (to which Pericles belonged, and with which no sane person could have imagined the Sausage-Seller to be connected) was said to be accursed on account of an alleged act of sacrilege some two centuries earlier.

39. That is, Hippias, the last 'tyrant' of Athens. To say that a man's ancestors had served the tyrants in such a capacity was a truly deadly charge, equivalent to the allegation of having belonged to the Tsarist secret police. In the Greek text the Sausage-Seller, to give the accusation a whiff of verisimilitude, mentions not Hippias but his wife Myrsine, whom he calls Byrsine to suggest a connection with oxhides (*byrsai*), Cleon's stock-in-trade.

40. Cheese was a staple product of Boeotia.

41. Fighting-cocks were primed with garlic before a contest. Demosthenes' next speech continues the metaphor.

42. Aristophanes' previous plays had been produced by others; *The Knights* was the first for which he 'applied for a Chorus' in his own name.

43. These are the titles of five of Magnes' comedies.

44. These will have been two songs from Cratinus's plays. The word 'figwood' (*sykon*) was constantly used by comic poets to refer via a pun to malicious informers or prosecutors (*sykophantai*).

45. A prizewinning musician who had fallen on hard times but continued to wear the faded garlands he had won years before.

46. Another variant on Cleon's dining rights (cf. note 15), suggested by Cratinus' bibulousness.

47. That is, the statue of Dionysus which was placed in the theatre during the festivals. As the god of both drama and alcohol Dionysus was clearly Cratinus' peculiar patron.

48. Aristophanes' first reference to his baldness.

49. It is not quite clear what this refers to: possibly warships sent out to collect tribute from recalcitrant subject allies (cf. page 76).

50. Poseidon had temples at Sunium, the southern tip of Attica, and at Geraestus, the southern tip of Euboea.

51. The admiral who in the early years of the war drove the Spartan and allied navies from the seas. In my translation I accept Rogers' supposition that he had died not long before the production of *The Knights*.

52. The embroidered robe presented by the people of Athens to their patron goddess every year at the Panathenaic festival.

53. Cf. note 15. 'Front seats' (next line) at the major festivals were also among the honours awarded to Cleon after Pylos.

54. What follows is based on an Athenian expedition which had recently attacked Corinthian territory under Nicias. The expedition led to no decisive result, but it included a hard-fought battle in which the cavalry were instrumental in securing victory for the Athenians.

55. It is not clear whether this is the Theorus, a minor politician and satellite of Cleon, who appears in *The Acharnians* and is mentioned again disparagingly in *The Clouds* and *The Wasps*; and it is even less clear, if it is the same Theorus, why he should have been mentioned here.

56. *Music:* 'Let's give three cheers' (Sullivan, *H.M.S. Pinafore*).

57. In the Greek *pseudatraphaxys*, an invented word compounded of *pseudos* (lie) and the name of a very fast-growing plant.

58. The annual sacrifice to Artemis in honour of the victory of Marathon consisted only of five hundred goats! These large sacrifices were popular because they meant free meat for all and sundry.

59. See note 53.

60. This wreath (*eiresionē*) was an olive-branch decorated with wool and various items of produce (fruit, cakes, small jars of honey, oil and wine), dedicated to Apollo at the autumn harvest festival (the Pyanepsia) and then hung on or near the door until the next year's harvest.

61. This is a hit at Hyperbolus (cf. pp. 84–5).

62. The 'dolphin' was a lump of lead, dolphin-shaped, which could be hoisted up to the mast of a ship to be dropped on to the deck of an enemy vessel.

63. For Lysicles see note 14. The two ladies were high-class prostitutes.

64. Caused by rowing at high speed while sitting on fixed wooden benches.

65. Harmodius, with Aristogeiton, had assassinated the brother of Hippias (see note 39) and sacrificed his own life in so doing. The pair were ever afterwards remembered (somewhat inaccurately) as the 'tyrannicides' who struck the first blow for democracy in Athens.

66. Owing to frequent Spartan invasions the entire population of Attica had to live within the city walls during the war.

67. In this unlikely event, Athens would have become the first state ever to conquer Arcadia, mountainous and isolated in the centre of the Peloponnese. The proposed rate of pay was nearly double the normal scale.

68. Themistocles (d. c. 460) had been mainly responsible for the defeat of the Persians in 480, the reconstruction of the walls of Athens and the building of the port of Peiraeus, among other services.

69. A deliberately ill-matched and inappropriate pair of catch-phrases from Euripides.

70. It is not known what this refers to; perhaps a plan for dividing the wards of the city by walls.

71. See note 23. The meaning is presumably that Cleon took bribes to conceal the defalcations of dishonest magistrates.

72. 'Ostracism' was the procedure whereby an unpopular politician could be exiled for ten years.

73. The strip between the Long Walls linking Athens and the Peiraeus, through which passed the imported corn on which the City's food supply depended.

74. In the Greek 'a man from Copros', a deme whose name meant 'dung'.

75. The command of a warship, like the sponsorship of a dramatic production, was a compulsory public service, and carried responsibility for the maintenance of the ship. The state paid the crew and supplied sails, oars, rigging and the like.

76. *Music*: 'Sir Rupert Murgatroyd' (Sullivan, *Ruddigore*).

77. See note 31.

78. In the Greek the sandwich is of beef-fat (*demos*), with a pun on Thepeople's Greek name Demos. I have borrowed from the opening scene (see note 4) a reference to Thepeople's fondness for beans.

79. In the Greek 'cormorant'; the same term is used of Cleon in *The Clouds*.

80. Cleonymus was a notorious glutton, and a political ally of Cleon's. In *Peace* we shall meet him in a third capacity.

81. This refers to a famous Delphic oracle that Athens, 'like a wineskin, would ride the stormy seas and never sink'.

82. Smicythes' name, in both Greek and English, is of ambiguous gender. So apparently was Smicythes himself, and therefore, like a married woman, he is to be sued conjointly with his 'husband'.

83. *Music*: 'The soldiers of our Queen' (Sullivan, *Patience*).

84. In the Greek the pun is on the 'Dorian mode' and *dorodokia* (bribery).

85. See note 12.

86. This famous oracle about Athens is misapplied by the Oracle Man in *The Birds*.

87. A familiar nickname of Cleon's, apparently; it is used again by the First Dog in *The Wasps*, who represents Cleon.

88. With these words we return abruptly from the dog to Cleon. 'The Islands', as on p. 42, means the Athenian empire generally.

89. In the Greek 'Antileon', an early tyrant of Chalcis.

90. i.e. in the stocks.

91. This saying originally referred to a dispute between various cities named Pylos over which of them had been the Homeric city over which Nestor had ruled, a dispute only settled by the discovery in the present century of a Mycenaean palace some four miles from the Pylos captured in 425.

92. In the Greek there is a pun on *Pylos* and *pyelos* (bathtub).

93. Philostratus was a brothel-keeper. He is referred to again under the nickname 'Dogfox' in *Lysistrata*.

94. A harbour in the north-west of the Peloponnese. I have imported the palms for the purpose of the pun, which in the Greek is on *Cyllene* and *kylle* (the hollow of the hand).

95. An oracle-monger whose hand was ever open for donations.

96. A minor state official, according to an ancient commentator, and evidently a partisan of Cleon's.

97. This 'funnel' appears to have been attached to the voting-urns in the courts. The juryman placed his hand in it and either did or did not release his voting-pebble; then he did the same at the other urn, so that the secrecy of the vote was preserved.

98. He is thinking of the ivory and gold statue of Athena which Pheidias made for the Parthenon. The divine titles in the next few lines are all appellations of Athena, though the reference to Pylos is merely another case of the Paphlagonian's familiar parrot cry.

99. Here begins a whole series of puns all of which I have had to adapt. The present one is on the word *peplos*, which means the robe presented to Athena (see note 52) and also the outer covering of a haggis.

100. Evidently tragic parody, but the source is unknown.

101. In the original this line is in Doric Greek; again presumably a parody of some familiar poetic phrase.

102. Quoted from the lost *Bellerophon* of Euripides.

103. Parodied from Euripides' *Alcestis* (line 182).

104. We meet Phanus' name in company with that of Cleon in *The Wasps*. He apparently specialized in prosecuting his chief's enemies.

105. A member of high society and a notorious practical joker, mentioned also in *The Acharnians* and *The Wasps*. In poverty he seems to have rivalled Thumantis.

106. The Greek has 'know white from the Orthian melody', a surprise for 'know white from black'. This family comes in for further extended treatment in *The Wasps*, where we hear that there was another brother who was an actor.

107. See note 80.

108. Afterwards Cleon's successor as the most influential speaker in the Assembly (cf. *Peace*, p. 120) and the most frequent victim of the comic poets. He was exiled by ostracism in 417 or 416 and assassinated in 411.

109. Both these sanctuaries conferred absolute asylum on all who took refuge in them. (But it would be quite impossible literally to sail to either.)

110. Hyperbolus is frequently reproached (so again in *Peace*, p. 121) with having made his money in the lamp business.

111. This treatment was first applied by Medea to a ram, with success; Jason's cousins were thus persuaded to cook their father Pelias, but (as Medea had fully intended) they got the formula wrong and killed him.

112. Just one year before, in *The Acharnians*, Aristophanes had criticized the Athenians for being too easily flattered when foreigners used this famous epithet of Pindar's about their city, and had described 'rich and shining' (below) as 'an epithet more fit for a sardine'. It is not only the Paphlagonian and the Sausage-Seller who can display impudence.

113. Miltiades was the victor of Marathon, and Aristides the founder of the confederacy that became the Athenian empire.

114. sc. because a heavy fine is needed in order to provide pay for the jurymen.

115. Two effeminates, who appear in *The Acharnians* masquerading as Persian eunuchs. Cleisthenes is mentioned in almost every one of Aristophanes' plays for the next twenty years; in *The Poet and the Women* he is described as 'the women's protector', being pretty much of a woman himself.

116. A few years after this Phaeax was a prominent politician, although irritatingly little is known about him.

117. The practice of rich men being accompanied by attendants with folding stools was typical of the Persian war period.

118. Since the beginning of the war the inhabitants of rural Attica had to live in the city owing to Spartan invasions.

119. This is the only extant play of Aristophanes which does not end with at least a short sung passage, and many have thought that such a passage has been lost in the transmission of the text. Whether this is so or not, it seems possible that Thepeople's final speech (which in the manuscripts ends with 'to see him') has lost a line or two, and I have supplied a makeshift conclusion for it.

PEACE

1. The Greek word is very nearly ambiguous between 'the Hurler of the Thunderbolt' and 'the Eater of Dung'.

2. Dung was a prominent component of the Aristophanic underworld; it is mentioned again in this context in *The Frogs*.

3. The Etna region was famous for its horses. The ensuing scene is freely based on the hero's flight to heaven on Pegasus in Euripides' lost tragedy *Bellerophon*.

4. Aristophanes refers more than once elsewhere to the probability that the Medes (= Persians) will take advantage of the Greeks' internal divisions.

5. This plea is parodied from the lost *Aeolus* of Euripides.

6. The eagle had stolen the beetle's young.

7. The name *kantharos* (beetle) was given to a type of small boat made on the island of Naxos.

8. It was a stock joke about Euripides that his plays were full of cripples. Bellerophon (who had fallen off the original Pegasus) was one of these.

9. When an Athenian citizen was killed on the territory of any 'allied' state, the state in question had to pay a collective fine of 30,000 drachmas. It is likely that there had been a recent case of this kind involving Chios.

10. These lines are repeated almost word for word in *The Frogs* (lines 465–6); I have borrowed the translation from David Barrett's version of that passage.

11. i.e. Castor and Polydeuces.

12. See Introductory Note to *The Knights*.

13. Prasiae, a town in Spartan territory, is here represented by leeks (*prasa*) merely because of its name. Megara, Sicily and Athens are each represented by one of their staple products.

14. This appeal would no doubt be addressed to the statue of Dionysus in the theatre (see note 47 to *The Knights*).

15. The 'pestle' is Cleon. (The Greek text here has a line describing him as 'the tanner who threw Greece into confusion', but this is probably an interpolation.) On his death and that of the Spartan 'pestle', Brasidas, see the Introductory Note.

16. The Cabeiri, worshipped in Samothrace, were the special protectors of sailors, and it may be for this reason that their Mysteries are invoked.

17. Castor and Polydeuces, the patron gods of Sparta (cf. p. 105 with note 11).

18. The name is that of a Persian general, but one ancient authority states that it was also the name (or nickname) of one of the sons of Carcinus (cf. p. 124). In the original he uses the passive form of a verb that could not be used in the passive; I have made him use 'pleasant' for 'pleased'.

19. The Greek text here is corrupt, but some pun of this kind is apparently intended. As to 'Good Fortune', cf. *The Knights*, p. 39; the libation poured to this deity was always of unmixed wine.

20. Officers, both at Athens and at Sparta, wore red cloaks. Lamachus (two lines below) was a prominent general, who appears in *The Acharnians* where he is represented, as here, as hotly in favour of war. In fact, however, when peace was concluded a few days after the production of *Peace*, the name of Lamachus appeared on the treaty as one of seventeen Athenians who took the oath to observe it.

21. Cleon, of course (cf. *The Knights*, p. 75).

22. See note 51 to *The Knights*.

23. Just outside Athens; afterwards famous as the site of Aristotle's school.

24. Cillicon appears to have been a fifth columnist who gave this answer on being interrogated by his government about his activities.

25. Text and interpretation are uncertain, but Hermes was the patron god of lotteries and luck.

26. Trygaeus equates death with military service.

27. At the Eleusinian Mysteries, where each prospective initiate had to offer a piglet. The Mysteries were the only official Greek cult mainly concerned with securing a happy after-life.

28. This man was later a prominent politician, one of the leaders of the oligarchy which ruled Athens briefly in 411.

29. Hermes was the god of thieving.

30. In *The Clouds*, the Moon is made to complain that the months have

got out of step with her phases. It may be that in an attempt to put this right some days had recently been omitted from the calendar.

31. The Greek has a pun on *phialē* (cup) and *ephialein* (get down to the job).

32. See note 80 to *The Knights*. Cleonymus had committed this act of cowardice in 424.

33. In the Greek Trygaeus complains that the traditional invocation of Apollo, *iē paiōn*, sounds too much like *paiein* (smiting), and the Leader changes the invocation to simply *iē*.

34. See note 20.

35. Argos had remained neutral and prosperous throughout the war.

36. i.e. those who had been captured at Pylos.

37. During the war Athens had cut off most of Megara's trade and devastated her territory in regular invasions. In *The Acharnians* a starving Megarian tries to sell his daughters to get some garlic and salt (normally Megara's staple products).

38. Cf. p. 106; also note 41 to *The Knights*. With Platnauer, I have assumed that the advice to the Athenians which follows is a hint that territorial concessions should be made for the sake of peace.

39. Euripides, in the lost *Telephus* – except that the last word was 'child'.

40. The famous sculptor had apparently been prosecuted for some financial misdemeanour; the accusation was probably meant as an indirect attack on Pericles. There is, however, no reason to suppose any connection between this and the origin of the war.

41. A trade embargo against Megara, treated by Sparta as a gross provocation.

42. Sparta was notorious for arbitrary expulsion of foreign visitors.

43. It was Hermes' job to escort spirits to Hades.

44. For Cleonymus see note 32, and note 80 to *The Knights*. The joke in Greek is based on the similarity of the words for 'one who throws something away' and 'a child substituted for another'.

45. See note 108 to *The Knights*.

46. Simonides had been notorious for the high fees he charged for his poems; but Sophocles is the last person one would expect to be accused of this fault. Had he perhaps been instrumental in securing a rise in the remuneration of tragic poets which the comic poets had failed to get?

47. Since the comic poet Cratinus (cf. *The Knights*, pp. 56–7) is known to have been alive in 423, and there had been no Spartan invasion since then, we can hardly take this passage as evidence that he was dead by 421.

48. It was from the Council that delegates were chosen to attend Pan-hellenic festivals.

49. The concluding words of the hated mobilization orders.

50. The beautiful boy whom Zeus had once taken a fancy to and made his cupbearer.

51. This passage is repeated verbatim from *The Wasps* (lines 1030–36). Cynna was a well-known woman of pleasure.

52. Cf. *The Knights*, p. 57 with note 48.

53. Up to this point the song is borrowed from Stesichorus (Himera, Sicily, sixth century B.C.).

54. The sons of the tragic poet Carcinus appeared as dancers in the finale of *The Wasps* – not, it would seem, to Aristophanes' satisfaction.

55. These four lines are also from Stesichorus. For Morsimus see *The Knights*, p. 52; his brother Melanthius, also a tragic poet, turns up again in this play (p. 132) and in *The Birds*.

56. A prolific and versatile author and poet, who had won first prize for tragedy at Athens.

57. See note 54. The sons of Carcinus, as is evident from *The Wasps*, specialized in dizzying pirouettes.

58. This refers to the quadrennial festival held at the Attic village of Brauron in honour of Artemis, of which a girls' procession was a notable feature.

59. Inns being few and small, visitors to the games normally put up tents, marking out the space for them well in advance 'to avoid disappointment'.

60. Compare *The Knights*, p. 84.

61. Literally 'to hold the Anarrhysis', the name of one of the days of the Apaturian festival; but the Greek phrase can also mean 'to draw (them) back'. Trygaeus' next speech is also to be understood throughout in two senses.

62. A rather poor pun on *bous* (an ox) and *boēthein* (to send reinforcements to an army).

63. A leading politician, mentioned again (usually for pomposity and boasting about imaginary wealth) in *The Wasps*, *The Birds* and *Lysistrata*.

64. In the Greek *oi* (a sheep), which was also an exclamation of terror.

65. This flute-player is also execrated in *The Acharnians* and *The Birds*.

66. No animal could be sacrificed against its will; hence the victim was regularly induced to shake its head, this being taken as signifying consent.

67. The word *krithē* meant both 'barley grain' and 'male organ'. This passage unfortunately gives no decisive evidence whether women could attend the dramatic performances.

68. The standard congregational response to 'Who is here?' was 'Good men in plenty'.

69. Trygaeus may be reckoning from the beginning of the war between Corinth and Corcyra in 435, out of which the Peloponnesian war grew. Two lines below, Peace is given in the Greek the name *Lysimache*, literally 'Ender of Battles'; it is probably significant that this name was borne at the time by one of the most honoured women in Athens, the priestess of Athena Polias.

70. See page 125.

71. The Greek text names Stilbides, one of the leading members of this profession.

72. Peace would reduce the demand for his services, since knowledge of the future is always more eagerly sought in times of uncertainty and danger.

73. This part had to be specially examined for signs of good or bad omen.

74. This line has been suspected, but Hierocles is evidently hamming. For Bakis see *The Knights*, pp. 40 and 74.

75. It is not clear whether this piece of nonsense is to be assigned to Aristophanes or to textual corruption: probably the former.

76. 'We' here means Athens and Sparta: here, as later in *Lysistrata*, Aristophanes is thinking of the joint hegemony which broke down very shortly after the Persian war. An Athenian-Spartan alliance was indeed formed in 421, but came to nothing.

77. Quite untrue, although the lines contain several Homeric formulae.

78. See note 8 to *The Knights*.

79. This is a genuine quotation (*Iliad* IX, lines 63–4).

80. This mythical beast, a creation apparently of Aeschylus', is constantly being made fun of in comedy. Aeschylus himself is made to say in *The Frogs* that he got the idea from the figurehead of a ship.

81. The statue, in the market-place, of the ancestral hero of the Pandionid 'tribe': the call-up list would be posted there, since the army was organized on a tribal basis. The 'brigadier' (*taxiarchos*) was the commander of the tribal contingent.

82. Language and metre suggest that this is a tragic quotation, but the source is unknown.

83. i.e. when serving as commander of a warship (cf. note 75 to *The Knights*), with the object of fraudulently keeping the money provided by the state for the missing oarsmen's pay.

84. In this game (called *kottabos*) a small disc would be balanced on top of the rod, and the players, with the wine left in their cups after drinking, would try to upset it.

85. 'The Egyptians ... purge themselves for three days in succession each month' (Herodotus).
86. The helmets could then be used as bowls.
87. The beginning of *The Epigoni*, an early epic sometimes ascribed to Homer (now lost). The rest of this boy's songs are adapted from the *Iliad*.
88. See note 20; in the Greek Trygaeus' pun which follows is on the -*machus* element in the name, which means 'battle'.
89. Cf. page 113 and note 32.
90. The beginning of an elegiac poem by Archilochus (seventh century).

THE BIRDS

1. Execestides is mentioned three times in this play. He seems to have been a slave from Caria, in Asia Minor, who had somehow managed to acquire Athenian citizenship.
2. 'Go to the crows!' was the Greek equivalent of 'Go to blazes!'
3. Acestor (said to have been a tragic poet) was evidently another foreigner who had obtained, or was trying to obtain, Athenain citizenship. He is referred to here by his nickname Sakas ('the Scythian').
4. The Tereus of legend (and of Sophocles' play) raped his sister-in-law Philomela and cut out her tongue. She and his wife Procne took their revenge by serving up his son, Itys, for his dinner. Further slaughter was averted by divine intervention, Tereus being turned into a hoopoe, Procne into a nightingale and Philomela into a swallow (in other versions it was she who became the nightingale). None of these bloodcurdling events seems to have cast its shadow over the happy married life of Aristophanes' gentle Hoopoe and his consort, and Procne's lament for Itys is described in most sympathetic terms by the Hoopoe himself (p. 162).
5. Except for his splendid mask and headdress, and a pair of wings, the Hoopoe is dressed like a man.
6. A fast galley reserved for important state missions. Only a few months before, this vessel had been sent to Sicily to arrest Alcibiades and bring him back for trial.
7. A notorious informer. He had only one eye, hence the name coined for him later in the play (p. 197).
8. Philocles, a nephew of Aeschylus, had written a play about Tereus which Aristophanes clearly regarded as a feeble imitation of the one

by Sophocles. The Hoopoe identifies himself with the Tereus of Sophocles, not the 'derivative' Tereus of Philocles' play. The dancing Hoopoe, as the *son* of the latter, is, as it were, two generations removed from our friend who is speaking. Athenians were often named after their grandfathers, as in the Hoopoe's illustration. The logic of the joke should not be pushed too far: its main purpose is to introduce the name of Callias, an Athenian of illustrious birth who had squandered the family fortunes.

9. Cleonymus is known to us chiefly through the constant references to him – always malicious – in Aristophanes' plays, in which he is derided for (a) his obesity; (b) his gluttony and avarice; (c) his cowardice (he was supposed to have fled from the battlefield at Delium, throwing away his shield). The song about him later in this play (p. 204) also implies that he has enriched himself through the lawcourts, i.e. by informing.

10. The ancient myths relating to this bird connect it very closely with the sea, as indeed does its name (which at some period, rather inappropriately, became attached to the kingfisher). In classical times – in poetry at any rate – the halcyon was still associated with the sea, and it seems likely that the name originally applied to some seabird like the tern or (as Rogers suggests) the shearwater. The phrase 'halcyon days' (a reference to the myth) is used by Poseidon later in the play (p. 208).

11. The Greek equivalent of 'carrying coals to Newcastle'. The Little Owl was sacred to Athene, and appeared on Athenian coins.

12. Procne (see note 4) was the daughter of Pandion, king of Athens.

13. Perhaps the snub-nosed Lysicrates with dyed hair mentioned twice in *The Assemblywomen*. Whoever he was, this passage indicates that he took bribes. It has been suggested that the name may also have been an accepted epithet for Priam (it means 'dissolver of power'), but there is no evidence for this and it is not essential for the joke.

14. One of the most eminent pundits of the day; he would have been regarded as an authority on such a subject as this.

15. A notorious highwayman: See note 26.

16. See note 1.

17. One of the two generals currently commanding the Athenian cavalry. Ancient commentators inform us that he had made his money as a manufacturer of wicker sheaths for wine flasks: the handles of these were called 'wings', as were the flapping tails of a cavalry officer's cloak (*chlamys*).

18. Both often mocked for their boastful manner of speech, along with a third braggart, Proxenides.

19. Diagoras had been outlawed for atheism and blasphemy, and the proclamation quoted is probably genuine. The reward for tyrant-killing was still included in the formula for certain public ceremonies, even though there had not been a 'tyrant' (dictator) in Athens for a hundred years.

20. See note 18.

21. The Porphyrion of ancient legend was one of the giants who led the attack on the gods of Olympus. The bird, *Porphyrio porphyrio*, is the Purple Gallinule, a small water bird related to the Coot.

22. 'Quail-flipping' was a popular market-place pastime. A well-trained quail would not retreat when flipped on the bill with a forefinger; the owner would take bets from anyone who wanted to try.

23. A village in Achaea (Northern Peloponnese) where woollen cloaks were made.

24. See note 17.

25. See note 9.

26. A notorious footpad, who operated in the poorly lit streets on the outskirts of Athens. Namesake of one of the 'heroes' of legend, who were believed to enjoy immortality.

27. See note 1.

28. He had been punished for stealing the Fire which Zeus had hidden, and bringing it to earth for the benefit of mankind.

29. A pupil of Socrates (we meet him in Plato's dialogues too), said to have been very pale and corpse-like in appearance.

30. Laespodias, one of the generals who held office round about the time of *The Birds*, is said to have had a withered or deformed shin, which he concealed by wearing his toga in a particular way.

31. Citizens were enrolled soon after birth in the *phratry* ('clan' or 'kinship group') to which the father belonged. In modern terms this would be the equivalent of having one's birth entered in the parish register. When older, he would also have to be registered as a member of his *deme* (electoral district).

THE ASSEMBLYWOMEN

1. Attended by women only.

2. The text is uncertain, and ancient commentators give conflicting accounts of Phyromachus and of his unfortunate remark or slip of the tongue. The joke seems to revolve round the word for 'companions, fellow conspirators', which in its feminine form (used here)

becomes ambiguous, the normal meaning being 'female companions', i.e. courtesans. In adapting the joke to English, the translator has had to do what he can with 'in on the plot'.

3. The Greek *himation*.

4. Chickpeas were served with wine – much as we now nibble salted peanuts.

5. Lamias: obviously a well-known official, of whom vigilance was to be expected – perhaps he was chief watchman, or governor of the prison. The joke cannot be satisfactorily explained, and has been shortened and paraphrased here.

6. A leading demagogue who had recently increased his popularity by securing an increase in the payment for attendance at the Assembly. But the comic poets had an old grudge against him: many years before, he had been responsible for a reduction in their emoluments.

7. The Greek domestic mouser was not actually a cat at all, but a domesticated polecat.

8. Head-wreaths, normally of myrtle leaves, were worn at drinking-parties, as well as by speakers on public occasions.

9. See note 6.

10. The reference is probably to the anti-Spartan pact between Athens, Thebes and Locris, 395 B.C. Nothing is known of its exiled proposer.

11. Thrasybulus (referred to by name in the text).

12. Cephalus, a potter by trade, was a leader of the 'democratic' party and an accomplished orator.

13. In tragedy, dramatic convention did not allow the Chorus to intervene actively at moments of crisis: this did not prevent authors from giving them lines like 'I fear that all is not well: don't you think we should do something about it?' The Greeks saw the funny side of this.

14. This instruction is probably merely a cue for the theme of the song which follows; it should not be taken to imply that the women are to keep up the role of rustics throughout the operation. They are, after all, wearing their husbands' town clothes; and Chremes describes them later as looking like shoemakers, not farmers. The country voters, indeed, show hostility to Praxagora's motion (lines 426 ff., p. 236).

15. A successful Athenian general of the preceding century.

16. The poet Cinesias, a favourite butt of the comedians, had once been in serious trouble for having 'defiled' a sacred precinct. He was never allowed to forget it.

17. The topical reference is obscure.

18. Before the introduction of pay for attendance, citizens loitering to

gossip instead of hurrying to the Assembly sometimes had to be 'roped in' to a session by constables carrying a rope smeared with vermilion. On this occasion, however, the rope seems to have been used to disperse the crowds still trying to get in.

19. Blepyrus misquotes Aeschylus.

20. See notes 4 and 8.

21. These were used for the allocation of jurors to the various courts.

22. See note 7.

23. The name suggests an old man, which gives point to the words 'another young fellow'.

24. His words imply (quite strongly, in the Greek) that he has thought of a brilliant scheme, the frustration of which one would expect to be the subject of a later episode in the play. Has a scene been lost, or did Aristophanes change his mind?

25. These lines must have been put in at the last moment, after the order of performance of the competing plays had been decided by lot.

WEALTH

1. This line in the Greek has a tragic tone.

2. 'Gets off', because in these circumstances the husband was entitled by law to kill the adulterer on the spot.

3. Citizens were now paid three obols for attending the Assembly.

4. This mercenary force had been raised some years previously by the Athenian general Conon, and had been operating successfully against the Spartans from its base at Corinth, now an ally of Athens.

5. Pamphilus was a politician and general who had just been campaigning unsuccessfully against Aegina. The prophecy here made came true: he was prosecuted for embezzlement and his estate confiscated.

6. A leading politician with tax-farming and banking interests. He had won great popularity by increasing the payment for attending the assembly, and in 389 was elected a general.

7. It is not known exactly to what this refers. Egypt was still nominally under Persian rule, but was now, as often, in revolt.

8. The Corinthian Lais was one of the most beautiful women of the age. She had recently become the mistress of Philonides, who is universally described as exceptionally ugly, stupid, and rich.

9. Timotheus had recently inherited the fortune of Conon (cf. note 4), and built himself an ostentatious house with a tower. He ran through his entire patrimony in the next fifteen years, but meanwhile played

a leading role in the revival of Athenian power and influence in the Aegean.

10. Literally 'than Lynceus', one of the Argonauts, whose eyesight was proverbial.

11. The shaking of the bay-trees is often referred to as a sign of the presence of Apollo when a response was being uttered.

12. At this time jurymen were assigned to their courts by lot every day: they drew a ball from an urn, and their court was determined by the letter marked on the ball (the Greek here means literally 'your letter, having been allotted, is judging in the coffin'). A juror who had duly sat and voted on a case was given a ticket, exchangeable for his daily pay, by the magistrate (*archon*) presiding over the court; here, by what is apparently intended for a pun, *archon* is replaced by *Charon* who ran the ferry service to Hades.

13. The 'comrades' are only introduced in order to keep up the equations Circe = Lais (see note 8), Philonides = Odysseus.

14. Aristyllus, however (who is not otherwise known), would have enjoyed this; his sexual perversion(s) are mentioned in *The Assemblywomen*.

15. See note 3; late-comers to the Assembly were not paid.

16. An excess of this liquid (which has given its name to 'melancholy') was thought to be responsible for certain kinds of insanity.

17. For the expression compare *Peace*, p. 119; it was normal to carry small change in one's mouth.

18. This painting, based on Euripides' tragedy of the same name, was to be seen (according to the ancient commentators) in the Painted Portico (Stoa Poikile). It had probably not been painted long, as Pamphilus is known to have been active over twenty years later.

19. I translate the passage as it stands; but the transition is rather abrupt and illogical (even more so in the Greek), and I suspect that three or four lines may have dropped out before this speech.

20. That is, by your crimes.

21. Greek doctors were often state employees who practised in any city which made it financially worth their while: Athens in 388 could not or would not afford to.

22. The tragic scene referred to is unknown. Blepsidemus' next remark sounds like an offer of violence, but the text seems to rule out the possibility of his actually having used violence at this point; and Poverty's question is odd when an opinion has already been expressed about her identity ('you' is plural in the Greek). Perhaps we ought to delete from 'A Fury' to 'look out!'

23. The public baths were a habitual refuge for the poor and heatless in winter.

24. Thrasybulus had overthrown the oligarchic régime at Athens in 403, and for the next fifteen years was a prominent politician, a strong but not an extreme democrat. Not long before the production of *Wealth* he was murdered on campaign. Dionysius was 'tyrant' of Syracuse and at this time overlord of most of Sicily.

25. These offerings were left at shrines of Hecate sited at crossroads; they generally consisted of food too poor for the household to eat.

26. Compare *The Knights*, p. 66.

27. Pauson, the painter (who must have been getting on in years), is mentioned in *The Acharnians* as one of the pests of the Market Square, and in *The Poet and the Women* as never having anything to eat.

28. This whole passage is mock-tragic. Probably the model for the parody is some contemporary play; but Carion's next speech (from 'He's blind no more . . .') is quoted from Sophocles' *Phineus*.

29. Greek doctors sometimes called themselves 'sons of Asclepius'.

30. The usual comic assumption that all women love drink.

31. The play on words in the Greek is based on *prāgma* (ambiguous in the same way as 'matter') and on the imprecation *es kephalēn soi* '(may it fall) on your head!'

32. A few years earlier, in *The Assemblywomen*, Neocleides had been merely 'bleary-eyed'.

33. She and Panacea were daughters of Asclepius; their names are from different roots both meaning 'to heal'.

34. The point of the joke is in the Greek somewhat obscure. I follow the suggestion of an ancient commentator that the reference is to examination of excreta by doctors, already a common practice.

35. Text and interpretation are uncertain, but there seems to be an allusion to the procedure of *hypomosia*, a challenge to a motion made in the Assembly on the ground that it (the motion) was against the public interest: such a challenge, if made on oath, entailed a second vote on the original motion.

36. Actually sweetmeats, dried figs and the like, normally used for welcoming newly-acquired *slaves*.

37. The beginning of Wealth's next speech is literally 'Yes, and I also first of all make obeisance . . .', as if he was answering someone. I therefore assume that whatever the Chorus do in their other interludes, here they *sing*, ending with an exhortation to the incoming Wealth, perhaps to thank the gods for his cure. Here and here only in the play the two main manuscripts, instead of just 'Chorus', have the note 'Short stanza (*kommation*) by Chorus'.

38. On this occasion a new white robe was worn, which was normally not used thereafter and frequently dedicated in a temple. Carion is light-heartedly pretending to accuse his visitor of sacrilege.

39. Either, as the ancient commentators say, in order to avoid military service, or because lawsuits involving merchants were heard only in a special court and only in the winter months, so that a person representing himself as a merchant might be able to get the trial advanced or delayed to suit his interest.

40. The significance of this expression will appear presently; but it is not clear whether Aristophanes expected his audience to understand it right away. If he did, the joke is unduly prolonged; if he didn't, it is odd that he makes Carion understand immediately.

41. Votive offerings were often attached to wild olive trees in sacred precincts.

42. In the Greek 'a comrade, even a figwood one': figwood was proverbially weak, 'figwood assistance' meaning much the same as our 'broken reed', but it was also the eponymous emblem of the informer, whose designation (*sȳkophantēs*) meant literally 'revealer of figs'.

43. See note 12. Here the reference is to the preliminary daily selection (again by lot) of the jurors required by the courts from the usually larger number who had volunteered to serve: surplus jurors might try to slip into court for the sake of the payment (perhaps by using forged or borrowed identification). And what jury service is to the Athenian male, alcohol (according to Aristophanes) is to the Athenian female.

44. Proverbial for anything and everything that had had its day.

45. Demeter and Persephone.

46. The Greek word (*tēliā*) seems to mean a round table or board with a raised rim, on which corn was displayed in the market.

47. Literally, 'like an old harvest-wreath' (*eiresiōnē*); cf. note 60 to *The Knights*: the wreath remained hanging on the door long after it withered and dried.

48. The game was to bet how many nuts one's opponent held in his closed hand – a more elaborate variant of 'odd-and-even'.

49. In the Greek Chremylus swears by Hecate, an oath normally used only by women.

50. The play in Greek is on two words each of which refers both to sex and to the sealing of wine-jars with pitch to prevent air leaking into them.

51. Compare *Peace*, p. 134. The tongues of sacrificial victims were sacred to Hermes as the herald and spokesman of the gods; in the

present passage the double meaning will be captured if 'you a' is pronounced rather like 'your'.

52. This was the day on which Hermes was supposed to have been born. Carion's reply is quoted from an unknown tragedy.

53. The Greek has a pun on *kōlē* (ham) and *askōliazein* (to play the game of hopping about on a bladder).

54. Literally 'captured Phyle', as Thrasybulus (note 24) did at the start of the campaign that ended in the overthrow of the Thirty. After the restoration of democracy there was a general amnesty for all political offences, only the Thirty themselves and a few of their closest associates being excepted.

55. Quoted from an unknown tragedy.

56. See notes 12 and 43. The preliminary selection of jurors was on the basis of a permanent division into ten sections, so it was advantageous to get oneself (fraudulently) enrolled in more than one of these.

57. This was the home of the major State treasury, very much depleted since the revenues of the old empire had been lost.

58. Compare *Peace*, p. 130.

SELECT BIBLIOGRAPHY

1. Editions of Aristophanes

All the eleven comedies of Aristophanes have been edited, with translation and commentary, by A. H. Sommerstein (Warminster, 1980–2001). The final volume (*Wealth*) contains updates to all the preceding volumes.

There are excellent separate editions (Greek text and commentary) of *Peace* by S. Douglas Olson (Oxford, 1998), of *Birds* by Nan Dunbar (Oxford, 1995), and of *The Assemblywomen* by R. G. Ussher (Oxford, 1973). An edition of *The Knights* by Jeffrey Henderson, in the same series, is in preparation.

2. Aristophanes and his work

K. J. Dover, *Aristophanic Comedy* (London, 1972).

K. J. Reckford, *Aristophanes' Old-and-New Comedy I: Six Essays in Perspective* (Chapel Hill, 1987).

P. A. Cartledge, *Aristophanes and His Theatre of the Absurd* (3rd ed., Bristol, 1995).

D. M. MacDowell, *Aristophanes and Athens* (Oxford, 1995).

M. S. Silk, *Aristophanes and the Definition of Comedy* (Oxford, 2000).

N. W. Slater, *Spectator Politics: Metatheater and Performance in Aristophanes* (Philadelphia, 2002).

3. Greek theatre production

C. W. Dearden, *The Stage of Aristophanes* (London, 1976).

L. M. Stone, *Costume in Aristophanic Comedy* (New York, 1981).

A. W. Pickard-Cambridge, *The Dramatic Festivals of Athens* (3rd ed., revised by J. Gould and D. M. Lewis) (Oxford, 1988).

C. F. Russo, *Aristophanes: An Author for the Stage* (London, 1994).

E. G. Csapo and W. J. Slater, *The Context of Ancient Drama* (Ann Arbor, 1994).

J. R. Green, *Theatre in Ancient Greek Society* (London, 1995).